1985

COACH'S
PUBLIC SPEAKING
PORTFOLIO

COACH'S PUBLIC SPEAKING PORTFOLIO:
With Model Speeches and Anecdotes

P. Susan Mamchak
and
Steven R. Mamchak

PARKER PUBLISHING COMPANY, INC.
West Nyack, New York

Library of Congress Cataloging-in Publication Data

Mamchak, P. Susan
  Coach's public speaking portfolio.

  Includes index.
  1. Speeches, addresses, etc. 2. Public speaking.
3. Coaching (Athletics) I. Mamchak, Steven R.
II. Title.
PN4193.04M35 1986   796'.07'7   85–
12239

ISBN 0-13-139049-X

We dedicate this book to the coaches in our lives who have inspired, encouraged, lifted spirits, and given invaluable direction. We gratefully acknowledge your able assistance, and we dedicate this book to you:

Coach Tony "Doc" Bevacqui
Coach Kevin Graham
Coach Norm Kauff
Coach Bill Moore
Coach Matt Roth
Coach Andy Russo
Coach Mark Sessa

HOW TO USE THIS BOOK TO YOUR BEST ADVANTAGE

As a coach, you are faced with never-ending demands on your time and energy. Few of us would disagree with that statement. Indeed, we know only too well that a coach's day begins early, ends late, and is a continuous succession of matters that require here-and-now attention.

Yes, it is an evident fact that the coach is in demand. This is true not only on the practice and playing fields, but in other areas as well. The coach is constantly being pressed to serve on committees, aid in community projects, and express opinions on a variety of subjects and in a variety of situations.

Indeed, as part of his professional life, the coach is often asked to act as host on a myriad of formal and semiformal occasions; to actively participate in honors for players or professional colleagues; to deliver his own as well as the organizational philosophy concerning sports and athletics; to address team members, parents, and press; to act as spokesman for the team; to inform; to congratulate; to appease; to educate.

In each of these and similar situations, the coach's tool is speech, and the problem is time. The coach is, after all, a leader and shaper of young lives, and that must remain the number one priority. Often, however, the demands of that priority are so exacting that there is little time left to effectively prepare those speeches, addresses, and commentaries that are required of them. Yet, coaches must meet these needs and meet them well as an essential part of their educational and professional responsibilities, as well as their duty to their team members and the community.

Tonight, an auditorium filled with parents will await your greeting and your insights about the sport in which their children are participating. Tomorrow evening you will speak at a dinner to honor a coach who is retiring after thirty years of service to the community. Next week, you are expected to host an evening of testimonials for team members. The alumni association wants you to speak at their annual dinner. There is so much to prepare for.

Where do you find the time? There are drills and practices to conduct. You must find time to formulate strategies for the upcoming games. There is also that meeting with your assistant coaches and budget requests are due by next Tuesday.

You'll be lucky to find time for lunch, let alone the time to research, write, and revise a dynamic and effective speech for each occasion.

It is precisely at times like these that everyone has dreamed of a magic source to which they could go and in which they would find models of the *exact* speeches they need. Moreover, they would be models that could be easily adapted, perhaps with little more than the change of a name, to *their* particular circumstances. As long as it is just a dream, they also would be speeches that were dignified, intelligent, and appropriate not only to the situation and the topic, but to their positions as professional coaches as well.

It was exactly this sort of dream that led to the creation of this book. *Coach's Public Speaking Portfolio: With Model Speeches and Anecdotes* isn't magic, but it will provide that source of model speeches that will save you hours, perhaps days, of tedious preparation time. Here is a volume that is filled with speeches specifically tailored to the professional coach and written for those occasions he most frequently encounters. These speeches may be used as is or adapted to meet the coach's most exacting requirements; they are perfected, polished, and professional; they will express exactly what you want to say in the exact way you want to say it.

If you're looking for the perfect speech to give to those parents, you'll find a variety of them in Section Four (speeches for nonsports audiences) and Section Nine (speeches for special events). Section Seven (speeches for retirements and testimonials) will provide you with the exact speech for that retirement dinner, no matter what the status of the retiring coach. You can fire up your team or your team's supporters to new heights of achievement with any of the speeches in Section Six (speeches that inspire).

In addition, you'll find models of icebreakers that will set everyone at ease; you'll find models of introductions for all occasions; you'll find the perfect speech for opening or closing any activity; you'll find dignified eulogies and memorial speeches; and you'll find speeches about the history and development of every major sport in America.

After every model speech you'll find a Special Data section that gives specific details about the speech such as the time of delivery, the precise circumstances under which the speech is most effectively used, and audience-tested hints that will ensure the best possible delivery.

Finally, for those exceptional occasions when you must spend time preparing a speech, there is a step-by-step guide derived from years of experience that will make the task easier and ensure a superior product. There is even a section that will tell you the secrets of dealing successfully with those problems that pop up occasionally in public speaking. Add to this a special Locatomatic Index which allows the coach to find the topic or subject area he or she needs in a matter of seconds, and you have a volume worthy of attention.

All in all, this is a book that you will use often. The special nature of the model speeches that are geared to the needs of the coach; the ease with which these speeches may be adapted to all occasions; the data and specifics on each speech; and the wide variety and number of speeches from which to choose make this a reference that you will use again and again to save time and energy in developing and delivering quality speeches. For the active and involved coach, this book is a reference that will occupy a prominent space on the coaching bookshelf; a book that will be used for successful public speaking throughout the season and the year.

P. Susan Mamchak
Steven R. Mamchak

CONTENTS

part
ONE

═══════

Model Speeches and Anecdotes for All Occasions

Part One of this book contains model speeches and anecdotes that have been specially crafted for the working coach.
Here, you should be able to find the right speech for the occasion
you *have in mind.*

This part is divided into ten sections which cover general
areas of speaking that affect the coach. Check the one appropriate to your wants and needs, then look in the Contents for
more exact listings. Finally, check the Locatomatic Index for
even more comprehensive listings by topic.

We hope that these speeches serve you as well as they have
served us.

SECTION 1

A Coach's Collection
of Usable Anecdotes
and Icebreakers

Nothing has a greater impact on an audience than the use of appropriate humor in a speech. When people laugh, they are almost immediately put at ease. For the speaker, this piece of information has been used to advantage on innumerable occasions. There is a poem which begins, "Laugh and the world laughs with you." Well, the speaker recognizes that this is only a part of the truth. The audience that laughs with you is also more apt to be well disposed to your ideas and suggestions, and, generally, to come away with a feeling of warmth and friendship for you.

While humor may be used anywhere in a speech, it is usually most effective when used at the beginning or the end of your presentation. Obviously, any serious matter that you have to present should be delivered seriously and be presented without interruption. After all, asking an audience to shift moods quickly or frequently can be confusing. However, a speech that begins with humor, eases into a serious matter, and ends on an upbeat note that leaves a smile on everyone's lips, is one that is likely to be remembered and appreciated by any audience.

Remember that merely getting up before an audience and telling jokes will not do. The anecdotes or icebreakers that you use should be appropriately suited to your audience, your speech, and your personality. They should have meaning within the context of what you are saying, and they should not be offensive to any member of the audience.

Within the following pages you will find a number of anecdotes and icebreakers on a variety of subjects appropriate for any audience. Use them to get your audience on your side, to prove or exemplify a point, or merely to put the audience at ease. Try to personalize them by changing the names and places to those with which the audience is familiar. If the words as written don't flow smoothly from your mouth, change them around until they sound like you. In short, make them personal and you will make your audience smile.

One final suggestion: Don't forget to laugh along with your audience. If you enjoy yourself, the audience will enjoy you.

1

TOPIC: *Quick Thinking; Ingenuity.*

AUDIENCE: *Appropriate for all audiences.*

When I was going to school, I had a coach who was renowned through-out our area for his ability to get his players to use their minds as well as their bodies. Training and physical conditioning were a great part of it, of course, but this coach placed an equally heavy emphasis on outthinking the opponent.

This coach's name was Jones and, one day before I graduated, I asked him what had convinced him to place so much emphasis on creative thought.

"Son," he told me, "once when I was your age, I played on a high school football team. During the second quarter of one of our games, I was warming the bench along with several other players when I noticed a blur of action out of the corner of my eye. The blur took shape, and there was the biggest skunk I had ever seen. The creature walked out from under the bench and sat down about three feet in front of me.

"I was sitting there with my mouth hanging open when my coach, who had witnessed the skunk's approach, upended a large galvanized wash tub that we used to keep ice in, and planted it upside down over the black and white furry thing.

" 'Coach!' I yelled, 'what great quick thinking!'

" 'That was nothing, Jones,' my coach said as he led me over to the tub and plumped me down on top of it. 'All I did was give you a place to sit down while you figure out how you're going to get rid of it!'

"Ever since that day, I've had this compelling need to train people to think fast!"

SPECIAL DATA: *Time of anecdote: a little over a minute. This might be used effectively to lead into the fact that mere brawn is not enough for today's athlete; that games are played with the mind as well as the body; or anything along these lines. You might want to change the name of the coach to one who is well known to your audience.*

9

$$\boxed{2}$$

TOPIC: *Dullness of Thought; a perfect "roast" for a fellow coach.*

AUDIENCE: *Adults; particularly fellow coaches and/or athletes.*

Recently, Coach Jones and his two assistants, Coach Smith and Coach Brown, decided to attend an olympic-type sports event that was being held in a nearby town. When they arrived by train at the local station, they found that they had forgotten to bring enough money with them, and between the three of them, they couldn't come up with enough for bus fare to the stadium where the event was to take place.

They were standing around wondering what to do next, when they spotted a bus which bore a large sign stating, "BUS TO STADIUM—FOR ATHLETES AND THEIR EQUIPMENT ONLY."

All at once, Coach Brown's eyes widened, and he ran into a local department store. A few moments later, he emerged carrying a long-handled broom. He removed the head of the broom, and, carrying only the handle, he approached the bus.

He went up the driver and said, "Brown—pole vault!" The driver let him on the bus.

At this point, Coach Smith smiled broadly and disappeared into a nearby auto parts store. When he came out a minute later, he was holding a large, shiny hub cap. Carrying this prominently under one arm, he, too, made for the special bus.

"Smith—discus throw!" he told the driver, and was allowed on the bus as well.

This left Coach Jones standing alone in the town square. He thought and thought. Suddenly his face brightened, and he rushed into a local hardware store.

Brown and Smith were seated on the bus anxiously waiting as five minutes and then ten minutes went by without the appearance of Coach Jones.

Finally, they saw him emerge from the hardware store. Even at a distance they could see that something was wrong. Coach Jones appeared to be limping badly.

As Coach Jones neared the bus they saw to their horror that Jones was covered from neck to ankles in twisted barbed wire! Not only was it making movement difficult, but he was clearly bleeding in several places where the wire was cutting into him.

Breathing heavily and obviously in pain, Jones hobbled up to the bus driver.

"Jones," he said, "fencing!"

SPECIAL DATA: *Time of anecdote: about two minutes. This is the type of story that goes over very well at dinners or testimonials for a local coach. You would, of course, substitute the name of the coach for Jones in the story. Told with a twinkle in the eye that assures the audience that it is all in fun, this is an excellent "roast" for a coach. Usually, the coach laughs loudest of all.*

┌───┐
│ 3 │
└───┘

TOPIC: *The Coach and the Press.*

AUDIENCE: *Suitable for all audiences, particularly if members of the press are present.*

When Coach Jones had lost four games in a row, several members of the local press began to speculate openly in the sports pages about the wisdom of some of the plays he had called.

Halfway through the fifth game of the season, things were going no better than they had previously, and the outlook for victory was dim.

As his team played valiantly but vainly on the field, Coach Jones studied the player roster intently. Finally, he turned to his assistant.

"I want you to send in these players," he said. "Cznyk, Wskelevskelewicz, and Mozkelupoulopolis!"

(PRONUNCIATION: CHIN-ICK, WAZ-KEY-LEV-SKI-LE-VITCH, MOS-KEY-LOO-PO-LOP-O-LISS)

"Coach," said his assistant, "those guys are third-stringers. How can they help us win the game?"

"They can't," answered the coach. "I just want to get even with the reporters who are going to have to write up the game!"

SPECIAL DATA: *Time of anecdote: less than a minute. This goes over very well if members of the press are present. If they are, however, make certain that you follow this story with some kind remarks about them and the valuable service they provide. Told with a smile in your voice, however, this can be an effective anecdote for everyone.*

$$\boxed{4}$$

TOPIC: *Stress and the Coach.*

AUDIENCE: *Suitable for all adult audiences.*

Coach Jones was not feeling well. There was nothing specific that he could complain of—just some vague aches and pains, and a general feeling of not being quite right. Finally, he decided to pay a visit to his doctor.

The physician examined him thoroughly, and proclaimed him to be in excellent health.

"Then why do I feel so poorly all the time?" the coach asked.

"Well," answered the doctor, "you have a very stressful job. We're just beginning to learn that stress can produce some very bad effects on people. I would say that the stress you undergo every day is taking a toll on your physical well-being. That's why you don't feel well."

"If that's the case," asked the coach, "what can I do about it?"

The doctor smiled kindly and said, "It's really very simple. For the next few weeks, I want you to relax completely. Forget about coaching; forget about the team; forget about winning and losing. Just stay calm and avoid all situations that could upset you or cause you any kind of stress."

"Thank you, Doctor," said Coach Jones. "I'll try. I'm not going to get upset, and I'll avoid all unpleasant situations."

"Good!" smiled the doctor. "Oh, by the way, there's one more thing I'd like to ask you."

"Certainly, Doctor," said the coach. "What is it?"

"Well," said the doctor as he frowned deeply, "during the game last Saturday when we were fourth and seven on our own thirty-five-yard line, why did you go for it! Are you some kind of idiot!"

SPECIAL DATA: *Time of anecdote: about a minute and a half. The stress felt by every coach is a very real thing, and this story humorously exemplifies that it comes from every quarter. This story is also effective if the coach tells it on himself, as "I wasn't feeling too well . . ." It is a good lead in to a speech about taking responsibility for one's decisions, or the necessity of making decisions even if they don't always turn out to be the right ones.*

$$\boxed{5}$$

TOPIC: *The Difficulty of Being a Coach.*

AUDIENCE: *Suitable for all audiences, particularly if fellow coaches are in attendance.*

Recently, I visited New York City (*NOTE: Change this to any large metropolitan area near your home base*), and I watched in awe and wonder as a group of workers were constructing one of those skyscrapers. I was particularly impressed by the men who worked on what they call the "high steel," the skeleton girders of the upper floors of the building. These men would walk across six-inch-wide beams, hundreds of feet above the ground, without any support on either side, and with only lines attaching them to the structure. It made me dizzy just to watch them.

One fellow in particular caught my eye. This man jumped from beam to beam without apparent concern; he swung out on a single line; he hung by one hand in open space; he was absolutely fearless.

I was so impressed by his daring, that when the whistle blew and the men came down from their shift, I sought him out.

"I had to tell you," I said, "that I think you are marvelous up there! I was watching all afternoon, and I can't get over the risks you take. Tell me, what did you do beforehand that prepared you for a job like this?"

"Well," he said, "I used to be a coach at a local high school, but I had to give it up—I lost my nerve!"

SPECIAL DATA: *Time of anecdote: about one minute. Everyone likes to have the difficulty of his or her job acknowledged and*

to be told that he or she is doing a good job. This story
does just that. It will be very well received, particularly
if told before a group of sports professionals, such as
coaches. Be certain to personalize it by changing the
name of the city and by changing the phrase "local high
school" to whatever is appropriate.

6

TOPIC: *Exaggeration and the Coach.*

AUDIENCE: *Suitable for all audiences.*

As you all probably know, Coach Jones is an avid fisherman. Indeed, several of us have been regaled with stories of his adventures on the high seas that could be subtitled "Fish I Have Known and Loved!"

One weekend he told me that he was going trout fishing at the lake. As luck would have it, I happened to be passing Coach Jones' home the next evening as the coach pulled into his driveway and began to unload his gear.

I strolled up and asked, "Well, Coach, how many did you catch?"

My question went unanswered, and, guessing that perhaps the great fisherman had gone without a catch, I pressed it a bit.

"Don't tell me that you spent all day and didn't get a thing!" I said.

"Actually," the coach said, "I did catch one fish."

"Really," I remarked. "Was it large?"

"You might say that," the coach replied. "When I finally landed him after a five-hour struggle, he was too big for my boat, so I had to call over five other boats and we laid him across all five and brought him in. Then, of course, we could never have gotten him up on the dock if we hadn't borrowed the crane from a nearby construction site. Finally, we didn't have a scale large enough to weigh him, so one of the fishermen there took a Polaroid picture. He had to step back about half a mile to get the entire fish into the frame."

"Sure," I said. "How about showing me that snapshot."

"Gladly," said Coach Jones. "I'll show it to you just as soon as it arrives. They're shipping it to me by parcel post. You see, the fish was so big, that the Polaroid weighed 23½ pounds!"

SPECIAL DATA: *Time of anecdote: slightly over two minutes. This is the type of good-natured kidding that can make for an enjoyable evening at a sports dinner. On the serious side, it could be used to lead in to a speech about the difference between exaggeration and the enthusiasm which plays such a key role in all sports.*

$$\boxed{7}$$

TOPIC: *Golf and the Coach; Being a Fanatic.*

AUDIENCE: *Suitable for all adult audiences.*

You all know how much Coach Jones loves golf. In fact, almost every spare moment he has is spent on the links. It is less well known, however, that his wife does not share the coach's enthusiasm for the game.

One Saturday morning, as the coach shouldered his golf bag and headed out the door, he was stopped by his wife.

"Remember," she told him, "that we are having company for dinner tonight. Now, I've had it with your being late because you're out on the golf course. You be home on time—or else!"

The coach affirmed that he would be on time and left for the course. His wife went about preparing for their guests.

Six o'clock came and went, and the coach had not arrived. The guests came, and still the coach was nowhere to be seen. Dinner was ready and served, and still Coach Jones was not home. Finally, the guests, sensing Mrs. Jones' growing anger, excused themselves and departed. Around ten o'clock that evening, it was a furious Mrs. Jones who heard the coach pull into the garage.

The moment Coach Jones entered the room, he raised his hand as if to stave off the attack that he knew would come.

"I know I'm late," he said. "I know it. But, this is a special case. Do you remember my golf partner, Harry Watson?"

"Certainly I know Harry Watson," fumed his wife. "What about him?"

"Well," Coach Jones said as he sat wearily on the couch, "today, Harry and I were teeing up on the second hole, when all at once, Harry let out a cry and fell over. I rushed to his side, but it was too late. Harry must have had a heart attack. He was dead, right there on the second green!"

"Oh, no!" exclaimed the coach's wife, all her anger gone. "It must have been terrible for you!"

"I'll say it was," answered the coach. "After that, it was nothing but hit the ball, drag Harry, hit the ball, drag Harry . . ."

SPECIAL DATA: *Time of anecdote: about a minute and a half. Like the last story, this is just plain fun which cannot be taken seriously. Don't be afraid to use gestures with this story, such as miming someone about to tee off in a game. These actions often add a great deal of humor to a presentation.*

$$\boxed{8}$$

TOPIC: *Misunderstanding; Lack of Communication.*

AUDIENCE: *Suitable for all adult audiences.*

While we are all familiar with Coach Jones' ability as a coach, it is a little-known fact that he was also a fantastic athlete as a youth.

When he was playing ball for (*here insert the name of the college your coach attended*), he was known for his toughness and stamina, as well as for the fact that whatever his coach demanded of him, he delivered.

During one particularly crucial game, the team's defense was being torn apart by the opponent's aggressive and burly linesmen. Consequently, it wasn't long before Jones' coach called him aside.

"Jones," said the coach, "we have to do something. I want you to get in there, get belligerent, and get vindictive. Do you understand?"

"Sure thing, Coach," shouted Jones, and, grabbing his helmet, he charged out on the field.

Nothing happened. For several plays, Jones did nothing. He didn't block; he didn't charge; instead, he seemed to be roaming the field, looking first one way and then the other, almost in desperation.

Finally, the coach sent in a replacement, and when Jones trotted back to the bench, the coach was furious.

"What is the matter with you?" the coach screamed at Jones. "I thought I told you to get out there and get belligerent and vindictive!"

"I tried," Jones complained. "I really did! But, honest, Coach, I looked real hard, and I couldn't find those names on any of the jerseys out there!"

SPECIAL DATA: *Time of anecdote: a little over a minute. It is fine to tell this story about a coach who is being honored or about yourself, when everyone knows that it is nothing more than good, clean fun. Please do not tell this story about one of the players on your team, however, as we feel that there have been enough "dumb athlete" stories to last us forever. Today's athlete is intelligent and perceptive, and we feel you should never give an audience the implication that it might be otherwise.*

9

TOPIC: *Baseball; Visitors From Other Countries; Misunderstanding; Kindness*

AUDIENCE: *Suitable for all audiences.*

I recently had the pleasant task of entertaining a guest from Spain. It was his first visit to the United States, and he was very anxious to see all those activities that symbolize America to the world. Naturally, I wanted to take him to a baseball game. I figured you couldn't get much more American than that.

Therefore, I got tickets for a game at (*Name the major league stadium closest to you*). On the day of the game, I bundled José into my car and set out for the stadium in what I figured would be more than enough time.

I had not counted on the traffic, however, and by the time we finally pulled into a parking space, it was very nearly time for the game to start.

"Come on, José," I told my friend, "we're going to have to hurry!"

And hurry we did. We all but ran through the corridors and were just sinking into our seats when the crowd rose for the national anthem.

As the organist played and the fans broke into song, I looked over at my friend, José, and found that his eyes had filled with tears and his chin was quivering.

When the anthem was finished and the crowd was seated once more, I leaned over to my friend and asked if anything was wrong.

"Oh, no," he said. "It is just that I am overcome by the great hospitality of the American people."

"What do you mean?" I asked.

"First," said José, "when I come into this place, everybody stands up to greet me. Then, they have even hired a musician to play for my entrance. Then, the people serenade me. But, what really made my heart leap up was that everyone was so concerned that I had a good seat for the game. You heard them; everybody here was asking, 'José, can you see?' "

SPECIAL DATA: *Time of anecdote: a little over a minute. Of course, the event could be a football game or any other sporting event. Also, that last paragraph is geared for a number of laughs from your audience. Pause slightly after each sentence, and "build" with your voice in enthusiasm and pitch up to the final punch line. In that way, the laughter will start small and end big.*

$$\boxed{10}$$

TOPIC: *The Value of the Coach; the Coach as Local Hero.*

AUDIENCE: *Suitable for all audiences.*

Recently, I was driving to school on a dank, wet morning with heavy, gray clouds hugging the earth and a fine mist spraying my windshield, when I noticed a car pulled over to the side of the road. Standing beside the car was one of our cheerleaders looking damp and uncomfortable, and staring forlornly at a very flat tire.

Cursing my fate a bit, I pulled over and offered my assistance. The young lady was very grateful; she told me that she had no idea of how to change the tire and was late for her classes already.

I told her to sit in my car and get out of the rain as I went about the task. I have changed a few tires in my life, but never was there a more miserable job than that one. In rain and mud, I labored with wet and slippery tools to get it done. By the time I was finished, I was splattered with dirt and soaked to the skin.

I put away the tools, stashed the flat tire in her trunk, and wearily walked back to my car. I sank into my seat behind the wheel thoroughly exhausted.

"Oh, thank you so much," the young lady said. "I don't know what I'd have done without you."

"It was nothing," I lied, trying to be very cavalier about the matter. "If I hadn't come along, somebody else would have."

"No," she insisted, "you don't understand. I'm driving Coach Jones to school this morning. He's asleep in the back seat, and if you hadn't come along when you did, I would have had to wake him up!"

SPECIAL DATA: *Time of anecdote: about a minute. This is the perfect anecdote to use if you are speaking about a coach who is very popular or one who has just had a successful season. At such times, we have found that the coach's stock is very high. This anecdote acknowledges that fact in a humorous manner. Naturally, if there is any matter of contention about the coach of whom you are speaking, this would not be appropriate.*

$$\boxed{11}$$

TOPIC: *Humorous Lines to Use When You Are Introduced.*

AUDIENCE: *Suitable for any audience.*

SPECIAL NOTE: The following are one-liners that you would use before you began your speech. They should appear to be off the cuff, spontaneous reactions to the introduction you have just been given.

If you are given a particularly flowery introduction:

Thank you, Mr. Smith, for that great introduction. Now I know what the toast feels like after the butter and jam have been smeared on.

After an introduction filled with praise:

Come up to the podium looking puzzled and shaking your head. Pause for a moment, look out at the audience, and say, Whom was he talking about? Is there another speaker on the program?

After an introduction listing your accomplishments:

He forgot to mention that I also take out the garbage on Tuesdays and Saturdays.

After a warm and glowing introduction:

Mr. Smith, I am overwhelmed by your introduction. Imagine what you'd have said if I had given you the free tickets you asked for!

After an introduction before a group of friends and colleagues:

Walk up to the podium, glance over at the person who introduced you, shake your head, look out at the audience and say, Well, I can't do any better than that! *and turn around and sit down. As the laughter dies, get up and return to the podium, smiling all the way.*

SPECIAL DATA: *Time of remarks: a few seconds each. Often, these so-called spontaneous remarks are remembered long after the speech. In any event, it is a good idea to memorize them and keep them as part of your speaking game plan. One word of caution: You must always suit your remarks to your audience, so don't use the last one with a group of people who do not know you well. Also, depending on the group you are addressing, you may not wish to use any of them. You are in the best position to know when these remarks will be appropriate.*

$$\boxed{12}$$

TOPIC: *Lines to Use When You Have Made a Mistake During Your Speech.*

AUDIENCE: *Suitable for all audiences.*

SPECIAL NOTE: Mistakes happen, even to the most experienced speaker. When they do, you can turn a potentially embarrassing moment (not only for you, but for the audience as well) into a moment of shared laughter by the use of the following "spontaneous" remarks. They have been audience-tested and have stood up well.

If you forget your speech:

Bear with me, ladies and gentlemen, and we shall all grow old together.

or

You know, folks, as I grow older, I find that I have difficulty remembering three things—dates, telephone numbers, and the third is . . . er . . . the third . . .

or

Ladies and gentlemen, I've grown so absent-minded that yesterday I was taking a shower and I couldn't remember in which pocket I had left the soap.

or

If you are wearing glasses, take them off and pretend to polish them on your coat; or, take your glasses out of your pocket and very dramatically put them on; or, if you don't wear glasses, rub your eyes with your balled fists. Then, take your written speech (or note cards), hold it prominently in front of you and squint as you move it backwards and forwards, finally ending up with it at arm's length. Say, Oh, so that's where I am! *and continue with your speech.*

If someone in the audience is roaming around or doing something that is distracting you and the other members of the audience:

Excuse me, sir, but I think what you want is out that way and down the hall. It's the door marked Men Only.

If your AV equipment fails:

That's the last time I buy anything during a clearance sale!

or

Well, I'm glad to see that our projector works as well as the government!

or

As I said, let me describe in vivid detail some of the pictures you're *not* about to see!

If you are interrupted by a loud noise:

Lord, did I say something you didn't like?

or

Come on in! There's immediate seating down front.

SPECIAL DATA: *Time of remarks: a few seconds each. Whenever anything goes wrong during your speech, whatever else you do or say, remember to smile. The audience is on your side and wants you to succeed. If you are embarrassed, they will be, too. If, however, you take it in your stride with a smile on your lips and an attitude that assures your audience that everything is all right, then they will not only be at ease, but we would not be surprised if you received a tremendous round of applause for your calmness and good bearing.*

$$\boxed{13}$$

TOPIC: *Dedication and the Coach.*

AUDIENCE: *Suitable for adult audiences and older students.*

I have known Coach Jones for many years, and I am well aware of how dedicated he is to the game. I think one story will show you very dramatically what I mean.

Long before he met Mrs. Jones, the Coach often treated himself to a night on the town. One particular evening, he was seated in a local bistro when a very beautiful and admirably proportioned young lady came in and sat down. They got to talking, and, within a short time, they had established a very nice rapport.

The evening wore on, and the young lady suggested they go up to her place for a nightcap. Coach Jones agreed.

When they got there, the young lady put some romantic music on the stereo, turned down a few lights, and excused herself while she changed into "something more comfortable."

Now, of course, I was not there, but all of this Coach Jones described to me in vivid detail.

According to Coach Jones, the next thing that happened was that the lady in question came out of her bedroom wearing a silk negligee. She walked over and sat down on the couch very close to the coach.

All at once, there was a loud knocking at the door, it burst open, and there stood a giant of a young man, six feet, nine inches tall and covered with solid muscle.

"It's my brother!" shouted the young lady as the monstrous lad stamped into the room.

"Good Lord," I asked Coach Jones, "what did you do?"

"What else could I do?" he told me. "I looked up at this six-foot-nine-inch monster and signed him on the spot for our basketball team. We spent the rest of the night talking about how we were going to the state championship with him playing center."

SPECIAL DATA: *Time of anecdote: slightly over a minute. This is a funny story that always gets a laugh, but it is not for every audience. While far from blue material, which you would never wish to use with any audience, it is a bit suggestive up to the punch line. Therefore, we'd keep it for use* *with a college audience or a group composed mainly of friends.*

$$\boxed{14}$$

TOPIC: *The Coach's Dream—The Perfect Athlete.*

AUDIENCE: *Suitable for all audiences.*

Coach Jones had just started spring training for the baseball team when he noticed a well-muscled youngster standing by the side of the field observing the players at their workout. The coach recognized the lad as a student who had recently transferred to the school from a small town somewhere in the hills.

"Mister," said the boy as Coach Jones approached, "what're those kids doin'?"

"They're training for baseball," answered the coach. "You must know what baseball is."

"Can't say as I've ever heard of it," the youth replied.

With that, the coach explained simply that baseball is a game in which one team tries to hit the ball and the other team tries to catch it. Figuring this was enough of a lesson for one day, the coach asked the boy if he would like to try his hand at it, and the boy replied that he would.

Leading the lad to the batter's cage, the coach handed him a bat, and showed him how to hold it.

The other students on the team smiled and gathered around to witness this first attempt. The pitcher winked at his teammates and went into his windup.

He threw a sizzling fast ball at the plate, and the young man with the bat instinctively took a step into the pitch and swung.

The loud crack sounded like a pistol shot and the ball took off as if it had been fired from a cannon. It flew over the infield, whistled by the outfielders, cleared the outfield fence by a mile and landed at least fifty yards into the field beyond.

The boy stood there at home plate, watching the ball disappear.

"Run!" shouted the Coach.

"Run!" shouted the amazed pitcher.

"Run! Run!! RUN!!! shouted the other members of the team.

With that, the young man threw the bat on the ground and raised his hands to silence the shouting.

"Fellers," he said, "I appreciate your not wanting me to get in trouble my first day at this school, but I've always been taught to be honest. Mr. Coach, if I lost your ball for you, I promise to buy you another one!"

SPECIAL DATA: *Time of anecdote: one and a half to two minutes. This is the kind of story that gets a chuckle and may be used to flow into a discussion of the natural athlete; the contention that athletes are made as well as born; how a coach would go about harnessing such a raw power; or anything along those lines. Told as a joke, it could also be used by a coach when talking about the team's star player.*

15

TOPIC: *Ten Short Remarks and Stories About Sports and Coaches.*

AUDIENCE: *Suitable for all audiences.*

Coach Jones is so honest that when he was in high school, he was thrown off the baseball team because he refused to steal bases.

* * * * * * *

He once told me that he could tell the score of a game before it started. I said, "That's impossible. I'll bet you five dollars that you can't tell me the score of Saturday's game before it starts."

"You're on," he said. "If you go to the stadium on Saturday and look at the scoreboard before the game starts, the score will be zero to zero!"

* * * * * * *

Coach Jones took his wife to a double-header at the stadium. During the second inning of the second game, she nudged him in the ribs with her elbow.

"Come on," she said, "let's go. This is where we came in."

* * * * * * *

Jones is such a dedicated athlete that when he was ill, he refused to let the doctor treat him.

"Come on, Jones," said the doctor. "Let me give you this medicine. You have a fever of 103 degrees."

"Not yet, Doc," moaned Jones. "I want to go for the record!"

* * * * * * *

"I'm sorry," said Mrs. Jones, "but my husband can't come to the phone. He's laid up with a football injury."

"Oh," said the caller, "I didn't know Jones still played football."

"He doesn't," answered Mrs. Jones. "He sprained his larynx at last Saturday's game!"

* * * * * * *

"Coach," I told Jones, "What your team needs is life!"

"I don't think that's necessary," Coach Jones told me, "but I wouldn't mind seeing them get ninety days in the county jail!"

* * * * * * *

Coach Jones took his wife to a professional football game. First, Mrs. Jones was late leaving the house, and then they got caught in a traffic jam. By the time they got to their seats in the stadium there were five minutes left to go in the final quarter and the score was tied nothing to nothing.

"You see," said Mrs. Jones as she indicated the scoreboard, "we haven't missed a thing!"

* * * * * * *

It's a little-known fact that at one time Jones coached the fencing team, but the judges kept throwing him out.

It seems that every time his team made a point, Jones couldn't resist yelling, "Aha! Foiled again!"

* * * * * * *

When Jones was in college, he was an amateur boxer for a while.

I won't tell you how good he was, but once he remarked to his coach that it was a very long way from the locker room to the ring.

"Don't worry about it," his coach told him. "I'm sure you won't have to walk back!"

* * * * * * *

A coach was receiving quite a reputation for his constant arguing with and abuse of the game officials. Indeed, so bad had the situation gotten that the Athletic Director of the school had cautioned the coach on his remarks.

"I want you to show some respect for the officials," said the Director. "I'm going to make it a point to be at your next press conference, and I want to hear you make some positive remarks about them."

At the very next press conference, the coach stood tall and addressed the reporters.

"I honestly believe," said the coach, "that our officials are outstanding human beings; I believe that they are sharp, knowledgeable individuals whose grasp of the game is unquestionable; I believe that the calls they make are reasonable and based upon sound judgment . . ."

The coach's voice trailed off, and, for a moment, he lowered his head. After a few seconds, his head came up and he gazed at the audience.

"But, then," continued the coach, "I also believe in the Tooth Fairy and the Easter Bunny!"

SPECIAL DATA: *Time of stories: from 5 to 45 seconds each. These are short jokes that can be used to advantage in any sports-oriented speech. Be careful how you use the ones about Mrs. Jones, however. Many women are not only actively engaged in sports themselves, but are more knowledgeable about sports than many men. Therefore, make certain that your audience knows that these stories are all in good fun, and that you are not serious. If you are at all in doubt, we'd suggest changing Mrs. Jones to a male friend of Coach Jones.*

| 16 |

TOPIC: *Sports and Gambling; Point of View.*

AUDIENCE: *Suitable for adult audiences.*

Recently, Coach Jones attended a coaching clinic. He was on his way home that evening when he passed a race track. On a whim, he decided to stop.

After he had paid for his admission, he discovered he had only a five-dollar bill. In the third race, there was a horse called Coach's Delight, and on an impulse, he placed the five dollars on the horse to win.

Not only did it win, but it paid 20 to 1, and Coach Jones now had $100. In the fourth race a horse called Perfect Team was running, and Jones placed all $100 on this horse to win.

Perfect Team paid 10 to 1, and the Coach now had $1,000. Coach

Jones bet the entire amount on a horse in the fifth race named Player of the Year. It won and paid an amazing 10 to 1. The coach now had $10,000!

In the sixth race a horse named The Coach Will Win was running. Coach Jones' eyes widened when he read the name, and, by special arrangement with the track, he placed all $10,000 on the horse, who went off at 50 to 1.

The Coach Will Win led the field by two lengths—up to the three-quarters pole. Then it slowed visibly and all but trotted across the finish line dead last!

Later that day, the coach drove into his driveway, and his wife was waiting for him.

"You're late," she said. "Did you stop by the race track?"

"Yes," said the coach, "I did."

"How did you make out?" asked Mrs. Jones.

"Not too badly," answered the coach. "I lost only five bucks."

SPECIAL DATA: *Time of anecdote: about two minutes. This anecdote concerns gambling, so you will have to use your discretion when deciding if you should use it with a particular audience. However, it is much more than that. It also shows the importance of keeping a positive attitude in life and, by projection, on the playing field. This was the way we originally heard it used, as a lead-in to a very inspirational speech on the importance of outlook and attitude to good performance. You might consider using it in this way as well.*

$$\boxed{17}$$

TOPIC: *Ideas and Creative Thinking.*

AUDIENCE: *Suitable for all audiences, particularly coaches.*

I had an idea just the other night;
     A fantastic idea it was, too.
Magnificent, wonderful, clear, and concise;
     Ingeniously smart through and through.
It was just unforgettable, wondrously bright,

Immortal and eternal, too;
And once I remember it, then I just might
Be able to share it with you.

SPECIAL DATA: *Time of poem: about 45 seconds. We wrote this poem for a speech on creative thinking. For the coach, you might want to alter the first two lines to read:*

I thought of a play just the other night;
And, Oh, the great things it could do.

The rest of the poem would still be appropriate. The point of this poem is that while many people have good ideas for solutions to problems, they sometimes fail to share those ideas or act on them. Consequently, what might have been an ideal solution is lost. The rest of your speech might exhort those involved to share their ideas in the hope of mounting a true team effort toward a winning season.

18

TOPIC: *The Coach and Discipline.*

AUDIENCE: *Suitable for all audiences.*

Coach Jones was furious with the lackadaisical and listless performance of his team at practice. Finally, he blew his whistle and addressed the group.

"Before you retire to the showers, gentlemen," he snapped, "I want you to do ten laps around the track for your terrible practice this afternoon!"

"Coach," said the captain of the team as he stepped forward, "when you played on a team, did your coach make you run punishment laps?"

"You bet he did!" answered Coach Jones.

"And, when your coach was playing," continued the captain, "did his coach make him run laps?"

"Yes," Coach Jones answered, "my coach told me that he did."

"And, when that coach was playing," the captain went on, "did he have to run laps?"

"I'm sure that he did and his coach before him," said Jones. "What are you getting at?"

"That's just my point, Coach," said the Captain. "Don't you think it's time we put an end to this inherited brutality?"

SPECIAL DATA: *Time of anecdote: about a minute and a half. The coach's task, in part, is to build a team, and discipline, especially self-discipline, is a necessary part of that process. You might use this story as a lead-in to a speech about that topic.*

19

TOPIC: *Two Poems on Humor and the Value of Laughter.*

AUDIENCE: *Suitable for all audiences.*

The value, the worth, and the power of mirth
Can help each of us to get through
When the going is rough and incredibly tough,
And even the sunshine looks blue.
For once you give in to a chuckle or grin,
Your spirits just naturally lift,
And life is worthwhile each time that you smile,
For a laugh is a God-given gift!

S. R. Mamchak

*   *   *   *   *   *   *

Laugh, and the world laughs with you;
Weep, and you weep alone;
  For the sad old earth
  Must borrow its mirth,
But has trouble enough of its own.

Ella Wheeler Wilcox

SPECIAL DATA: *Time of poems: under a minute each. It seems appropriate to end this first section with these two poems. Professionals have long known that humor is an essential element in any endeavor. It can enliven classes or meetings; it can make a point in such a way that the listener just has to agree; it can make the most trying of times and the most insurmountable of problems a little easier to bear. Humor has a place in our speeches, just as it has in our daily lives.*

Afterthoughts

While we have been exhorting you throughout this section to use humor in your speeches, it is also wise to remember that you are professional coaches and not stand-up comedians. Indeed, while humor is a very tasty dish, you must remember that it is a garnish and not the main course. We could think of no worse mistake for a coach than to give a speech consisting solely of one joke or humorous anecdote after another. If we are going to speak, our very positions demand that we give speeches of sum and substance.

Of course we should use humor when it is appropriate. Used at the beginning of a speech to set the tone, relax the audience, or lead into your topic, it is an outstanding device. It is fine to use humor during your speech to occasionally make a point, or as an example. Nothing is as effective as humor at the conclusion of your speech to leave your audience in a favorable mood to accept what you have said. Combine these techniques with a speech in whose body rests workable, practical, and sincere ideas, observations, and suggestions, and you will give a speech that any audience will long remember.

SECTION 2

A Coach's Blueprint
for
Introductions,
Transitions, and
Benedictions

Not all the public speaking you do as a coach will be in the form of full-length speeches. Certainly, you will have your share of invitations to speak formally before many types of gatherings, but there will also be those occasions on which your main speaking task will be to fill in. We speak, here, of those times when you are acting as Master of Ceremonies and must introduce other speakers and/or activities; when you must announce a transition from one activity to another or one part of a program to another part; or when you are called upon to offer a benediction over an activity, meal, or event.

As a general rule, introductions should be kept short. After all, the speaker is the main attraction. Nevertheless, introductions cannot be sloughed off. They must be precise, and they must prepare the audience for the speaker or event that is to follow. Humor may be used in introductions when appropriate (for example, when the audience realizes that you and the speaker are close friends), but it should not be overdone.

Transitions are, perhaps, the most difficult of the informal speaking tasks to handle. Moving an audience from one hall to another, for example, can be disastrous unless it is done properly. Here, preciseness of language, a good sense of humor, and a sense of leadership and command enable you to effectively handle the situation.

Benedictions can also be very tricky. We live in a pluralistic society, and numerous religious viewpoints and beliefs may be represented in any single audience. Therefore, care must be taken to phrase benedictions in such a manner that no individual member of the audience feels offended in any way or left out.

In this section, you will find relatively short but highly effective introductions for a variety of individuals; practical and tested transitions for a wide range of situations; and dignified but nonsectarian benedictions and blessings for many occasions.

We are certain that you will find what you are looking for.

INTRODUCTIONS

$$\boxed{20}$$

TOPIC: *General Introduction of a Coach.*

AUDIENCE: *Suitable for all audiences.*

Ladies and Gentlemen.

Of all the services that we, as parents, perform, perhaps the most pressing and most important is that of preparing our children for the world they will face as adults. In times past, this meant that a father taught his son a trade or a mother taught her daughter the intricacies of housework. We are well aware, however, that with changing times and the proliferation of information that we have witnessed in our lifetimes, this is no longer feasible or desirable. Instead, we have schools and colleges, and we entrust our children to educators in the hope that, with the help of these people, they will gain knowledge while we nurture their personalities at home.

Because education is so vital to every child, when we meet an educator who goes above and beyond the daily requirements of the job; who seeks out the spark in each child and kindles and fans it until it blazes forth in curiosity and a thirst for knowledge; who sees in each child the man or woman he or she will become and leads that child down a path toward a happy and productive adult life—when we meet such an educator, we can do nothing less than give him our thanks, our admiration, and our applause for a job well done.

We have such a man with us tonight. A coach who, for the past twenty years, has worked with our children, not only building their physical health and developing their bodies; not only teaching them to think in critical situations; not only honing their skills; but also a man who has worked with their minds and hearts to teach them trust and fairness, courage and honor. We have with us a man who can teach these virtues because he lives them every day of his life.

I speak, of course, of Coach Bill Jones. I hope that he knows how much we thank him in our hearts. I'm sure that he can feel the admiration of this group tonight; and I know that by our applause, we will all say, "Well done, Bill. Well done!"

Ladies and gentlemen, I give you our speaker for this evening, Coach Bill Jones!

SPECIAL DATA: *Time of introduction: about two minutes. This type of introduction would be used at a very formal occasion such as a testimonial dinner, or if the coach were to be the keynote speaker at some event. It also implies that the coach has worked with young people for a long time. With a few minor changes, this could fit a female coach equally well.*

$$\boxed{21}$$

TOPIC: *Specific Introduction of a Coach.*

AUDIENCE: *Suitable for all audiences.*

Ladies and gentlemen.

What do you call a man who, after college, served his country for three years, earning, in that time, a Purple Heart and a Silver Star Medal? What do you call a man who, when he returned to civilian life, dedicated himself to helping the youth of his community? What do you call a man who has coached basketball, wrestling, and soccer, and given our children the inspiration and the drive to attain local and state championships? What do you call such a man?

What do you call a man who, when his strenuous day's work is done, volunteers his services to help children who are less privileged than those he coaches in the school? What do you call a man who has organized the youth of our community into teams that give them direction and a constructive use of their spare time? What do you call such a man?

I call him a fine example of a human being. I call him a member of the community to whom we can look with pride and gratitude. I call him our speaker for this evening whom we are privileged and happy to have with us.

Ladies and gentlemen, I give you Coach Bill Jones!

SPECIAL DATA: *Time of introduction: about a minute. Let us assure you that, should you ever have to introduce anyone, a listing of that person's accomplishments is always cor-*

rect, always fits the situation, and always makes an effective introduction. Incidentally, the repetitive technique used in this introduction is extremely effective and dramatic for any formal speaking task.

$$\boxed{22}$$

TOPIC: *Introduction of a Principal or Administrator.*

AUDIENCE: *Suitable for all adult audiences.*

When a game is played and won, when victory is ours, who gets the credit? The answer is that it must be split many ways. Certainly the players deserve praise, but so does the support personnel on the team; so do the cheerleaders who inspired the team; so do the fans who cheered and praised, and played each game in spirit; so do the parents of the players for their undying and endless support. In a few isolated cases, even the coach gets *some* credit! (*This is a very funny line and will get some laughs if you are a coach delivering this introduction.*)

There is, however, one person whom we have forgotten. This may be because this person does not seek the credit or the limelight. This may be because this person is content to do his job out of the spotlight and without the cheering crowd to provide continual support. Whatever the reason, we too soon forget that a great deal of the credit for any sports program goes to the principal of our school.

Here is a man whose job it is to oversee not one team, but every team in the school. This is a man who takes the final responsibility for everything that happens both on and off the field. This is a man without whose encouragement, support, and leadership, the teams and programs simply would not function.

Yet, he is a quiet man who takes his credit in the knowledge that he has helped; in the feeling of accomplishment as he sees the students of our school work and play and strive and win. He is a man who has dedicated his life to work for others without the attention, without the glory, without the newspaper articles and headlines.

Ladies and gentlemen, I am privileged and honored to introduce this man to you, and I know you will want to tell him, by your applause, exactly how you feel about him.

Ladies and gentlemen our principal, Mr. Howard Smith!

SPECIAL DATA: *Time of introduction: a minute and a half. While this introduction is written for the principal of a school, there is no reason why, with very small changes, it could not be used for a Director of Athletics, a Community Youth Administrator, or even the Mayor of a town. In general, administrators do perform vital and relatively thankless jobs, and it is fitting and proper to acknowledge their contributions.*

23

TOPIC: *Introduction of a New Coach.*

AUDIENCE: *Suitable for most audiences.*

Ladies and gentlemen.

I am about to introduce to you the man who, in a very few days, will take over the coaching of our football team. As you are all aware, this is a far from easy task and requires a person of very special talents indeed. I think we have before us just such a person.

After a brilliant college career as a player at State University, he went to Smalltown, where he coached their football team for three years and brought them up to a divisional championship. Following that, he served as coach at Anyville for six seasons, during which they brought home four divisional titles and a state championship. With these successes behind him, he spent three years at Techtown and organized the school's first football team, leaving them with a very impressive record.

Now he comes to us, and, considering the fact that he can't seem to hold down a steady job, I think he'll be perfect for us.

Ladies and gentlemen, help me welcome our new football coach, Mr. Bill Jones!

SPECIAL DATA: *Time of introduction: about one minute. The new coach rarely has an easy time of it, especially if he is replacing a coach who was well liked and admired. Your listing of the new coach's impressive record along with the small joke that sets everyone at ease and tells the audience that you like him can go a long way toward smoothing that person's path.*

$$\boxed{24}$$

TOPIC: *Introduction of a Friend.*

AUDIENCE: *Suitable for all audiences.*

When I was eight or nine years old, I would get together with a friend of the same age, and we would tell jokes like: What has eighteen legs and catches flies? Answer: A baseball team. Then, we would roll around for a while, not only laughing at the joke, I think, but rejoicing in the happiness of being together.

Over the years our faces and bodies changed, but our friendship remained the same. No, that's a lie. It didn't stay the same; it deepened. As we grew and our taste in jokes improved, so did our knowledge of the world around us. We experienced wonder, disillusionment, and pain, but our friendship was always there to share the wonder, to provide a firm and solid foundation in the face of disillusionment, and to ease the pain.

I came to know my friend as someone I could depend on in all situations. I came to know him as a person of consummate skill, lively intelligence, unquestioned honor, and deep sensitivity.

While life took us down different pathways, our friendship has always been a bond that joins us over the miles as well as the days. Tonight, I am proud to have my friend on this stage with me. I know that you will come to admire him as much as I do.

Ladies and gentlemen, let us welcome my friend, Coach Bill Jones!

SPECIAL DATA: *Time of introduction: slightly over a minute. Obviously, you may wish to say some special things about a personal friend whom you are introducing, and this introduction is an excellent framework to hang them on. Please, never tell anything about your friend that he, himself, would not want published in the local newspaper. This is not the time to tell the audience that his nickname was Stinky or that you stole apples from Farmer*

*MacGregor's tree. Always keep the introduction of a
friend warm, personal, and wholesome!*

$$\boxed{25}$$

TOPIC: *Introduction of an Athlete.*

AUDIENCE: *Suitable for students and adults; team members and laymen.*

Coaches may give pep talks and compliments, parents may point with
pride to a helmeted player on the field, cheerleaders may exhort a crowd
to cheer and sing out an individual's name and number, but once the game
has started, the player is alone on that field with his teammates. The coach
fades in the distance, the noise of the crowd fades to a whisper, and even
the cheerleaders are a blur along the sidelines. Once that game starts, the
athlete and his fellow players must concentrate on pitting their strength,
skill, and intelligence against an opponent who is equally as anxious and
ready to win.

In such a situation, leaders inevitably emerge. On every team I have
ever coached, there has been that player who goes the extra step in out-
witting the opposition; who supports his teammates and gives them the
courage and faith to carry on when all looks dark and hopeless; who is
always ready to do what is required and more; who accepts the blame or
the credit with equal grace and dignity.

This is the true athlete; the one who is admired because he has
achieved the integration of mind and body that is the model for all players;
because he is not only a fine athlete, but an outstanding human being as
well.

It is just such a player whom we have with us this evening. He is a
young man whom I have personally known for the past four years both on
and off the field. He is a person whom I would gladly call one of my best
players and one of my friends. I am overjoyed to have him as both.

It is with great pride that I introduce a truly fine human being, Mr.
Tom Henderson!

SPECIAL DATA: *Time of introduction: a minute and a half. This is the
type of introduction that may be given for any fine
athlete, although it may be amended by adding a per-*

sonal anecdote about your relationship to the individual if you wish. Remember, however, that this will add time, and your audience is there for the speaker, not for you.

26

TOPIC: *Humorous Introduction of a Fellow Coach.*

AUDIENCE: *Suitable for an audience composed of colleagues and friends.*

Ladies and gentlemen.

There is absolutely no truth to the rumor that Coach Jones has been signed to coach jai-alai next season in Tijuana.

We need Bill Jones here. He is an essential part of our athletic machine. If he didn't scrub out the locker room after each game, can you imagine how that place would look?

His team loves him. Just the other day, I was passing by the locker room, and do you know that his players have placed Coach Jones' photograph on the wall? That's right, and let me tell you, some of those kids are getting pretty good at the darts they keep throwing at it!

I have known Bill Jones for years. I remember the day he started coaching football. He wanted to get everything right, so he came to me with a plan for getting a touchdown by using the ground rule double rules. Whatever happened to that plan, Bill?

Bill is an inspiration to his team. He's always out there leading them to the field, leading them to victory, leading them to the showers during the third quarter!

There's one more thing about Bill Jones—he loves to laugh. This is exemplified by the fact that he has allowed me to share a little fun with you at his expense. It is very typical of the man that you want to laugh with him and could never think of laughing at him. He doesn't need me to sing his praises; his record and his personal integrity do that every day. He doesn't need me to tell you what a fine and warm human being he is; each of us in this room has reason to know that on a personal basis.

In fact, the only thing he needs me for is to say, ladies and gentlemen, I give you our friend, Coach Bill Jones!

SPECIAL DATA: *Time of introduction: about two minutes, depending on audience reaction. If you are giving a humorous introduction, always pause and wait for the laughter to die down from one line before you begin the next. Also, whenever you are going to use humor in an introduction (and it should only be with a very good friend) it is always wise to clear it with the person first. If the person has any objections, don't use it.*

27

TOPIC: *Three Humorous Lines for Acknowledging an Introduction.*

AUDIENCE: *Suitable for all audiences.*

(SPECIAL NOTE: These lines should follow your introduction and come before the formal opening of your speech. If possible, they should sound spontaneous.)

For a humorous introduction from a friend:

I want to thank you for that introduction, George, and I just want you to know that if it takes my entire life, I'll get you for this!

For an introduction filled with praise:

You'll have to excuse me, but I'm a little shaken up. Harry, that was a beautiful introduction, but just before I came here this evening, I was reading some of my press clippings, and, Harry, I don't know how to tell you this, but some of those reporters don't see it the same way you do!

For a truly glowing introduction:

Gosh, thanks, Tom. Now all I have to do is live up to that!

SPECIAL DATA: *Time of remarks: several seconds each. These remarks are very useful in getting the audience to laugh, break the ice, and put the audience in a receptive mood, particularly if the introduction has been highly complimentary, as they usually are. Memorize them until they are natural to you and use one of them or the ones* *in the first section the next time you are introduced. We think you'll see some very positive results.*

Afterthoughts

In ending this part on introductions, let us bring your attention to the fact that, in all introductions, the name of the speaker is reserved for the very end. This is an excellent technique, as it ends your introduction on a positive note. Your voice should rise a bit toward the end, and the name of the speaker or person you are introducing should be pronounced loudly and clearly. It is also wise if you, as the person doing the introducing, lead the applause for the person. Just say the person's name and start applauding. The audience will naturally join you. Turn toward the speaker, acknowledge him with a slight nod, and then back away from the podium. Never turn your back on the audience or the speaker.

TRANSITIONS

$$\boxed{28}$$

TOPIC: *Moving an Audience of Adults to a New Location.*

AUDIENCE: *Adults; parents, colleagues, and perhaps team members.*

. . . and that brings us to the close of this section of tonight's program. In a few moments, I'm going to ask for your cooperation, but first, I'd like to ask you a very important question.

How many people here believe that using logic and reason is better than ranting and raving?

(You will find that all hands will go up. In a group situation such as this, no one is going to admit that he or she is emotional. Review the sea of hands for a moment.)

Well, this is really something! It looks as if everybody here believes in reason. I think that's tremendous!

Why did I ask you that question? Well, the next part of tonight's program is going to require that this entire audience get up, move through the two exits to my right *(raise your right hand as you say this)* and take seats in the auditorium down the hall.

Considering the size of this audience and the size of our hallways, if we all try to do this at once, there is going to be a lot of the ranting and raving I spoke about a moment ago and that you just told me that you don't like.

But, you do like reason, or so you said, so I'm going to ask you to be reasonable—and do it my way! *(Smile)*

Therefore, what I'd really like is for everyone on the right side of the center aisle *(hold up your right hand again)* to leave slowly by Exit A, which is right over there *(indicate Exit A)*, turn left, and enter the auditorium through the doors you will find that are marked AUDITORIUM. *(Smile)* At the same time, I'd like everyone on the left side of the center aisle *(hold up your left hand)* to leave slowly through Exit B, which is the door in the back of the hall *(indicate Exit B)*, turn right, and enter the auditorium through the other door marked AUDITORIUM.

All right, now I have another question. Would someone in this audience be kind enough to give me five hundred thousand dollars? No? Well, would any person who has that half-million dollars to give me please stay seated, and all the rest of you please rise.

(Smile as you say this. You may have to encourage the audience by repeating the last line. When they are all standing, smile broadly, and keep smiling as you say . . .)

Well, as nobody wants to give me money, and as you're all on your feet anyway, let's leave here the way I just described and assemble in the auditorium, all right?

Oh, and one more thing—thanks for the cooperation; I really appreciate it.

I'll see you inside . . .

SPECIAL DATA: *Time of transition: two to three minutes. This is a case where you are dealing with a large group of adults and must move them to another location. Notice that nowhere was the audience ordered to do anything. Rather, through the use of humor, they were gently guided into the move. Naturally, the topography of your auditorium will differ from the one used above, but if the move is well planned in advance, and the entire speech is delivered with a smile on your lips and the proverbial*

*"twinkle in your eye," the audience will not only go
along with it, but will admire your cleverness. Be certain to follow the directions in the speech, as you must
make certain that the audience knows exactly where to
go and how to proceed.*

29

TOPIC: *Transition from Off-Season to Preseason.*

AUDIENCE: *Potential team members; team personnel; colleagues.*

Welcome.

Well, it's that time again. For several months, you have gone your
separate ways, and I'll wager that you enjoyed it. After all, it's great to
have free time to be able to spend with your families and engage in those
activities that we like to do by ourselves. There is a certain satisfaction in
being able to sleep late on a weekend morning; to eat what we want without
worrying about waistlines; to have a day that is unstructured, with no one
to tell us what to do or where to go. Yes, those days are very valuable,
and we all need them from time to time.

But that has passed, for today you sit here at the start of our preseason.
Many of you know from experience, and those who don't have probably
been told, that over the next few weeks your time will be structured; you
will have to watch your diets; and you will be in for a great deal of hard
work, sweat, frustration, and, yes, pain. Out of that work will come our
team for this year, and some of you, in spite of the hard work, will not be
there.

Why, then, have you come here today? Why have you chosen, of
your own free will, to put yourselves in this situation where you will have
to give up so much that is enjoyable in return for hours of sore muscles,
cuts and scrapes, and someone who looks like me watching your every
move and telling you, in a slightly raised voice, that you have all the grace
and control of an elephant on a surfboard? Why have you done this?

I don't think I can give an answer for the entire group; each of you
has an answer in his heart that suits him, personally. But, if I know you

as I think I do—if my years of experience as a coach have taught me about you—then I know the answer has to do with a personal commitment to do something with your life that is constructive; it has to do with proving something to yourself; it has to do with giving of yourself for the good of others; it has to do with honor.

Whatever *your* reason; whatever combination of those I just mentioned, I congratulate you on your decision. Yes, over the next weeks, you will be tested as you have never been before, but I'm going to guarantee you that you will be the better for it. You are going to develop from a group of individuals into a team with all the spirit and brotherhood that that word implies. You are going to look into a mirror and see someone who can stand up anywhere and be proud of a job well done!

You are *all* winners because you have chosen to be here today. I am proud of each and every one of you. If you believe in yourself and work toward your goal, I have no doubt that you will be able to achieve it.

I know you have the intelligence; I know you have the drive; I know you have the courage. I know you are winners!

It starts now!

Come on, winners, let's go!

SPECIAL DATA: *Time of transitional speech: about four minutes. Whether it's a sandlot team or semipros, this is the type of speech that will have them on their feet and ready to go during those first crucial days of preseason. It also does not hurt to plant some inspiration and self-esteem in your players. A speech such as this is long remembered and appreciated.*

$$\boxed{30}$$

TOPIC: *Transition from Preseason to Season.*

AUDIENCE: *Team members; team personnel; colleagues; interested adults.*

You have worked hard.

Perhaps that is the greatest understatement since Noah said, "It looks like we're in for a little rain." I have been with you, and I have seen you sweat; I have seen you so tired it was all you could do to lie on your back and try to breathe; I have seen you fail and fall only to get up and go at it again and again until you succeeded.

I have witnessed all of this, and I feel proud and privileged to have been a part of it. Over these past weeks, I have seen dedication, courage, generosity, and spirit as I have seen it in few other places and at few other times. I have watched a group of fairly undisciplined individuals pull themselves together into a functioning, cohesive unit that is our team. I have seen people accomplish physical feats they would not have believed possible only a few weeks ago. All this I have seen, and I am prouder of you than my words can possibly express.

Now, that time is a part of your past. It is a time to be cherished, of course, but it is a time to be remembered as we look toward the future. Behind us lie the weeks of preseason, but before us lies the season itself, a time when we will be tested, not on the practice field with our friends and teammates, but on the field of athletic competition, facing another team that has worked and sweated, and that also wants to win.

Listen to me now, and listen well: There is not a single doubt in my mind that each of you will meet that test and conquer it. I could not have been with you this long without coming to know you, and I *know* that each person here will work for the team; will be supported by the team; will give to the team; and will march with the team to ultimate victory.

If we have tried; if we have given everything it is within us to give; if we have stayed with it and never given up; if we have worked as the team we have become, then whatever the score, *we* will be the true winners!

I was going to offer you my wishes for good luck, but I'm not going to do that. You don't need luck. You have your individual intelligence and skill; you have commitment and drive and purpose; and, as the team you are, you have each other.

That is enough for anybody!

SPECIAL DATA: *Time of transitional speech: about four minutes. This is the type of speech that could be given before the first game of the season, or the night before that game, or at a school or community function before the season starts. At any of these latter events, it is quite common to have the press present, and remarks such as these must be delivered with that in mind. The active support and belief of the coach is a most important factor in* *team success, and this speech assures the players of exactly that.*

$$\boxed{31}$$

TOPIC: *Transition from Season to Off-season.*

AUDIENCE: *Team members and personnel; adults and community members.*

My grandmother had an old expression that she was fond of. She used to say, "A baby cries and someone dies." I think that what she was expressing was the fact that life goes on. One phase ends, and another begins. It is a never-ending cycle of changes that takes us from our births through the ultimate change.

In a very small way, we have just experienced one of those changes. From a loose group of people, some in better condition than others, we have pulled ourselves together into a functioning and a winning team. We have come to know each other and depend on each other as brothers. We had our disagreements, as all families do, but we were one. We were one in practice; we were one in spirit; we were one on the field; and we were one whether the outcome was defeat or victory.

Now, that season, that phase of our lives, has come to an end. For some of you, it has ended for a few months; for others, this is the start of your life without this team of which you have become a part.

There is sadness in this, certainly. There is always sadness when we must leave those we have come to know and cherish, if only for a little while. I know that I will personally miss each and every one of you, and I hope that, for many of you, this is a mutual feeling.

However, the time we have spent together has been of value. We have learned from each other as we have learned from the experiences we shared. We go our separate ways now, but the unity and strength that we forged together over the past months will serve us well in whatever we will face in the future.

We have grown; we have learned; we will remember and be strong!

From the bottom of my heart, I thank you for the time we had together.

Enjoy your time off—you deserve it!

SPECIAL DATA: *Time of transitional speech: about two and one-half minutes. It is our personal belief that any activity in which people have spent some time and effort should be brought to a close with both a look backward and a look ahead. To merely have something end, without a word said, can be disheartening. Therefore, this speech puts a definite topper on the season and gives players and anyone else who may be present a good summary of what has been accomplished both on and off the field.*

$$\boxed{32}$$

TOPIC: *Transition from One Coach to a New Coach.*

AUDIENCE: *Players, personnel, colleagues, administrators, general public.*

In a few days I will begin what I see as one of the most exciting and challenging periods in my life. I will be taking on the responsibility for coaching *(name the institution or the team).*

I know this will entail a great deal of hard work and will require not only my full attention and concentration, but the aid and assistance of all members of the team and the coaching staff. I am aware that it is a difficult assignment, but it is one that I look forward to with the enthusiasm inspired in me by the words and deeds of John Smith, the coach I am replacing.

Now, I just said that I am replacing Coach Smith, but that's not true. I have seen Coach Smith's record; I have heard several of you speaking about him; I know of the admiration, loyalty, and respect that he inspired in all those who knew him. Therefore, I know that no one can replace him, certainly not I.

Rather, I shall be carrying on the work that he started. It is Coach Smith who is responsible for the groundwork that has resulted in the dynamic and vital organization that faces me. It is he who has inspired, led, trained, and shaped a winning athletic machine. It is he who gives me the courage to carry on his work and the confidence of knowing that I have on my side the finest group of athletes and support personnel.

I know that this is something I cannot do alone. I know that it will require the cooperation of everyone here today. I know that I shall make mistakes that will require your understanding. I know, too, that I can reach out to this organization and receive the cooperation and understanding that will be so vital to the success of each and every one of us.

I ask for that cooperation; I ask for that understanding. With it, I intend to earn your respect.

We have the heritage of Coach Smith to guide us and sustain us in the days ahead; we have the power and fortitude that comes from dedication and resolve; we have the will, the desire, and the skills. Together, we will carry on; together, we will strive; together, we will succeed.

I am proud to be a part of you!

SPECIAL DATA: *Time of transitional speech: about two and one-half minutes. It is never easy being the "new kid on the block." This is especially true if you are taking over the coaching duties from someone who was loved and admired. It is wise, therefore, to acknowledge and honor the coach whom you are replacing. This speech not only does that but also aims to establish a feeling of unity by starting out as an individual and ending as a part of the team. This is extremely effective in these situations.*

Afterthoughts

In any speech where a transition is involved—between one place and another; between one time and another; between one situation and another—the key elements in your transitional speech should be threefold. First, there should be recognition of the past. That is, you, as speaker, should acknowledge what has been done previously or the situation that existed previously—the off-season just past; the work of the previous coach; the season just completed; and so on.

Next, there should be a recognition of the feelings of the audience. Those feelings may be positive (after a winning season), or they may be negative (when the team is reluctant to return to a strict regimen after an off-season or feels natural antipathy to a new coach). Whatever the feelings, the speaker must acknowledge that they exist. Tell your audience that you understand how difficult it is to give up the freedom of the off-season for hard work and practice, or that you know that the previous coach was special and engendered special feelings. This lets the audience know that you understand them and their emotions.

Finally, there must be a "looking forward" and a rationalization of the new phase to come. This can be as simple as explaining the procedures for moving from one place to another, or as complex as providing the rationale for a new policy, but it must be done so the audience will understand the next move in the scheme of things.

If you handle it in this manner, the audience will understand and appreciate whatever transition is to come. They may not always like or approve of it, but they will understand its necessity and will be better disposed to cooperate.

BENEDICTIONS

$$\boxed{33}$$

TOPIC: *Benediction for a Sports or Athletic Activity.*

AUDIENCE: *Mixed audience; students, players, adults.*

Dear Lord . . .

In a few moments, these fine young people will engage in a contest of their skill, their knowledge, and their physical ability.

We ask You to bless their actions. We ask that they may play well, striving on the athletic field as they will strive in life. May they strive for excellence using the knowledge they have gained, and do their best at all times, even if everything looks hopeless. Most important, may they play as they will live—with honor, with fairness, with sportsmanship, and with an appreciation for the worth of others.

We ask You to look after their well-being and to protect them on the field.

We ask You to bless this endeavor. Whatever the outcome, may we have given our best and take consolation in the fact that, win or lose, we have given all that we had to give.

We thank You for this opportunity as we thank You for each other. May we continue to grow ever closer, and may that unity be pleasing in Your sight.

SPECIAL DATA: *Time of benediction: slightly over one minute. If you are ever asked to give an invocation or blessing before* *a game, whatever you say, don't ask God to let your team win. We know of one person who got into trouble when he gave an invocation in which he asked God to defeat the opposing team. You can well imagine what the local press did to him, not to mention the alumni association of the opposing school. The purpose of the activity is the playing of the game, not winning or losing. This should be reflected in the benediction you give.*

$$\boxed{34}$$

TOPIC: *Benediction for a Dinner, I*

AUDIENCE: *Suitable for all audiences.*

We have come together this evening to share our food and our fellowship. As that food nourishes our bodies, may the closeness and fellowship nourish our minds and our hearts. May we grow ever closer in mutual friendship, love, and respect for one another.

As we share this evening, let us share our lives with everyone we meet. Let us give of ourselves as nourishment to others. Let us help to sustain each other through joyous times, such as this evening, and times that are less joyous as well.

May our joy in each other be unconfined; may the memory of this evening enrich our lives for some time to come; and, may what we feel for each other at this moment be reflected in our relationships throughout our lives.

SPECIAL DATA: *Time of benediction: about one minute. Blessings before meals should be kept short and to the point. This one is adaptable to all audiences from a team breakfast or dinner to any affair composed solely of adults. It is completely nonsectarian, says some very basic but very sound things about living and life, and may be used any time you are asked to provide the blessing.*

$$\boxed{35}$$

TOPIC: *Benediction for a Dinner, II*

AUDIENCE: *Suitable for most audiences.*

Dear Lord . . .

We are your children, for You are the Father of all.

We have gathered here this evening to share our love as soon we shall share our food. We ask you, Father, to bless that food and to bless this assembly. As we partake of Your bounty, may we come to know each others as brothers and sisters in Your divine love.

We thank You for the blessings we receive tonight, and for each other. May both gifts be worthy in Your sight, and may we be worthy of them.

SPECIAL DATA: *Time of blessing: about forty-five seconds. You undoubtedly noticed some similarity between this and the previous benediction. The chief difference is the invocation of the Supreme Being. We sincerely doubt that there is anything in this that could offend a member of any religion, but it does mention God prominently. You will have to be the judge, therefore, whether or not it is suitable for your audience. We have used it several times, and haven't had any objections.*

$$\boxed{36}$$

TOPIC: *Benediction for the Dedication of an Athletic Facility.*

AUDIENCE: *Anyone who attends dedications: adults, students, team members, press, general public, etc.*

We have come together today to dedicate this building, but before we do, it is fitting that we ask the Lord's blessing.

We all know that a building, of itself, is nothing more than stone and glass and paint and brick. We know that a building is only a shell. However, we also know that after today's dedication, it will become much more than that. It will become a place of learning, a place to train our young men and women as athletes, and a place where they will grow in spirit as well as in body.

We pray, therefore, that the young athletes who will use this place will find in it the skill and concern of their coaches so that they may develop their skills until they are as sharp and fine as they are capable of becoming. We pray that they may find in this building the knowledge that will help them not only on the field of athletic competition but in life as well. We pray that in this place they will come to know themselves and to know others and will develop the respect, honor, and love that will carry them through life as worthy human beings.

We ask you, Lord, to bless this building, and we ask that its use may always be favorable in Your sight. We ask, also, that You grant that today will be but the beginning of many tomorrows filled with personal growth, true and honest sportsmanship, courage, honor, and unity for all who use it.

Bless us as well, Lord, and grant that we may always use this place in accordance with Your divine will.

SPECIAL DATA: *Time of benediction: about a minute and a half. A speech such as this can often set the tone for what is to come, particularly if you are the head coach or even one of the coaches who will use it. As many influential people are usually present at a dedication, as well as members of the press, a speech such as this should be well prepared and well delivered. It can state your philosophy as well as asking God's blessing for the building.*

37

TOPIC: *Benediction for an Activity Involving Patriotism.*

AUDIENCE: *Suitable for all audiences.*

". . . one nation, under God, indivisible . . ."
Let us take those words to heart and learn to live by them, for they

are so much more than mere words. They are a belief, a creed, that has shaped the course of our nation as it has shaped the lives of everyone present here today.

For we *are* one nation. We are united in our belief in the quality of life. We, who are concerned with the youth of our country, strive constantly with this ideal in mind, providing guidance to each person so that he or she can become the best that he or she is capable of becoming.

We are also "under God," for we know that with the help of the Lord, we will continue to grow as a nation, continue to offer the best we have, continue to grow closer into one people with the common goal of achieving the best possible society to nourish and support each and every citizen.

We also know that "under God" we are indivisible. Working together, with God's blessing, we will become a solid force for peace and democracy in the world; a stronghold of freedom of which we may all be justly proud.

Therefore, we ask God's blessing on the activity that we are about to begin. May our efforts here today bind us together as Americans, as one people, now and for all our tomorrows.

SPECIAL DATA: *Time of benediction: about one and one-half minutes. Many athletic events are held during times closely associated with patriotic holidays, such as Thanksgiving, Memorial Day, Veteran's Day, and the Fourth of July, just to mention a few. Audiences seem well disposed to patriotic messages, especially at sporting events. We have much to be proud of as Americans, and it is right and proper to state this every now and then.*

38

TOPIC: *General, All-purpose Benediction.*

AUDIENCE: *Any audience, any time, anywhere.*

> We have gathered at this place and time
> >In fellowship and pride,
> And this gathering is a tribute
> >To the love we feel inside.
> And, by that love we know we're blessed

In very special ways
That give a purpose to our lives
And meaning to our days.

Oh, may we always have the chance
To join, as friends will do,
In fellowship and unity
That no one can undo.

And may our lives illuminate
The world and all its parts,
As being here together brings
A sunrise to our hearts.

S. R. Mamchak

SPECIAL DATA: *Time of poem: less than one minute. If you do not have the time to make up a benediction, or none of the others in this section seem appropriate for your particular occasion, we recommend this one. It is short, simple yet sincere, completely nonsectarian, and fits any occasion people have gathered for, be it a sporting event or a dinner. This is easily memorized, and you will always have an appropriate benediction should you be asked.*

39

TOPIC: *Benediction for an Awards Ceremony.*

AUDIENCE: *Suitable for all audiences.*

In a few moments, we shall be honoring those individuals who have proven themselves outstanding on the athletic field. These people have excelled above and beyond our expectation; given all they had to give and then, somehow, found a deeper reserve of strength and courage, skill and determination, intelligence and fortitude from which to draw.

It is right and proper that we present them with these tokens to tell them that we are proud of them, and that we recognize the contributions that they have made.

But, I wish them something else this evening. I wish them the award of a life well lived. I wish them the respect of their fellow human beings for their good deeds and their selflessness. I wish them the sense of accomplishment that comes from giving of themselves. I wish them the love of many that will warm them through their coldest days. I wish them a time of reflection so that they may realize that the world is better for their having been in it.

What they have accomplished so far, as this occasion testifies, is ample proof that all of these wishes are within their grasp. May they continue to strive for perfection to benefit us, as their accomplishments have filled us with pride and thankfulness that they have been a part of our lives.

SPECIAL DATA: *Time of benediction: about one minute. This is really a mixture of a benediction and a transitional speech like the ones we saw earlier in this section. It doesn't only convey good wishes and give a sense of purpose to the occasion; it also gives a look backward and a look ahead for the awards recipients, which is what a transitional speech should do. This combination makes it ideally suited to any function where an individual or group of individuals will receive awards.*

Afterthoughts

There is something important to keep in mind when you are called upon to deliver a benediction or a blessing. The vast majority of athletic events in this country are school-related in some way. The policy of separation of church and state mandates that no prayer of any kind be allowed in public schools. However, the general public quite often requests benedictions at occasions such as those reflected in this section. Quite often this task falls not to a clergyman, but to you.

When this happens, there are some general rules to be followed. For example, blessings or benedictions should always be kept short. It is far better to say one or two lines and sit down than to ramble on and risk losing your audience.

Moreover, you must always remember that, as we said at the beginning of this section, in our pluralistic society it should be the speaker's goal to see to it that no one in the audience is slighted, offended, or made to feel inferior or left out because of the content of the benediction. Therefore, it is important to be certain that the benediction is either one that makes no particular religious references or is worded so that no one of any religious faith will feel slighted.

The benedictions in the last part of this section are specially tailored to meet those requirements. Even the ones that ask God's blessings directly are written in such a way that no religious group could possibly object.

Remember, also, that a benediction is a serious address and humor is not appropriate. The sincerity, honesty, and forthrightness of the speaker will inevitably carry it off.

SECTION 3

A Game Plan
for
Opening and Closing
Speeches

An *important* part of every coach's life is his participation in the various programs that are held throughout the year. These can range from activities directly connected to his institution, to informational programs for the general public, as well as conferences or panel discussions for the sports professional.

Frequently, someone is asked to open or close the program with a speech, especially when the program consists of a number of speakers or a single expert who will speak at length or a panel discussion of some sort. This is not a task that can be taken lightly, and the chances are very good that sooner or later, it will fall to the coach to be the speaker.

The speaker who opens a program sets the tone or theme for the evening. The speech is not expected to be long (after all, the people came to see the program), but it should be lengthier than an introduction. This kind of speech usually gives an overview of the subject to which the speakers who follow will address their remarks. It should focus the attention of the audience on the evening's subject matter and make them anticipate what is to come.

When a speaker closes a program, generally he or she is expected to summarize what happened during the program. The audience has listened to the entire presentation, and the closing speaker should bring the program into perspective for them. If he can also give the audience a greater understanding of what has been said, then so much the better.

There is an old saying among speakers: "Tell them that you are going to tell them; tell them; tell them that you've told them." Your job as opening or closing speaker lies at both ends of that statement. You tell the audience what is coming and set the tone, the program is performed, and then you tell the audience what has been learned over the course of the evening.

The first half of this section contains opening speeches on a wide variety of common topics. The second half contains closing speeches on the same topics. In this way, you can see exactly what is required for each occasion.

OPENING SPEECHES

$$\boxed{40}$$

TOPIC: *Opening Speech for a Sports Night Activity*

AUDIENCE: *Mixed audience; students, faculty, parents, alumni, etc.*

Good evening, ladies and gentlemen, and please forgive me.

Forgive me, because I am about to tell you a joke that I once heard and it will undoubtedly offend everyone here. All I ask is that you bear with me, because it does have its point.

The story goes that at a conference-leading college, they had a first string wide receiver who was renowned for his spectacular catches and equally well known for his miserable grades. Just before the "big game," the math professor announced that the boy would not be able to play, as he was flunking that subject so badly, he couldn't even pass a basic examination. The coach pleaded with the professor to give the boy a make-up examination, and, after much pleading, the professor agreed.

On the day of the exam, the coach brought the wide receiver to the math professor's office.

"All right, young man," the professor said, "we'll make this an oral exam. For your first question, please tell me how much is six plus five?"

The football player frowned and thought and finally looked up and said, "Er . . . twenty-three?"

"This is impossible!" the professor roared. "That's it; this boy has flunked the course!"

"Aw, come on, Professor," the coach pleaded, "give the kid another chance. After all, he only missed it by one!"

(In spite of the way in which you have prepared your audience for this story, there will be laughter. Wait for it to die down, and then continue.)

You did laugh, didn't you? That's because it's funny; it's the type of funny story that has been told about athletes and coaches for years and years. The image of the big, looming, and incredibly dumb athlete with his equally simple-minded coach has been giving comedians and writers fuel for decades. There's only one problem with it—it simply isn't true!

Sports are part of every school curriculum, basically because we realize that the ancient goal of a healthy mind in a healthy body is not a fantasy but a realistic and attainable goal. The playing fields of today have a place for strength, it is true, but, as anyone who has ever taken the time to find out knows and knows well, they have no place for mindless strength. Sports, as they are practiced in our world today, require quick, intelligent minds as well as healthy, trained, and conditioned bodies.

You here tonight are the living proof of that. Indeed, none of you would be on our teams if you did not carry adequate academic averages. We know that participation in sports requires the type of quick thinking, analysis, and decision making that only someone who has trained his or her mind can accomplish. An athlete who must size up the situation on the field, analyze all the possibilities, choose the correct option of play, and act decisively to execute that option, all in a split-second's time, simply cannot be a mindless brute who is unable to add six plus five and come up with the right answer.

So, perhaps it is fitting that we laughed at that story; laughed at it as an example of a false idea that is dead forever; laughed at it as living proof that it is false; laughed at it because, in our hearts, we realize that it was intelligence—a great deal of intelligence—combined with dedication and skill, which has brought us to this very night.

I salute you all. I salute you for your prowess on the playing field and I salute you for your academic status and the work that went into it; I salute you for your bodies, and *your* minds!

This is truly your night, and it is my sincere wish that you enjoy every minute of it. I cannot think of anyone who deserves it more!

Thank you.

SPECIAL DATA: *Time of speech: about five minutes. Everything in this speech is true and it is very well received by any group engaged in sports or sporting activities. The stereotype of the dumb athlete has haunted the scene for too long, and this speech deals with it directly and positively.*

41

TOPIC: *Opening Speech for a News Conference*

AUDIENCE: *Adults; mainly members of the press.*

Ladies and gentlemen of the press . . .

In a few moments, my colleagues and I will be answering your questions. I am certain that you must have many of them, and I assure you that everyone shall have his or her turn.

I have always admired journalists. Although it isn't very widely known, I tried writing for my college newspaper. Even then, I was very sports oriented, so, naturally, my editor sent me to cover a concert given by the college orchestra. The first, and last, piece I ever wrote ran something like this: "Last night, our college orchestra played Beethoven. In a hard-fought contest, Beethoven lost, four to zip!"

In my short-lived career, however, I did get a brief taste of the difficulty of your task. That is why I want you to know that we appreciate your skills, and we will certainly do anything we can do to make your life a little easier where we are concerned.

The public is anxious for news of sports and sports activities. Whether that news is their consuming passion or brings a few relaxing moments into their day, they have a desire as well as a right to know. It is also your right as well as your duty to report that news; to bring into their homes the factual information, the sidelights, and the insights that make sports an exciting and vibrant concern of so many.

In this task, I would like to believe that we are partners. Certainly, I have my job to perform and you have yours, but working together in an honest and open relationship, I hope that we can produce the type of news that will enhance the lives of all your readers and all our fans.

I promise you honesty, and I promise you candor. I promise that you will know when I am pleased as well as when I am displeased. I promise that if you ask a question, it will get an answer—not an answer clouded in doubletalk, but a straightforward, honest answer that states the facts as I see them.

In return, I ask only that you ask. Has there been speculation about the prospects of one of our players? Don't guess; ask, and you will get the answer. Are we contemplating a major change in our team? Don't ask others, ask us. We will tell you; we will keep you informed; we will see to it that you get the true story you need to keep your sports-minded public informed and current.

An honest question deserves an honest answer, and that is why we are here this evening. Let us start our partnership of truth now, right now, and hope that throughout the season, we may continue to grow together for our mutual benefit and for the benefit of the public as well.

SPECIAL DATA: *Time of speech: about three minutes. As a coach, you* *want the press on your side. That doesn't mean that they must always paint you as the reincarnation of Knute Rockne. Rather, it means that should something come up that might potentially throw a shadow on you or your team, they will seek out your views before they write an article. We feel that this is best achieved by honesty and by making yourself available to the press. Consequently, opening the first news conference of the year with statements such as these can only be beneficial.*

$$\boxed{42}$$

TOPIC: *Opening Speech for a Conference on Sports Medicine*

AUDIENCE: *Adults; coaches, trainers, people directly involved with the topic.*

When I was playing football, the coach once called me from my position of semipermanent bench-warmer and told me to go in for a particularly important play. I was ecstatic. I grabbed my helmet, waved enthusiastically to the crowd whom, I believed, had waited all game just to see me play, and trotted toward the field with the grace and speed of a young gazelle.

While I was still on the sidelines, I stepped in the water bucket, fell face forward, and broke my nose.

It was a terrible embarrassment at the time, but it has served me well in my later years, especially when my wife starts dropping hints about how nice it would be if I painted the house and I sigh deeply and tell her how happy I would be to do so if it weren't for my old football injury!

Actually, outside of that one broken nose and several cuts and bruises, which is a price paid happily by every athlete I know, I received no injuries; I have no lasting scars; I feel I am the healthier for the experience.

This is the experience of the majority of people who engage in sports. Outside of very minor, easily treated inconveniences, they have engaged in their sport, and they have been better for that involvement.

That is not the entire story, however. Unfortunately, the same sports experience that has meant health and vitality to so many has also meant pain, disability, and even permanent damage to others.

If we think back and remember hard enough, I dare say that everyone here this evening has heard of someone or been involved with someone who has suffered an injury that has permanently marred his life.

Yes, we can tell the stories of paraplegics and quadriplegics who will never walk again or even be able to handle a ball. We can tell of people who walk with permanent limps, who see with a single eye, who will carry a useless hand or arm for life. Most tragically, we can tell of young athletes for whom a particular game was their last act on earth. We can tell of these things, and our hearts swell with the sadness they convey.

Perhaps it is right that we pause to reflect on these things, but only for a moment, because we are doers. It is our job to be out with our players helping, encouraging, building them into the athletes they wish to become. That is why we are here today.

Throughout this program, we will hear of advances in training and health care for the athlete that are aimed at preventing injuries. We will learn what medical science can do for the injured athlete. We will hear and learn about viable plans and techniques that minimize the risks while maximizing the benefits.

Because we are the doers, the learners, the facilitators, we will walk away from this session with what we have learned and carry it with us back to the training and playing fields; we will implement our new-found knowledge; we will coach and teach with a new awareness, and that awareness will serve our athletes both now and throughout their happy and productive tomorrows.

For every coach I know, this is a goal well worth any time and effort, and I am certain that after tonight's program we will all agree that we have been privileged to attend something that will mark the beginning of a new and greater understanding for us all.

SPECIAL DATA: *Time of speech: about three minutes. There seems to be quite a concentration of late on the techniques of sports medicine, a field that was unheard of a decade ago. The advances made in this field, however, are nothing short of phenomenal, and conferences of this sort seem to abound. If you are ever asked to open such a program, this speech sets the groundwork for what is to come and also reminds the participants exactly why they are there.*

$$\boxed{43}$$

TOPIC: *Opening Speech for Any Conference or Program Where Some New Material Is to Be Presented.*

AUDIENCE: *Suitable for all audiences.*

If you enjoy nature and the out-of-doors as I do, perhaps you have shared the experience that I had when I stood on the bank of a mountain stream and watched it flowing in the golden, late-afternoon sunlight.

I stood for some time and watched the water as it bubbled and splashed over the rocks and stones that had been worn smooth by its passage. In places, it leaped and frothed, while elsewhere it whirled and eddied. Its passage was turbulent, and beyond the place where it was hidden behind a stand of trees, I knew that there were rapids, boulders, and cataracts. Nevertheless, its beauty held me in its grip, and the water that flowed through my fingers when I stroked its surface was clear and bright, and twinkled in the glare of the afternoon.

In that same area, however, there was a pool that had gathered from the seepage of the river, and I visited that as well. That, too, had its beauty, with majestic pines standing guard around it, and its surface calm and tranquil, devoid of the turmoil I had witnessed a few moments before at the bank of the raging river.

However, when I dipped my hand below the silent surface and lifted a palmful toward the sky, the water lay dark and lifeless, hazy with the growth of microbes and bacteria, stagnant and unappealing.

What was the difference? In the first case, the river moved; it flowed. True, it might have been filled with the crashing of rocks and the splash of whirlpools, but as long as it kept moving, it was alive and vibrant. In the meantime, the pool was calm and peaceful, but with the lack of movement the water had become brackish and stale.

In a very real way, we have a choice of being like either of those two bodies of water. We can choose to remain where we are, using only the knowledge that has brought us to this point in our lives, and avoid all that is new or anything that may challenge what we have come to rely on as comfortable routine. That's a safe move, and it has its own, particular comfort. Like the pool in the forest, however, the "water" that is your life and mine will begin to take on the color of dust; will become hazy with the endless stream of days too much the same; will atrophy and die long before our bodies pass the same way.

Or, we can choose to be like the river that crashed ahead, fresh and vibrant. We can accept the validity of what we know, while at the same time keeping an open mind to new ideas, methods, and techniques.

There is a danger in this, to be sure, for every new idea is a challenge; can mean a revision in our lives and routines; and may change the direction in which we thought we were going. However, while there will be rocks, boulders, and whirlpools to surmount and conquer, we, like the flowing river, will remain fresh and vibrant. We will look at ourselves, and know that we are alive!

We are about to hear some new ideas and insights. Let us flow like that sparkling, crystal stream. Let us open our minds to these new ideas and strategies. If we do, we will be confident that when we do discard a strategy or technique, we do so not because it is old, but because it no longer works. If we use a new technique, we know that we use it not because it is new, but because it *works*!

The very fact that we are here today indicates to me that we have opened our minds and wish to flow like that sparkling river, continuing to breathe life and vitality into all that we do, both now and throughout the years to come.

SPECIAL DATA: *Time of speech: about four minutes. This type of speech can be used to advantage for any program where new material is to be presented, whether it is of a philosophical nature or consists of actual training methods. This is also a particularly good opening speech for any program where the speaker or speakers are going to voice opinions that may be considered controversial. The speech asks for openness and understanding, and that is exactly what you would want under those circumstances.*

$$\boxed{44}$$

TOPIC: *Opening Speech for a Testimonial Program.*

AUDIENCE: *Adults; friends and colleagues, invited guests.*

Mark Twain once told the story of a man who had been seized by the townsfolk of a small midwestern city for some offense. He had been tarred and feathered, and, in the tradition of the early frontier, was being ridden out of town on a rail. Someone asked the culprit how he liked what was happening to him. Twain reports the gentleman answered that if it were not for the honor of the occasion, he would just as soon miss it.

Our guest this evening might well make the same comment, but, I hasten to add, under totally different circumstances. He has come here tonight to be honored by us in a highly public manner, and we all know how deserving of it he is. In the speeches that will follow, you will hear of his accomplishments, his heroism, his concern, and his humanity. You will hear these things from people who work closely with him and who are his friends, as well as from people whose lives he has touched in unique ways. Indeed, you will hear of the wonder of this man from everyone except one person—the man himself.

I am certain that if you asked him about his life-long contributions, he would tell you that he didn't do anything special; he just did his job. That is the type of person he is. It is that humility and that sense of selflessness when working for others that endears him to us.

Yes, we have gathered here to honor this man, but in a sense it is not he who is being honored. We will merely state the facts, and they will speak eloquently for themselves. Truly it is we who have been honored— honored by his presence with us; honored by the efforts of his lifetime; honored by the fact that we may say that we know such an outstanding human being.

Therefore, let us begin by hearing from a man who knows our guest very well . . .

SPECIAL DATA: *Time of speech: under two minutes. This is a typical opening speech for an activity where you are going to act as master of ceremonies and introduce successive speakers. This speech gives a definite beginning to the program, puts the audience in a receptive mood, reminds them why they are there (that never hurts), and ends in the introduction of the first formal speaker of the evening. In place of "this man" or "our guest" you would use the person's actual name. Unless you are a personal friend of the guest, use the person's full name (Bill Smith) or his name and title (Coach Jones; Mr. Jones), because you want to avoid anything that smacks of being contrived, like calling a person by a familiar name or nickname when the audience knows that you have a passing acquaintance at best. Also, when you* *come to the end of the last full paragraph (. . . such an outstanding human being), turn toward the guest and begin applauding. The audience will join in. This provides a small honor for the guest, gets the audience ready to applaud later, and provides a logical ending to your speech so that you may immediately introduce the first speaker.*

$$\boxed{45}$$

TOPIC: *Opening Speech for a Fund-Raising Activity.*

AUDIENCE: *Students and adults; generally supportive crowd.*

Ladies and gentlemen . . .

Welcome and thank you. Thank you for being here this evening; thank you for the support you have shown in the past and will show in the future; thank you for your enthusiasm and your concern.

I would like to tell you how happy I am to see you here this evening, but that would be an understatement. I am ecstatic, I am overjoyed, and, I am somewhat in awe of you.

I say that because I know that you are all busy individuals with lives to lead and many activities to pursue, and yet you have chosen to work and devote your time and energies to a cause in which you believe. You continue to give new meaning to the words devotion and dedication.

As a coach, it has been my privilege to witness outstanding acts of courage and heroism. I have seen individuals work and push themselves to their limits in order to attain a goal which they considered important. I have seen people sacrifice glory that might have been theirs alone so that the team might succeed. I have seen people reach the end of their endurance only to reach deep within themselves and find there a reserve of strength and courage. I have seen all this, and I have been proud to be a part of it.

I want you to know that in my heart, I am just as proud of each and every one of you. I see your courage; I see your work; I see your sacrifice; and I know that you are a team as fine, dedicated, and selfless as any that ever took a field to play a game. I know this. I am proud of it. I am proud of you!

However, just as every team member knows our plans and what ultimate victory will mean, so it is fitting that you understand just what your efforts will bring . . .

(At this point, detail what the funds raised will be used for, what these funds will mean to the people or institution that receives them, and the precise goal of the fund-raising activity in which they are participating.)

You are here because you understand the value of the goal toward which you are working. You are here because you have the drive, the enthusiasm, and the will to work unselfishly for a common goal. You are here as a team, as dedicated, courageous, and purposeful as any athletes who have come under my direction.

Are you ready to work together? (*) Is our goal worthwhile? (*) Can we do it?(*)

I have no doubts! I *know* that *we* can succeed! I *know* that *we* are ready! And, most important, I *know* that, working *together*, we—that's you, me, and everyone whose lives will be affected for the better by what we accomplish—*we will win!*

SPECIAL DATA: *Time of speech: three to five minutes depending on audience reaction and inserted material. This is a real barn burner of a speech. If, at the end of it, you don't find the audience cheering wildly, then perhaps you've been giving your speech to an empty parking lot. When you are asking the questions at the end, pause each time (we have indicated the pause with (*)) and wait for an audience response—it will be there. Then, with the final paragraph, emphasize the italicized words, and, when you come to the phrase "We will win!" throw up both arms in a typical victory stance. It really doesn't matter if you are raising money to get new uniforms or to build a new stadium, the people who are working to raise those funds are very special and very important. This speech recognizes that fact, gives them a sense of importance and purpose, and shows them that they are appreciated. It is an excellent opening speech for all activities of this type.*

Afterthoughts

As we said at the beginning of this section, opening speeches must set the tone for the program that is to follow. We hope you will agree that all of the preceding speeches do just that. Moreover, they have been crafted to keep that tone upbeat and positive. For the most part, they give praise and recognition to the individuals or groups who will be participating in the activity. All opening speeches should have these qualities if they are to be successful.

The speeches that follow are examples of closing speeches. They are for the same types of programs as the opening speeches just presented. This will allow you to have an opening and a closing speech for the most common programs in which you, as a coach, may be involved.

CLOSING SPEECHES

$$\boxed{46}$$

TOPIC: *Closing Speech for a Sports Night Activity.*

AUDIENCE: *Mixed audience; students, teachers, parents, alumni.*

Ladies and gentlemen . . .

The last award has been given out; the last student athlete has been honored; and the last speech of the evening is about to begin. This evening is drawing to a close.

Yet, as we all know, the end of each evening implies the beginning of a new day. What kind of day will tomorrow be?

Judging by what we have seen here this evening, tomorrow will be a bright and fair day filled with hope, because these fine young people whom we have honored this evening will be a part of it.

The British have a saying which claims that their military battles were won "on the playing fields of Eton." Eton is a school that has produced many of England's greatest military and naval heros. The saying refers to the fact that many of those leaders believed that they achieved knowledge and perfection in tactics, decisiveness, analysis of the situation, quick thinking, and leadership and command as part of the sports they played at their school.

There is much to be said for that. This evening, we have had a chance to observe our young athletes in a social situation, just as we have often had the opportunity to observe their prowess on the field. We can see the confidence, the poise, and the good-natured sportsmanship that their participation in sports has brought them. We cannot help but be impressed.

To them I say, "You do us proud!" Through your efforts; through your commitment; through your hard work, you have trained your minds along with your bodies; you have grown in every aspect of your lives. You are, indeed, a credit to your school, a credit to your parents, and a credit to yourselves.

Our thanks go to everyone who attended this evening and helped to make it the enjoyable experience it was—to our marvelous speakers, whose wit and insight entertained and stirred us all; to my fellow coaches, whose dedication to excellence and the ideals of sportsmanship and fair play have truly inspired us all; to our parents—our long-suffering, loving, nurturing parents—without whose support and encouragement none of this would have been possible; and, to our student athletes who, in the final analysis, made all of this worthwhile.

Thanks to you all.

Have a very pleasant evening, and good night.

SPECIAL DATA: *Time of speech: about three minutes. In speeches such as this, where the audience is composed of students and parents, your aim must be toward acknowledgment of student effort without forgetting the others who have contributed to it—parents, teachers, other coaches, and the like. This speech does just that, and it is well-received by such an audience. Sports banquets or awards activities are one of the most frequent functions at which a coach is likely to be asked to speak, and it is sensible to be prepared.*

47

TOPIC: *Closing Speech for a News Conference.*

AUDIENCE: *Adults; mainly members of the press.*

Thank you, ladies and gentlemen.

While this press conference is over, I wish to express my personal desire that this not be an ending, but that it be the beginning of an ongoing relationship between us—the team and all its constituent personnel, and you, the members of the press.

From the caliber of the questions asked this afternoon, it is evident to me that you are not only a perceptive and knowledgeable group, but you are people who wish to get to the truth and see us as we are. No one on this team has any objection to that, and I know I speak for everyone here when I tell you that in the future we will continue to welcome your questions and try to answer them with candor and openness.

I hope that this truthfulness and open atmosphere of communication between us will allow you and your readers to see us as we are: neither supermen who can do no wrong nor supervillains who can do no right, but, rather, as a group of people who are individuals striving to do the best possible job we can both on and off the field.

Certainly, we shall make mistakes, for that is the nature of the human animal, but we shall also do everything in our power to learn from those blunders and make certain that we do not repeat them. That is the glory of the human spirit.

I hope that you will have much to report about us that is good and to our credit, but we will not shirk from our responsibility to keep you informed about anything that keeps us from reaching of our goals, either. With the open atmosphere that has been established this afternoon, I hope that we may all share both our happiness and our sorrow and come out the better for the experience.

We all look forward to many more opportunities for communicating with you, both individually and as a group on occasions such as today's.

Thank you again for your time and attention.

Good afternoon.

SPECIAL DATA: *Time of speech: a little over two minutes. Take a good look at what this speech does. First, it cements a positive relationship between you and the press. Second, it acknowledges that you (and your team) are not flawless, but pleads a strong case for understanding when mistakes are made. Third, it forges a bond between you and the press where (without actually being stated) you have identified your team with them. Consequently, although no journalist is ever going to gloss over some glaring blunder, you can expect a fair treatment in the press and journalists will be more disposed to print your side of a controversy should one arise. Whether you are the coach of a Little League or Pop Warner*

*team or the coach of a major sport in a major college,
a good, sound working relationship with the press is
one of your strongest and most viable assets.*

48

TOPIC: *Closing Speech for a Conference on Sports Medicine.*

AUDIENCE: *Adults; coaches, trainers, people directly involved with the
topic.*

I am certain that I speak for everyone present tonight when I express
my heartfelt thanks to the members of this panel for their insights and the
invaluable information they have shared with us this evening. I know that
I learned a great deal, and I am sure that every member of this audience
has come away with, at the very least, a greater appreciation for the role
of sports medicine in both preventing and treating sports-related problems.

I'd like to give a special thanks to Dr. Thomas Martin for his insights
on proper warm-up techniques in order to prevent injuries during practice
and play . . .

*(As in the example above, thank everyone on the panel individually,
giving the participant's name, the topic about which he spoke, and a short
comment, preferably from notes you have taken, as to the value of their
speeches.)*

. . . thanks to your expertise, this has truly been a worthwhile and
profitable evening.

As I listened this evening, I could not help thinking of how many
tragedies might have been forestalled and how much pain and suffering
eliminated had this knowledge been available when my contemporaries in
the audience and I were playing our sports. Certainly many injuries would
have never occurred and many people with disabilities today would have
never experienced their limitations had this knowledge been available
then.

That, however, is the past, and our remembrance of it is only useful
when we can use it to build for the future. Today, thanks to medical
research and a proliferation of knowledge to meet a pressing need, we are
aware of methods and techniques for minimizing, preventing, and treating

injuries to ensure that our athletes may participate in their sports as healthy and productive individuals both now and in the future.

It is up to us now to use the knowledge we have learned, to implement the techniques and methods, to see to it that procedures are followed that ensure the continuing health and well-being of every participant.

Our lives are involved with sports, and we have all dedicated ourselves to helping young athletes achieve and better themselves. Consequently, we are dedicated to our players. Because of this, I know that we shall take with us tonight a new purpose, and resolve that, armed with knowledge, we will work even harder to ensure the physical health and safety of each and every person who is in our charge. We can do no less, because we care.

Again, thanks to our panel and thanks to you, our audience, for your concern and your desire to learn. Countless athletes, many yet unborn, will profit from your dedication.

Thank you, and good night.

SPECIAL DATA: *Time of speech: about three minutes, depending on how many people you thank and what you say about them (see body of speech). We've come to the conclusion that it is very often just as necessary to thank the audience for its participation as it is to thank the speakers. Here is a case where you want the audience to use and implement what they have learned from the program. Consequently, an appeal to their dedication may well ensure that helpful ideas presented will be tried and used by those who participated. This type of closing excites and challenges the audience to use what they have learned, and that is a worthy goal for you, as closing speaker.*

49

TOPIC: *Closing Speech for any Conference or Program Where Some New Material Has Been Presented.*

AUDIENCE: *Suitable for all audiences.*

Ladies and gentlemen, that brings to a close this evening's program. I thank you all for your attendance and I thank our speaker for his open and candid remarks and presentation.

Ideas are like sparks struck from pieces of flint. They can glow for a moment, a brief second, and then fade away into the air; or they can glow and ignite a flame which, fanned and tended, can ignite a fire. So much depends on the material on which those sparks fall and the person who is doing the striking and the fanning.

Tonight, we have heard many ideas that have glowed in our minds. Whether they produce a flame or a momentary flash will, in the final analysis, depend on you and how you receive them. I know that our speaker has provided all of us with much to think about and consider, as I am sure we all will over the coming days, and I thank him for that. We have listened, absorbed, asked questions, and used our minds, and I know that we are all the better for that.

If there is one mark of our democracy, one quality, that sets us above the darkness of repressive regimes throughout the world, it is our right to express our ideas, to talk openly and without fear about them, and to choose of our own free will, without coercion, whether or not we shall believe or act on those ideas. In that sense, we have all been privileged tonight to participate in an exercise in those fundamental ideas of democracy that have made us the beacon of freedom for the world.

It is up to you, as it always has been. I am certain that the process of absorbing new ideas, considering and weighing them, and making our own, individual decisions, will continue to make for healthy, active minds that will benefit us and our society both now and in the years to come.

Thank you for your participation.

Good night.

SPECIAL DATA: *Time of speech: about two minutes and thirty seconds. This is a particularly good closing speech for any program where the material presented might be considered as controversial. What you have said is that ideas cannot hurt them, that they have a choice, and that controversy has its place in any democratic situation. Particularly if the ideas expressed in the program have inspired a great deal of resistance in the audience, this exhortation to the open and free exchange and consideration of ideas will go a long way toward ending the evening on a positive and upbeat note.*

50

TOPIC: *Closing Speech for a Testimonial Program.*

AUDIENCE: *Adults; friends and colleagues, invited guests.*

Ladies and gentlemen . . .

When this evening began, I was fairly certain that I knew our guest of honor and knew him well. I was certain that I respected him as a fine and upstanding individual. I was certain that I honored him for his outstanding achievements throughout his brilliant career. I was certain of all these things. Now, I'm not so sure.

Did I really know this man? Tonight, along with all of you, I have heard people tell of the time he has devoted to others and the good that he has done, all of which I had never heard before, certainly not from his lips. This has given me a new understanding of this man and the type of person he is. True, I knew him as a quiet individual who did his good deeds in private, without the glare of the spotlight, but I never realized the extent of that humility and of those good works until I heard others tell of them this evening. In a way, it is like rereading a cherished book, turning a page, and finding that there is an entire chapter that you had missed before; a chapter just as marvelous and awe-inspiring as what you had come to know, but golden with possibilities for discovery.

Did I really respect this man? Like most feelings that are personal and deep, I knew what I felt for him over the years, but I had never put those feelings into words. Tonight, I know that the depth of that respect, rather than diminishing with time, has grown stronger over the years. We have heard of his contributions and the exemplary way in which he has conducted his private and professional life both on and off the playing field, and we stand in awe of his honesty, his courage, and his determination. We hold him as a model against which others must be judged. There is a term for that feeling—respect. Tonight, I know that I feel it more deeply and more personally than I ever have before.

Did I really honor this man? Yes, I knew what he had done; what he had accomplished both for others and in his own life, but did I ever tell him what I felt about that? He is so unassuming that it seems natural, when you are around him, to forget the greatness of the man and to see him as another figure in a daily parade of faces. In much the same way, I am certain that the people gathered for the dedication at Gettysburg may have thought that it was interesting to hear the president speak, even if it was rather short and unimportant. I will not make that mistake again. I will not wait until he is no longer there to realize what an honor it is to be with him for a day, an hour, a few minutes.

Knowledge. Respect. Honor. These are three words with which our guest is very familiar, because they are part and parcel of what he is as a human being; they are beacons that have guided his life; they are the qualities he instills in others whom his life has touched.

On this occasion, however, it is we who stand in awe of his accomplishments and who experience deep gratitude for his many contributions to us over the years who use those three words in regard to him. We know him for what he is; we respect him for what he has done and continues to do; we honor him for a lifetime of selflessness and devotion.

(The speaker should turn toward the subject and address the following paragraph to him.)

Knowledge. Respect. Honor. These are yours tonight, not because we have decided to hold a special program for you, but, rather, because you live those qualities; because you embody those virtues; because you are deserving of them each and every day of your life.

Ladies and gentlemen, I give you our guest this evening: a man we know, respect, and honor; a man who continues to enrich the lives of those about him each and every golden day.

SPECIAL DATA: *Time of speech: four to five minutes. It is more or less traditional for the guest of honor at these affairs to say something after the final speaker (that's you), so this speech ends with an introduction of the guest. You would start the applause yourself, while turning toward the guest. If he rises to speak, shake his hand and back away from the podium. If he chooses not to speak, thank the audience after the applause has died down, and say good night. When you are closing a program such as this, remember that you are representing the entire audience in summing up their feelings toward this individual. Please remember to call him or her by name rather than "this man" or "our guest" as we did in this sample. Make it personal and sincere, and you can't miss.*

$$\boxed{51}$$

TOPIC: *Closing Speech for a Fund-Raising Activity.*

AUDIENCE: *Students and adults; generally supportive crowd.*

> *SPECIAL NOTE: We are going to give you two closing speeches for a fund-raising activity. This first one is for the conclusion of the event that starts the fund-raising drive.*

You have a long, hard road ahead of you. It will be difficult. It will be beset by frustration, long hours, and difficult labor.

Tonight, you have heard the plans and you know the goal of our fundraiser. You know that what you do in the next few weeks will benefit yourselves and the many who will come after you. You know the importance of the goal for which you have chosen to work and devote your time.

Yes, it will be a long, hard road, but I have every confidence that I will see you all at the end of it. Yes, it will be difficult, but I know you, your dedication, and your resolve, and I know that difficulty is no deterrent to you. Yes, it will be beset by frustration, long hours, and labor, but I have worked with you and I know that you will turn frustration into victory; I have worked with you, and I know that long hours mean only more time in which to work and give of yourselves for others; I have worked with you, and I know that you understand that only through our own labor and the work of our individual lives can we accomplish our goal for the good of all, even those who do not choose to work with us now. I have lived and worked with you, and I know that that is the kind of group you are.

I have no doubt but that you will succeed.

I trust in your dedication and enthusiasm.

I am proud of each and every one of you, and I am prouder still to call myself a part of you.

Onward, my friends . . . onward to *our* victory!

* * * * * * *

> *SPECIAL NOTE: This second speech is an example of a closing speech where the closing is the conclusion of the fund-raising drive itself.*

What can I say other than this: "You did it!"

We have reached our goal. We have worked for something in which we all believed, and, because of our common effort, that goal has been reached. Others may think that this is the conclusion of the fund-raising drive, but you and I know that this is far from a conclusion. Rather, it is the beginning of our victory celebration!

Do you know what you have done? Do you know what you have achieved through your efforts? Let me tell you . . .

(At this point you would detail just exactly what their fund-raising efforts have meant, both in terms of cash and pledges raised and what the money will be used for. Let's assume that you have done this.)

. . . and that, my friends, is what your efforts, your work, and your dedication will mean to all of us!

Indeed, this is a time to celebrate, but it is also a time to pause, remember, and reflect. You have before you a prime example of what you can do when you are united by a common purpose; of what you can do when you each give of yourselves for the good of all; of what you can accomplish when you work together. It is something that you can all remember for the rest of your lives and point to with pride. It is good, it is worthwhile, and it is yours!

For years to come, yours will be an example of selfless dedication by which others will measure themselves. What you have done over these past few weeks is a credit to you and your spirit, and it is an accomplishment that will long be remembered by us all.

Certainly, you have my thanks for a job well done, and whether you will be aware of it or not, you will have the gratitude of those who will come after you and reap the rewards of your efforts. But, most important of all, you have the knowledge that through your individual efforts, you have achieved something worthwhile and grand.

And, that is something that will remain with you always!

Thank you, and good night!

SPECIAL DATA: *Time of speeches: between one and two minutes each, depending on audience reaction. The first closing speech ends the "kick-off" meeting of the fund-raiser, so it still remains inspirational in nature, exhorting the listeners to go on and work for their goal. The second closing speech is one that would be given at the conclusion of the fund raising when the final goal had been met. In both speeches you will notice that those who work on the fund raising are praised and complimented. We feel that this is very important, as everyone likes to have his or her efforts appreciated and acknowledged, and* *it is right and proper to do this when someone or some group has worked hard on behalf of your project. Moreover, word of this is likely to spread, and you will find people more disposed to working the next time some effort of this type is required.*

Afterthoughts

There is a maxim among comedians and stage performers that goes, "Always leave them laughing!" Well, if we may paraphrase that statement, perhaps your maxim for all closing speeches should be, "Always leave them thinking!"

As the leader and moderator of the program, as well as a coach who is used to controlling and guiding large groups, the audience expects you to set the tone of the evening. You do this with your opening remarks. At the conclusion of the program, they also expect you to say a few words. What you say during those closing remarks can be just as important as what has gone on during the entire evening.

A speaker who merely stands up, thanks the speakers, says goodnight, and sits down, leaves the audience with a highly impersonal feeling. Someone, however, who summarizes or encapsulates the evening, who thanks the speakers in the name of the audience and then thanks the audience and praises them for their participation, who reflects on the meaning of the evening's activity in some personal way and then sends the audience off with something to think about and appreciate is a speaker/coach who has created a warm and positive feeling in the audience, and is a speaker/ coach who will be appreciated and remembered.

SECTION 4

A Coach's Speeches for the "Non-Sports" Audience

There is not a profession in the world that does not develop its own jargon. Perhaps this is natural, working as we do with such a wide variety of topics and situations. We develop short cuts in language that others in our position would understand without complicated explanation. Consequently, we talk of a player "going long," of a "flea flicker," and how well someone executed a "squeeze play." In short, we use a host of expressions, words, and phrases with which we are familiar and that have become a part of our lives over the years.

This poses no problem when we are speaking with other coaches or even with a sports-minded group or individual who understands the language, but it can be confusing and frustrating to anyone not familiar with what we are talking about. Indeed, if you use that type of language with anyone not familiar with or engaged in sports, you will find that the person or group will "tune out," just as you might turn off a radio or TV program that was being broadcast in Mongolian!

Yet, the coach is often asked to address groups of people ranging from the parents of his athletes to a meeting of the general public to a woman's club to a civic association. The one thing that all of these engagements have in common is the fact that the audience may be composed of a variety of people who know little about sports terms and jargon or whose only association with sports may be a few minutes of a game on TV caught while changing channels.

Consequently, the coach must take particular care when presenting a speech before such groups. The language of the speech must be such that everyone in the audience understands without feeling that he or she is being talked down to. The coach must also project a warm, confident, and very positive image because quite often the audience will judge the sports program and its effectiveness on their reaction to the coach. Whether this is right or wrong does not concern us here, for we have seen it happen too often to negate it.

The speeches in this section are for just such occasions when the coach must face the "non-sports" audience. They are on a wide variety of topics that have been found to be of interest and concern to such audiences. Each speech has been used successfully, and will work for you.

TOPIC: *Parents and the Student Athlete*

AUDIENCE: *Adults; parents of team members.*

Good evening, ladies and gentlemen, and thank you for that warm reception.

Recently, I was doing some yard work around my home, when I overheard my seven-year-old son talking with some of his playmates. They couldn't see me, but I could hear them as they began to talk about their fathers and what their respective dads did for a living.

"My dad's a policeman," said one. "My daddy works in a bank," said another. "My father owns a gas station," said a third, and so it went until they came to my son. I can tell you that my ears pricked up, and I smiled in anticipation.

"What does your father do?" one of the boys asked my son.

"My father doesn't do anything," my son replied. "He's a coach, and all he does all day is play games!"

One of these days, I'm going to have to take that lad aside and set him straight.

Of course, that is the way a child would view it. At that age, most children have only a vague idea at best of what adult jobs and professions entail. When he is ready to understand, I think I'll tell him that playing games is only a small part of what his father does as a coach. I'll tell him that being a coach also involves helping people develop and become the best individuals they are capable of being. I'll tell him that it involves overcoming problems that hold back the individual from his or her best performance. I'll tell him that it involves building character, instilling in each individual a sense of his or her individual worth, and creating an attitude within the individual that allows the person to face problems not as insurmountable obstacles but as challenges to be met and conquered.

Yes, I'll tell him all of this, and I'll tell him one thing more.

I'll tell him that in my job as coach, I have an invaluable and indispensable helper; a helper who is always there when needed, who provides inspiration at exactly the right time and support throughout the process, who aids, encourages, teaches, and trains.

I'll tell him that this helper has a name; he's called a parent.

For, make no mistake about it, without the support and the care of parents, my task as coach would be intolerable and impossible, and the excellence that we have seen in our student athletes over the years would never have materialized.

I say this, not because you are an audience of parents; rather, I say it because, over the years, I have lived it, and I know that it is true.

When a student decides to go out for a team, he or she may do so for a variety of reasons. For a few, it is the mistaken idea that without effort they will achieve glory, becoming the hero who saves the day on the last play of the game. This person usually doesn't last through the first practice session. For the vast majority of students, however, what motivates them to join athletics is a sincere love of the sport, a desire to participate with others who are like-minded, and a belief, sometimes shaky, that they are both mentally and physically capable of becoming a team member and a valuable, contributing athlete.

If these are the students' motivations, and if there are no physical problems which stand in the way, then they are likely to achieve their goals. That is, they will achieve their goals if they have the proper training and guidance, for the basic truth remains that they cannot do it alone.

This is where you and I come in. The price of success is work, hard work, and the student athlete soon finds out just how true that is. They will come home to you from their practice sessions and they will be tired, dirty, and sore. On the field, I have told them the purpose of the exercise or drill they followed. Encourage your children to tell you. Let them talk about what they did. If they want to complain, that's all right, too. You reinforce at home what I have been telling them on the field, and together we'll find a young athlete who doesn't give up; one who tries and sticks at it and is better mentally and physically for the effort.

We all realize that it is practice that makes the difference between a concert pianist and somebody who "fools around at the piano." This is true in sports as well as the arts. Encourage your child to attend all practices. If he wants to practice on his own, why don't you join him? Even if it's nothing more than tossing him the ball and watching as he runs zigzag patterns across your back yard, you'll be involved, your child will know this, and it will add to his determination to excel. Who knows, you might also find that you like the exercise.

We must realize that sports are played with the mind as much as with the body. Insist that your child keep up with his schoolwork. Far from being too tired to study, the physical conditioning your child receives from participation in sports will give him new and vibrant energy which must be devoted to his or her studies. There is no place on a team for someone who can't think, just as there is no place in any successful career for someone without education. Keep up the work on the school subjects, and let that include the rules of the game, play sheets, and other vital information that his coaches may provide.

Keep me advised of any changes in physical condition as soon as they occur. Perhaps this should have come first, since the safety and well-being of the athlete is of paramount importance. "But, if you tell the coach that I sprained my ankle," your child may say, "he won't let me play in the game on Saturday." That's absolutely correct. I will tell you, however, that the sadness and letdown your child will feel sitting on the sidelines will pass away with your understanding and mine, but injuries, for the most part, happen when players are not in top physical form, and I will *not* take the chance of letting your child get hurt. Your child's future and well-being are simply too much to risk.

Finally, there will come defeat. No one wins all the time. You and I don't like to lose, and we're adults, supposedly able to rationalize such things and take them in our stride. How much more intense is the feeling for an adolescent who has worked and strived and given of himself only to have the other team score the winning goal. Try to remember when you were that age, and what it meant to you. When the other team wins, be there. Be there to understand, to sympathize, to make your child see it as one incident among many. Be there to guide the disappointment into a resolve to try again. Be there, and your child will learn from you the joy of competition along with the realities of life.

I propose a partnership starting right here, tonight. It is a partnership between you and me. We have our goal in view: your child as a student athlete, sound in mind and sound in body. I know that I cannot do it alone. I know that I can supply the mechanics, but I also know that the heart and soul must come from you. I will supply the knowledge and the drill. I will supply the program for physical conditioning and knowledge of the game, and you will supply the understanding and the heart that makes for greatness in life as well as on the field.

If we can see ourselves in this partnership, if we take the time and effort to care about the student athlete, then I have no doubt that there will be one, single overall beneficiary of our efforts, and that will be the student athlete himself.

With perseverance, with understanding, and, perhaps most important of all, with love and true concern for the student athlete's welfare, how can we help but succeed!

Thank you for your attention, and good evening.

SPECIAL DATA: *Time of Speech: about 10 minutes. We know of one coach who, at the start of every season, issues a very strong invitation to the parents of all team members to attend a special meeting. At that meeting, he gives a speech very similar to this one. The result is that his popularity and esteem in the community are over-whelming. This speech shows a caring attitude along with strength of conviction. It calls on parents to be partners rather than adversaries or strangers on the sidelines. It projects a plea for cooperation that simply cannot be denied. Your sincerity combined with the words of this speech will provide you with a firm foun-dation for parental support throughout the season.*

$$\boxed{53}$$

TOPIC: *Why Sports Are Popular.*

AUDIENCE: *Suitable for any adult audience and/or student athletes.*

Thank you, ladies and gentlemen, and good evening.

If any of you have ever flown a long distance in a commercial airliner, you will appreciate the fact that after the smiling flight attendant has served you a plastic-packaged, plastic meal, after a short lecture on where the emergency exits are and what to do if your plane should decide to crash, there is really not much to do while cruising at thirty-five or forty thousand feet. In fact, if you don't want to talk to your fellow passengers, you really have only two options. You can sleep, or you can look out the window.

Personally, I like the window. Looking down from that height, there isn't much you can readily distinguish. You can't, for example, see someone standing in a field waving up to you. You can distinguish highways and throughways, but usually you can't see the cars moving on them. You may know that you're passing over a city, but you certainly can't read the sign on the general store.

It's a type of strangeness, almost of alienation, as if the earth below you belonged to another world. Then, just as this feeling is about to sink in, you see something that tells you that this is your world. You see something that lets you know that's America down there, as much a part of you as the breath you take. You see something which conjures up images of home, no matter where over this great land you may be flying.

Do you know what that is? Do you know what I have seen popping up at me from the red clay of Georgia, from the verdant lushness of Louisiana, from the foothills of the Rocky Mountains in Colorado, and from the patchwork quilts of farmlands in Iowa and Nebraska? It's a baseball diamond. That's right, a field dedicated to the playing of baseball. Nothing else looks like it, and it could be nothing else. Even from forty thousand feet, almost seven miles straight up, they are unmistakable.

That sight does bring you back home, because baseball is a part of your life as it is a part of mine. Whether you play yourself, have a relative who does, or just watch the game, for an American youngster growing up, the sheer presence of the game is unmistakable and unavoidable. Indeed, it is as much a part of our communal culture as fireworks on the Fourth of July.

Nor is it only baseball that pervades our life. America has become sports conscious. Besides baseball, it is difficult at best *not* to be aware of basketball and football, both the professional and scholastic varieties. Soccer, once relegated to the European sports scene, now draws record crowds. Hockey has become a winter passion. Gymnastics, once considered too delicate and esoteric for the general public, now makes front-page sports news. The general adult audience may still plop down before the TV set, but now they have jogging shoes on their feet as they watch local marathon races being broadcast nationally by the major TV networks.

In 1984, the Association of Secondary School Principals conducted a survey of teenagers who had said that they liked school and felt that school was worthwhile. These teens were asked to give reasons their feelings were so positive. Almost one-third of those responding listed sports and sports activities as one of the reasons for positive school feelings.

We would have to be shut away on some rock in the middle of the sea not to realize that sports are popular in America and that their popularity is growing daily.

Why? That's a question we may well ask: Why are sports so popular?

To find our answer, let's look at a group of kids from a neighborhood who find themselves together on a summer afternoon. One of them may have a ball; perhaps a regulation hard ball or a rubber variety or even something unrecognizable because it has been repaired so often with tape.

Another has a bat; a "Louisville Slugger" or the handle of a discarded broom. They find a place; a regulation playing field attached to a school or playground or an open field or a city street that is not frequently traveled.

When these items come into proximity, do you know what you have? You have a game. You have a sport.

You also have much more. You have the sheer joy of companionship; of being part of the group; of belonging; of liking those around you and being liked by them. Sure, you may argue and scream at each other on every play, but even as you do so, you know in your mind and in your heart that you are very close to these people; that you are a part of them, and they are a part of you.

Your body, that marvelous, puzzling, wonderous machine pulls, stretches, pushes, and weaves; muscles tense and relax; legs move, seemingly by themselves, feet beat the earth. The wind whistles past your ears and tousles your hair. Your body cries out with joy, and you are alive as never before.

Your mind is also alert and functioning. You watch, calculate, and anticipate. Your concentration is at its fullest. For these moments, there are no troubles, there are no doubts; there is only this field and these players, and your mind on them and what they do. The sharpness and clarity of your mind at these moments can startle you.

Finally, there is the emotion. Nowhere else can you go from elation to despair and from sorrow to joy so often and in so short a period of time. You are part of a team. Its victory is your victory and its defeat is your defeat. The ball whizzed past you; you fell down; you let an opposing player get through. The emotion wells up inside you, and sometimes, because you are so involved, so much a part of it all, it lapses over into your eyes and down your cheeks. You catch the ball; you make the play; you stop the opponent from scoring, and the emotion is there again; different this time, but still there and perhaps still in the eyes and in the tears. In short, you are vitally, magnificently alive.

Nor do you have to actively play in order to feel these things; to experience the participation. Even as a spectator, you are part of it all. You support a team, and they become a part of you. When they win, a part of you has won as well. You have a stake in the outcome of the game, for you have invested a part of yourself in it. The outfielder makes an "impossible" catch; the receiver threads his way through a field dotted with opponents; the American gymnast scores a perfect 10; your team scores the winning goal with one second to go. When these things happen, your body may be in a seat at a stadium or before a TV set, but in your mind and soul, *you* have just caught the ball; *you* are standing on the balance beam; *you* jump over the last opponent and score the touchdown; *you* are shoving the ball into the basket as the final whistle sounds. It does not matter whether someone else's hands or yours accomplished these feats; the emotion, the elation, the sense of joy are just as great and just as real.

Therefore it doesn't matter if you are on the field or in the stands; whether you caught the ball or just willed the player to catch it; whether you are jumping and weeping for joy with your fellow teammates or with your fellow fans. We participate in sports in many and varied ways and the rewards of that participation are well worth the effort we put into it.

This is why sports are so popular; this is why participation in sports is constantly growing. In sports, we invest ourselves—our emotions, our minds, and our bodies. The returns are in terms of ourselves as well—the sadness and the joy; the clarity of concentration which allows our worries, fears and doubts to take at least a momentary rest; the health and vitality we feel in our bodies and souls. Where else can you give so much and get so much back in real assets that are important in our lives.

Do you doubt this? Let your mind go back to the last Olympic Games. Remember now the medal ceremonies following the conclusion of any one of the events. Think of one when the gold medal was placed around the neck of the American athlete. See him or her standing there on the highest of the three pedestals. Watch as Old Glory rises, the topmost of the three flags. Listen as the strains of our national anthem begin. Look at the athlete's face. See his eyes; see her eyes. Now look at your own eyes and listen to your own heart. Remember what you felt at that moment. Even if you can't put a name to it, you will recognize it.

Therein lies the future of sports in America. As long as people feel; as long as people strive; as long as people wish and dream and desire, there will be a place for sports in America, and that place will grow ever larger in our minds and in our hearts.

For, make no mistake about it, we are a nation of people who are not ashamed to feel deeply; we are a nation of people who strive to accomplish their goals and wishes and desires; and we are a nation of dreamers who have the ability to turn those dreams into golden reality.

It is no wonder, no surprise, therefore, that sports are a part of our heritage, are a part of our daily lives today, and will continue to be a vital part of our bright and golden future.

Thank you for listening. It was a pleasure being with you. Good evening.

SPECIAL DATA: *Time of speech: about fifteen minutes. The question with a speech such as this is not where can it be used, but where it cannot be used. This is an ideal speech for any civic organization, and it fits in extremely well at patriotic functions. You don't have to be a sports expert or fanatic to understand what the speaker is saying. The philosophy expressed is positive and of such a nature that hardly anyone in the audience can disagree. We very highly recommend this speech for any of your speaking engagements before "non-sports" audiences.*

$$\boxed{54}$$

TOPIC: *A Life in Sports.*

AUDIENCE: *Suitable for any adult audience.*

Thank you very much, ladies and gentlemen, and good evening.

It started with whooping cough.

Oh, perhaps I should explain. I mean by that statement that if it hadn't been for whooping cough, I might not have become a coach and I might not have spent a very rewarding life in sports, which is what I would like to talk to you about this evening.

So you see, I'm grateful to whooping cough, and I want you to understand that that's what got me started.

I got whooping cough when I was seven years old, and I had a pretty rough time with it. I don't remember everything about it, of course, for that was . . . well, let's say it was a number of years ago. I remember the doctor, and medicine, and seemingly endless days of lying in bed. I don't know when it was decided that I was over it, but when I was, my parents had a very pale, underweight, frail child on their hands.

It was my parents and sports that put the color back into the cheeks of that child; put weight and muscle onto his frame, and turned frailty into robust good health.

I won't bore you with the details. My parents began by tossing a ball with me; by taking me to a park filled with sunshine; by encouraging me to run—short distances at first and then longer; by teaching me sports; by helping me practice; by supporting me when I joined a team; and by loving me.

By the time I reached high school, I had acquired three things: an abiding love and respect for my parents that continues to this day; a physically sound body; and a love of sports.

The rest is fairly mundane. I played sports in high school, went to college, and, when it was time for me to decide how I would like to spend my adult life, I knew that what I wanted most was to help kids through sports. I really didn't have a choice. I went into physical education and coaching.

It has been many years since my first coaching job, and I have seen many student athletes come and go. Perhaps it is fitting that I pause for a moment and look back on those years and at the sea of faces that looked at me as I spoke and with whom I spent so much time, so many days.

Make no mistake, I remember them all. I remember the athletes who could not be held back; who shone like stars; who made even the most complicated plays seem effortless; who picked up everything as easily as you or I would pick up an evening paper. I remember those to whom everything was an arduous task requiring hours and hours of grueling work for the simplest of operations. I remember those who came expecting to find glory only to find mud, scratches, and sore muscles. I remember those who only wanted to give of themselves for the good of the team. I remember cases that lightened my heart and enriched my soul. I remember cases that broke my heart. Yes, I remember.

I remember one boy, let's call him Tom, who came to me one afternoon and, with great fervor in his voice, told me that he wanted to be on the team. He was a handsome young man, with twinkling eyes and a winning smile. He looked to be in good physical condition, obviously had the desire to play, and his right arm was missing from just below the elbow.

I will tell you honestly that I had serious doubts. I have always believed in honesty with my athletes, and I told him of my reservations. He answered that he understood, but that all he wanted was a chance to try. I told him that I could provide that, at least.

Tom had a prosthesis, an artificial hand and forearm, that he used with amazing skill. He wanted to be a kicker, and when the ball was snapped to him, he would use that artificial limb to trap it, steady it, and then kick the ball with amazing skill and accuracy. It wasn't easy for him, I don't want you to get that idea, but when this boy got knocked down he picked himself up and got back to it with an even fiercer determination to try harder.

In short, he made the team, not because he lacked an arm, but because he had aggressiveness, fortitude, courage, and a great deal of talent.

It was shortly into the first game of the season that he got a chance to try that skill. Five minutes into the game, it was fourth down and eighteen yards to go, a situation which called for a long punt. I called Tom from the sidelines and told him what to do, and he was off.

Unfortunately, our line did not hold, and several of the opposing linesmen were all over Tom. He got the ball off, but found himself under a pile of bodies. As they were untwisting themselves, one of the opposing linesmen reached down and offered Tom a hand up. Tom, whether on purpose or without thinking, extended his artificial limb to the boy, and the lad took it and pulled.

There was a snap, and the opposing player was standing there with Tom's hand clutched in his own while Tom, on the ground, shouted, "What have you done with my hand? Give it back!"

Whereupon, the linesman looked at Tom, looked at the object in his hand . . . and fainted dead away!

It took every official on the field, both coaches, and fifteen minutes of clamor and fast explaining before it finally got settled.

That was one of the times when we laughed until the tears filled our eyes, but not all the times were like that. There was, for instance, my first brush with the problem of drugs and drug abuse.

We'll call the student Johnny. It was his second year on the team. During his first season, he had shown unqualified promise, and I was looking forward to this year and what he would accomplish with one season's experience added to his vast array of skills. Frankly, I dreamed of what the boy could accomplish. I would never find out.

I remember with frightening clarity how we sat at a team meeting one day. As I was talking, explaining some play, I noticed Johnny out of the corner of my eye. His eyes were shut and he was weaving back and forth as he sat on the bench. "Excuse me, Sir," I said in a light manner, "am I boring you with this material?" There was no answer from Johnny, although several of the other players giggled. I walked the few feet to where he was sitting and took him by the shoulder. "Johnny," I said, "is something wrong?"

Johnny collapsed. I barely caught him, and, as I lowered him to the floor, I became aware of his shallow breathing, his caked lips, the bluish tinge to his ashen pallor. The trainers and I were on him at once, the emergency squad was called, and Johnny did not die that day. We discovered that an overdose of barbiturates had caused this problem.

His friends spoke to him; his parent spoke to him; ministers, psychologists, and case workers spoke to him; and I spoke to him. I told him the future he had before him. I spoke to him of what he could accomplish, on his own, without the crutch of drugs. I told him how we would be happy to welcome him back to the team when he was well.

I saw him only once after that. It was three years and four days from the day in the locker room when he collapsed into my arms. I stood and looked at him as he lay in his coffin, dead of a overdose in some dark corner where no one could get to him in time.

But I would not for the world have you think that Johnny's was a typical story. Far from it! Johnny was the exception to our fine young athletes; he was not the rule. The majority, and I mean 99.9 percent, of the players I coach live lives of dedication and devotion to their skills that make me proud to be among them.

There was, for example, a student we'll call Bill. Bill was easily the most talented player I ever coached. To say that he was an outstanding player is to do him a disservice. He had a brilliant mind; a strong, healthy, and highly trained body; and an ability to think on his feet that you see few times in your life. You only had to see him play once to know that here was someone very special, indeed, and someone who was headed for a lifelong career in professional sports.

Indeed, during his senior year, he was literally besieged by recruiters from major universities and some not so major. Quite frankly, he could have had his pick.

One late fall afternoon, he asked if he could speak to me after practice. I imagined that he was going to ask my advice concerning the offers he had received, and I had a thought or two on the subject that I wanted to share with him. I was not prepared for what he had to tell me.

He thanked me for my help, which I brushed off lightly, asking, in turn, if he had decided on a college. He told me that he had, and he mentioned the name of a place I had never heard of. I suppose my face must have registered surprise, for he added, "Don't worry; they have a coach there that I've always wanted to play for."

"Oh," I said, trying to make some sense out of what he was saying, "and who might this great coach be?"

He looked at me squarely and said only one word—"God."

After that, there was no argument. He went to that school and became a minister. He realized his dream, and he played on God's team. From all accounts, he was as marvelous on that field as he had ever been on mine.

Someone once said to me concerning Bill, "Look at all he gave up!" To which I answered, "No. Think of all he found." Indeed, whenever this world gets me down, I find that the memory of Bill helps me to view things in a slightly different, slightly happier perspective.

I suppose that it is natural, considering the fact that I work so closely with young people, that I am often asked my opinion about the future of this world and of mankind in general. I suppose people figure that because I get to know the young people who will make up that future, I am in a position to know.

Well, I guess I am, after all. I work with these boys, and I get to know them intimately. I get to see into their minds and hearts, I watch them as they strive and work, I am there as they battle and work together for common goals. Yes, I know them.

With that knowledge as my guide, I have no hesitation in telling you that the future is bright indeed. Yes, certainly there are the Johnnys who throw away their lives and their futures, but there are also the Toms who refuse to be held back by any handicap and who will give countless hours of effort to overcome whatever stumbling blocks are placed in their way, and there are the Bills who look at life and see higher goals, who shun the material rewards of this world to work for the greater good of all mankind.

I am sorry for the Johnnys of this world, but I have pride, love, and hope in the Toms and Bills who abound and flourish, and who will make our future, the future of all mankind, something bright, shining, and fine.

That I have shared their lives; that I have had a part, however small, in the shaping of those lives; that I live in a world, the future of which shall be shaped by them—this fills me with happiness as it should fill each and every one of you with hope and a vision of a tomorrow of which we may all be justly proud!

Thank you, and good evening.

SPECIAL DATA: *Time of speech: sixteen to twenty minutes. This is a longer speech and well suited to a woman's club, political organization, or civic society. Naturally, this speech reflects the life of one particular coach, but we think that any coach could use it as a framework for an autobiographical speech on his own career. Certainly, we are all aware of incidents just as dramatic, funny, and poignant as those in this speech. Suit the speech to your career and keep the same enthusiasm and positive attitude as the speaker above, and you*

will have a winning address for any "non-sports" au-
dience. This material is truly dynamic and it brought
a standing ovation the first time we saw it used.

$$\boxed{55}$$

TOPIC: *The Athlete: A Rather Twisted View*

AUDIENCE: *Suitable for all "non-sports" audiences.*

(NOTE: The following is a satiric speech. It conveys a very powerful
message in an often humorous and light manner. In this case, as in all
satiric speeches, it is your tongue in cheek attitude and delivery that
will convey to the audience that this is, indeed, satire, and that they
are to understand that your meaning is the opposite of your words.
More of this in the special note following the speech.)

Just the other day, I heard of a case that came before one of the judges
in a local court. It seems that some people were petitioning to have an
old man committed to an institution on the grounds that he was mentally
incompetent.

The judge asked the complainants on what facts they had based their
opinion. "Your Honor," they answered, "this old man loves pancakes."

"What!" shouted the judge, "You want this old man committed to a
mental institution on the grounds that he loves pancakes? That's the most
ridiculous thing I have ever heard. Case dismissed!"

As the court was clearing out, the judge called the old man to his
side.

"Sir," said the judge, "I don't want you to worry. I'll see to it that
these people don't bother you again."

"Thanks, Judge," said the old man, "I was worried."

"Well, it was just unbelievable," said the Judge. "Imagine wanting to
put you away just because you love pancakes. Why, I love pancakes myself!"

"You do?" beamed the old man. "Then you must come to visit me. I
have every one of my closets filled to the top with pancakes and three
trunks full in the attic!"

Now, I tell you this story in order to point out a theory I have. I fully believe that the world is being pervaded by lunacy, and it's high time we did something about it and put an end to this madness.

Of all the lunatics and fanatics in this world, undoubtedly the chief among them has to be the athlete—that's right, the athlete. In general, athletes are people who don't conform to the norm. They are impractical, and completely nonsensible people, and I can prove my case.

Everybody knows that asthma is a very serious affliction. Everybody knows that if you have asthma, you have to take it easy, you can't exert yourself. You should live a pampered life, free of excitement. Sure, everybody knows this, but there is an individual whose name is Bob Gibson. He has asthma, but is he sensible about it? No! He insists on being in professional baseball, as a pitcher no less! He's right out there where the stress and worry are the worst. Instead of being careful and watching his every step, this Gibson fellow got out there and played sports. Why they even gave him something called a Cy Young Award for his pitching. I tell you, it just doesn't make sense!

Then, there's this other fellow who has to wear glasses. Does he avoid all situations where he might be hit? Does he take a nice, safe job in an office? No, this man by the name of Grover Cleveland Alexander actually tries out for major league baseball and becomes the first person in the major leagues to wear glasses! What's more, he has a brilliant career as a pitcher! He doesn't take a position in sports where eyesight doesn't matter, like an umpire. No, he's right in there in the thick of the action! Insane!

I can give you even worse examples of insanity in sports. Take physical handicaps. You and I know that a person who is handicapped should be sensible about it. He should stay home and listen to music, read a book, or watch television. Certainly, no one with a handicap should ever consider sports. Well, just try to convince someone like Tom Dempsey of that. Here's a fellow who was born with half of an arm and half of a foot. Does he prove to be sensible and resign himself to the life of a handicapped person. Of course not. He's an athlete, and he becomes a place kicker with an NFL football team. Half an arm; half a foot, and he has the audacity to kick a 63-yard field goal! Can you believe how insane that is?

I could give you others. People like Rocky Blier who was seriously wounded in Vietnam. Does he sit back and take it easy like any sensible person would? Certainly not. In spite of wounds received in action, he becomes a running back for the Pittsburgh Steelers; that's a professional football team I understand. He refuses to let wounds hold him back. I tell you, it's absolutely insane!

But, there is one final case I want to tell you about. This is really the epitome of nonsensible behavior. This person was not handicapped. Indeed, he was physically fit in every way. He was a cadet in the United States Naval Academy. On their football team, he was so outstanding that he received the famous Heisman Trophy as an outstanding collegiate player. Naturally, when he graduated, every professional football team wanted him. They offered very lucrative contracts. This boy's future was assured.

Of course, there was the matter of his service in the Navy. Was he sensible? Did he hire lawyers to try to get him out of the service? File law suits? No, this nonsensical person talked about the "debt" he owed to his country and served his four years in the Navy. Then, when he had no further legal obligations, when no one could force him into staying in the service, he even signed up for an extra tour of duty in Vietnam because he figured that his country needed him. Can you imagine how crazy that is? Here's a person who places his country above his personal career!

This person's name is Roger Staubach, and you may have heard of him, because he did go into professional football after serving his country.

Where, I ask you, will all of this end? If we allow nonsensible, nonconforming athletes like Grover Cleveland Alexander, Bob Gibson, Tom Dempsey, and Rocky Blier to continue to strive in spite of the odds and to continue to excel despite their handicaps, then what might happen next. Instead of sensibly sitting home in a room, handicapped people might get the idea that they could get an education, that they could make careers for themselves in business and the arts and even in sports, that they could succeed on their own merits instead of letting the rest of us take care of them.

If this trend is allowed to continue, you might even turn on your TV set and see races for people in wheelchairs, just as if their handicaps didn't matter. You might even see some sort of "special" olympic games for people with other handicaps. Yes, if we do not stop this nonsensical attitude, you might even find regular, sensible people swayed away from a rational life of caring only about themselves and volunteering in the thousands to help with these "special" games for these "special" athletes. Oh yes, it could happen.

Consider also what would happen if we were to allow the patriotism and commitment of a Roger Staubach to affect the youth of our nation. Why, people might come to believe that there was something bigger than themselves; to believe that there were such things as ideals, honor and love of country. They might get the nonsensical idea that it was a good and proper thing to serve others, to give of themselves for others, to work for the good of mankind rather than to amass dollars in a bank.

If that is allowed to happen, then someday someone might even get the idea that everyone should be given the opportunity to develop to his or her own potential in spite of drawbacks and handicaps; that service to others is something worthwhile and valuable; even that we are all equal and engaged in a common struggle to live together and to make our world a better place to live.

Let me leave you with one final thought. If we do not curb this tendency toward irrationality; if we allow people like these athletes to overcome their handicaps and to dedicate themselves to service rather than to personal gain; if we allow these nonsensical athletes to become role models for our youth, then I tell you it will be only a short time until people begin believing that there is nothing that, together, we cannot accomplish, and that all men are truly brothers. If we do all these things, what will happen to the world?

It's a question that only you can answer, and you must answer it in your heart. When dreamers are allowed to dream and make those dreams reality; when people look beyond themselves and give of themselves to a common good; when honor is no longer a word but an everyday deed, then what is to become of the world, ladies and gentlemen?

What can the future hold?

SPECIAL DATA: *Time of speech: approximately eight minutes. Please do not sell this speech short. Properly delivered, it is a powerhouse that will draw a standing ovation. It is ideal for any patriotic function or civic group. We must caution you, however, that your delivery of this speech is extremely important to its success. You must give this speech very enthusiastically, as if you were truly angry. Don't worry, the audience will see the true message behind the words. Your acting it out will make it all the more powerful. You might, of course, wish to add some other examples you know of, but don't go overboard. For a speech of this nature, something between five and ten minutes is just right.*

$$\boxed{56}$$

TOPIC: *Why Do We Need Coaches?*

AUDIENCE: *Suitable to any "non-sports" audience.*

I think that we have all had the common experience of looking out and seeing a group of kids playing some sort of game. It might have been on a sand lot, in a pasture, on a vacant lot, or even on a city street, but put a group of kids together, and sooner or later, they are going to choose sides, and a game will begin.

If that remembrance brings a smile to your lips, you are not alone. We can all recall similar situations in our own youth, and usually the memory is warm and pleasant. I think we look back with at least a little envy to those carefree days, free of adult responsibilities and pressure.

I mentioned this to a friend of mine once, and, knowing that I was a coach and seeking to get a rise out of me, he remarked that it would be wonderful, indeed, if adults could just refrain from interfering with those kids. It would be so much better, he explained, if they could be left to play on their own, without coaches making rules, holding practice drills, and pushing, pushing, pushing at these kids.

I understood that my friend was saying this in fun, but I will tell you honestly that it set me to thinking. If you can take any group of kids, put them together in a single place, and they, unaided, can get a game going and combine exercise with a good time, why do we need coaches?

I thought about that for some time, and I have an answer that I would like to share with you this evening.

It was my son who gave me part of that answer. He is eight, and, like most eight-year-olds, he is unbounded energy wrapped up in a boy's body. He and his friends quite often get games started and play the day away. I had been meticulous in staying out of his sports life even when I saw him doing something wrong that could have been improved by practice.

One evening, after supper, he came to me to ask a question. "Dad," he said, "I'm having trouble sliding into bases. I get tagged every time. Can you show me what I'm doing wrong?"

Of course, I was delighted that he had asked my advice, but I asked him why he wanted to know? Wasn't he having fun just playing with the other kids?

"Sure," he answered, "it's a lot of fun. But, I know I can do better.

I'm doing something wrong, but I don't know what it is. I want to be able to slide into that base and be safe every time."

There was my answer. What my son wanted was to perfect his skill. Having fun and being with his friends was a large part of why he played. But, he also wanted to get better at it. Instinctively, he understood that he was doing something wrong, and he needed someone to help him to correct his mistake and become better at what he loved to do.

Naturally, I gave him some instruction and practice, and while he was not safe every time he slid into a base, his average did improve dramatically.

There was the answer. We need coaches because the human animal is not satisfied merely to do something; he wants to do it well; he wants to do it to the limit of his capacity.

There is also the knowledge that while some may do it on their own, very few people have the capacity to correct their own mistakes or improve their skills unless someone guides them, directs their efforts, and gives them the insight they need to go off and, with determination and resolve, learn to do it better.

Nor am I speaking only of sports. Doctors constantly read and take classes even though they have practiced medicine for twenty years. Concert musicians take "master" classes to continually perfect their technique even if they are performing regularly to packed houses. Teachers continue to take classes themselves in order to learn to better deal with the students they face each day.

The list goes on and on. Perhaps it is a characteristic of human beings that they are not satisfied all the time; that they seek and strive for perfection; that they see what can be and reach out for it. Perhaps it is also characteristic that most of us realize that we cannot do it alone; that we need guidance; that we need a direction for our efforts if we are ever to achieve our goals.

As a coach, I have seen kids come to me with enthusiasm bubbling to be unleashed; with raw talent that glittered with promise; with healthy bodies and positive minds. I have seen these same kids trip over their own feet. I have seen them in the middle of a field standing with their mouths open in disbelief when the opposing team scored because they did not know what to do.

The talent was there; the drive was there; what was missing was the direction.

The greatest, most powerful river in the world can be a source of power that will light and heat the homes of thousands, or it can be a rampaging flood that sweeps away everything in its path. The difference lies in how those waters are channeled.

That is what I see as my job; that is why we need coaches. A coach can take the human desire to excel, combined with the raw talent, and channel and direct it until we have a person who is justly proud of himself for what he has accomplished; a person who knows that he has done the best that he is capable of doing; a person who stands with confidence in himself and a respect for his talent and the talent of those around him.

It is not always an easy task. Quite often, it reaches a point where the individual feels that it is hopeless, and here, too, a coach is needed. The coach is there at that time to let the individual know that he *can* do it; that what he wants *is* within his grasp; that effort and hard work combined with knowledge *can* produce the results for which he is so strenuously working.

The coach is there to needle, to comfort, to infuriate, to assist, to encourage, to demand. The coach is there to give that single word of insight, that one clasp on the shoulder, that final shout that brings the individual to the point where he knows that his dream is within his grasp; that it is his for the taking; that he has worked for and earned every bit of it.

Finally, the coach is there to help the individual keep it all in perspective. To teach the player that he is not alone, but part of a group striving for a common goal. He is there to teach the player that he is part of a team, and, however good he may personally be, he owes allegiance to that team. That is not a bad lesson for anyone to take to heart, whether on the playing field or in life itself.

I can tell you that I see hundreds of boys each year, and I have seen this process work time after glorious time. I have dealt with kids who stood before me and virtually apologized for their presence, and I have seen them at the end of a season with confidence in their faces and their hearts whether that season was a winning or a losing one, because they were winners, they had conquered themselves. I have seen overweight kids drop the pounds and underweight kids gain them, along with new health, vigor, and self-assurance. I have seen cocky and arrogant kids lose the false pride as they came to rely on their teammates and their teammates began to rely on them. I have seen hundreds and hundreds of kids grow and mature and flourish. I have seen them start out weak or arrogant or uncertain or untrained, and I have been privileged to see them walk away a credit to themselves, their parents, and the community in which they live.

I feel very humble, very humble indeed, to have had a part in this transformation; in this triumph of the human spirit.

Please understand. It is not I who have affected these changes. It is not I, nor any coach, who has allowed the best in that human being to come out. That credit belongs to the individual who felt the need to learn; who had the desire and the fortitude to work for perfection; who spent the time and the sweat and the pain to gain what they have. It is not I, for no sculptor can carve a statue from stone that crumbles and flakes away.

Rather, I have been a guide along the path. I have been the coach who could supply some of the answers these people needed and wanted; who could direct their efforts down the right pathway for the destination they had in mind; who could stand by when the going got rough to give them the little extra they needed to see it through.

Why do we need coaches? We need them because the human spirit cries out for knowledge and perfection; we need them because we are all part of humanity struggling to be the best we can; we need them to encourage and train and shout and enliven our lives as we reach out to become the best person we are capable of becoming.

If we coaches have rewards, it is in the knowledge that we have, indeed, helped; it is in working and seeing the change that our work brings about in our charges; and, perhaps most important, it is in the faces of those we have coached who look at us with confidence and strength and ability and honor that give us all hope that tomorrow will be as bright as it is within the power of the human spirit to achieve.

SPECIAL DATA: *Time of speech: about twelve minutes. This speech contains some very sound and uplifting philosophy about coaching and coaches, but you will notice that it is geared to the "non-sports" audience as we have identified them. It is well suited to a program on careers, to a school function where something of an athletic nature is being honored or will occur, as a tribute to a fellow coach (change the pronouns and mention his name), or for any civic affair. Again, as with the last speech, your conviction and belief in the words of this speech are essential to its success.*

Afterthoughts

The speeches in this section have been longer and more involved than any up to now. This is because we are dealing with speeches that are the main part of an evening's program or entertainment. We feel that they address their topics well, make dynamic and dramatic points, and show a bit of humor along the way.

Moreover, these speeches are meant for people who have no direct relationship to sports or sports education. They avoid all technical terms and any terms that only the initiated might know. They speak plainly and in warm terms that everyone in the audience can identify with and understand. Whether you use one of these or make up one of your own for your "non-sports" audience, if you incorporate these values, you cannot go far wrong.

SECTION 5

A Coach's Guide
for Speeches
Before Colleagues

While it is a certainty that the coach is in demand to speak before audiences such as parent's groups and civic clubs, it is an equal certainty that he or she will be asked to address a group of his or her colleagues somewhere along the line. Whether that group consists of colleagues within a school or district or a group at the county, state, or even national level, the challenges are great, and the coach is expected to meet them.

Speaking to a group of fellow coaches or sports professionals can often be the most challenging public speaking situation for a coach. While "non-sports" audiences are quite often willing and anxious to accept what the coach has to say, a group of coaches may include individuals equally as knowledgeable about various aspects of sports and coaching, and each may have his or her own opinions on the subject.

Therefore, the coach faced with this challenge must deliver a speech that will capture his or her audience's attention; that speaks to the subject in a straightforward manner; that presents issues or opinions that are backed by facts; and that is entertaining. That last aspect is particularly important, for the best material and research in the world will be skimmed over lightly and discarded if it is delivered in a dry and lifeless manner.

The speeches in this section, therefore, are geared to meet the coach's needs in just these situations. They are geared to all levels, from the players on a team to a gathering of coaches of the topmost rank. They are on a variety of subjects that strike at the heart of coaching and affect us all. They are even backed up by the latest data available where needed. Also, every effort has been made to ensure that they are entertaining and will fully involve your audience.

No matter how good the speech, however, remember the paramount secret of speaking to an audience of your colleagues: enjoy being with them and speaking to them, and they will enjoy listening to you.

$$\boxed{57}$$

TOPIC: *Playing the Inner Game.*

AUDIENCE: *Suitable for an adult audience of sports professionals.*

I think that we are all aware that there are many things that go into the winning of any given game. Chief among these elements is the training a team receives. Certainly, we are aware of the need for healthy, well-conditioned athletes. However, I believe that this is only a part of what goes into the making of a winning team.

I believe that given two teams of equal skill, training, and physical condition, the team that has the better mental attitude; that is the more aggressive; that wants it more will win.

These elements—attitude, aggressiveness, desire—are mental rather than physical. They are part of what many professionals have begun to call the inner game—the game that is played not on a field against an opposing team, but within the mind of each and every athlete who comprises the team.

I am certain that each and every one of us has come across an athlete during our careers who really excelled; who stood out from the others and was that "something special" of which we all dream. Well, analyze that athlete for a moment and answer for yourself the question of what it was that made him or her so special. I think you will agree that it was not only his or her physical condition or physical skill, but it was that athlete's attitude, his or her mental outlook, that raised him or her above the rest. That individual had the desire to win. That individual was able to concentrate completely on what he or she was doing. That person could anticipate, move, evaluate.

I used to say that such a person could think on his feet. This was a person who never gave up. This was someone who thought about the game rather than the party afterwards or what he was going to have for supper. This was a person who knew what he had to do and did it, 100 percent of the time, while giving 100 percent of himself.

I say that this comes from within, from the attitude, aggressiveness, and desire that are part of the inner game and that affect the outer game so drastically.

Therefore, I feel that it is essential to give your team practice in mental preparation as well as physical preparation. I believe that this begins the first day of preseason and is an ongoing process in which every successful coach must be involved.

I begin with the small things. I tell my players that many times during practice we will do things which may seem trivial or unimportant to the individual player. However, I emphasize that the sum total or cumulative effect of all these little things add up to a successful team effort, because if each individual can improve even slightly, the total effect is considerable improvement of the team as a whole. I make certain that they realize that none of us—and I include myself in that statement—ever knows enough or is good enough. Basically, I try to convince them that if they emphasize the little things to themselves, they will find that the big things become easier to accomplish.

It is very important that every player has this sense of being part of the larger effort. Each person must feel that what he does is of vital importance to the team as a whole. Therefore, each person must give all that he can in every way, including practice for the good of the team. This sense of being part of something larger than oneself, where one's individual efforts are never wasted but contribute to the good of everyone, goes a long way towards establishing the mental attitude that is part of the successful inner game.

Next, we must convince our players never to take anything for granted. No player must ever assume that he is not needed on a certain play. They must all go until the whistle. This is extremely important, since a player who assumes that he knows enough and doesn't have to listen to his coach is a player who is going to cause difficulty for the entire team. We can all imagine what would happen if our players assumed that they were in great shape and that all their opponents were not and would be pushovers.

Toward this end, I like to point out to my players that it has been scientifically established that no one, not even the best of us, does anything to his full capacity. Indeed, even the most outstanding performers use only a fraction of their total capacity. Therefore, it must follow that there is always room for improvement. We can all work harder, run further, play harder than we think we can. We can all improve; we can all contribute.

I often tell my players that there are a lot of athletes with little ability and a great desire to excel; there are a lot of athletes with great ability and a limited desire to excel; there are few athletes with great ability and a great desire to excel. I ask them to ask themselves where they fit. I demand that they use their minds to analyze their own thoughts and see if they can drive themselves to work for a greater utilization of their capabilities.

I let my players know that organized sports have also been called organized confusion. To a large extent, I tell them, this is true. Things don't always happen the same way we draw them on the chalkboard. Certainly, we work very hard on techniques, but no two individuals do things exactly the same, and the situations in a game are not always the same as they were in practice. Therefore, it is the team with the greatest unity that can adjust the best; that makes the fewest mistakes; that shows the greatest poise; that has the least amount of internal confusion—this is the team that will win in the long run.

All of these things are an important part of establishing a mental outlook, an inner game, that aids each and every athlete as well as the team as a whole. We must convince our players that everything they do is of value; that they cannot take anything for granted; that they can do more and better than they think they can; that they must be alert and give their all at all times. If we can establish these beliefs in the minds and hearts of our players, then we have established an attitude geared toward being the best that each individual is capable of being. We have established aggressiveness as vitally important to the individual in performing his task from whistle to whistle with concentration and resolve. We have established the desire to excel as a part of each individual's mental makeup. These three elements, combined with the training in skills and physical conditioning that we supply, build teams that rise above the average— teams that win.

You know, I often tell my players that there is a great correlation between sports and life in general. When you are up, you will get knocked down. If you give up, others will swarm all over you and demolish you. If you hold on when you are down and keep trying, things will get better. You can be sure of it.

Yes, that is a matter of skill and prowess, but no one—*no one*—can deny that it is a matter of mental attitude and outlook as well. Given the absence of physical drawbacks, those who believe they can succeed, will succeed; those who have faith in themselves; who give of themselves as much as they are capable will discover that they have even more to give than they realized.

Let's give our athletes that headstart. Let's train them in the mental game—the inner game—as well as in the physical game, and the rewards will come not only in terms of games won and physical performance on the field, but also in terms of our athletes' growth within themselves and, by projection, in life itself.

This is a gift that we can give to our players, and, because we are coaches; because we care about our players; because we have seen the importance of mental attitude in sports as well as in life, I know that we can do no less than try.

SPECIAL DATA: *Time of speech: a little over ten minutes. This is very sound sports philosophy which will find very little dissent among your colleagues. It is, however, the type of thing that people tend to forget as the years pass. It is, therefore, good to take it out and look at it every once in a while, and a speech such as this is usually well-received by an audience of colleagues. Note here the differences between this speech and the speeches in the previous section for the "non-sports" audience. Here, the speaker assumes a basic knowledge of coaching and the fundamentals of group sport on the part of the audience. This speech could be used as part of a sports conference, teaching session, or even a sports banquet, because it borders on the inspirational in nature.*

$$\boxed{58}$$

TOPIC: *What You Will Receive from the Coaching Staff.*

AUDIENCE: *Athletes: potential members of a team.*

(NOTE: *This speech is geared to football, but there is no reason that it cannot be used with any other team sport. See the SPECIAL DATA following this speech for further suggestions on its use.*)

Good morning.

Very shortly we are going to take the field and begin our first real practice session. For many of you, this will be like coming home, since you have been here before. For others, it may be an eye-opening experience. For all of you, it is going to mean sore muscles and a great deal of hard work.

We are here, however, to form a football team, and that means that the coaching staff is going to expect a lot from you. Quite frankly, some of you are not going to make it, some of you will become average football players, and some of you will be outstanding. At the end of it all, we expect to have as fine a football team as we can get.

But, you, as athletes and players on this team also have a right to expect certain things from us, the staff who will be coaching you over the next several weeks. I think it is only right that you know what we can give to you.

Our main objective in coaching football is to improve you, the individual. We want you to become as fine a player *and* as fine a person as you are capable of becoming.

We feel that this can be accomplished in two ways. First, we can do this by direct contact with a player in discussing problems both at home and at school. This doesn't mean that we will solve them for you, but we are always available to talk, to advise, and to understand. Second, we will relate to you our experience and knowledge both on and off the football field.

You see, football is a game in which you must make sacrifices in order to succeed. You may have to give up that slice of chocolate cake. You may have to give up some time you wanted to spend elsewhere in order to practice or help the team. As we all make sacrifices in life, so we must make them in football if we are to succeed. The coaching staff will help you here as well, offering support, understanding, and guidance as you progress. We sincerely believe that our job goes far beyond just coaching football. We hope to give you our ideas, hopes, and desires, and to help you reach your own personal goals.

Now, an overall look at football shows this game to be a team sport. This is true, of course, but a closer look shows that it is also an individual sport. You, that's each and every one of you, have a particular job to do, and you must perform that job successfully if you as an individual as well as the team as a whole are going to survive and win. This is the area in which we hope to get the most accomplished—working with individuals.

But, these are all general things. What, specifically, can you expect?

You can expect constructive criticism on your performance on the field during practice sessions and during games. You must never assume that a coach who criticizes your performance is picking on you or trying to embarass you. Quite often, the player himself is in the worst possible position to see what he is doing wrong. The object of our criticism is to get you to correct your mistakes and to make you a better player. Therefore, you should expect criticism and accept it as an athlete. I tell you from long experience that constructive criticism is vital to the success of a player.

You can expect dedication to football and the football team. We, the coaching staff, will give 100 percent effort aimed toward the development of a winning football team. You should know that countless hours will be spent in preparation for games and improving an individual's performance on the field. Just as we do not expect you to take the field unprepared, you can expect that we have worked many hours toward our preparation for the sport.

You can expect communication from the coaching staff. You will always be able to discuss problems with the staff, whether those problems relate to home, school, or performance on the field. We firmly believe that a sense of true communication in a coach-player relationship will lay the foundation for a successful football team. We want you to know that we are here for you, and we are always willing to sit down and talk with you.

You can expect experience from the coaching staff. Everyone on this staff has played football beyond high school. We feel that experience is often the best teacher, and our experience is something that we can offer to you. We will share this experience with you, show you what has worked for us and for others, and show you what will work for you.

You can expect fairness to all players. This coaching staff will form unbiased opinions and work with the player *in the situation that occurs*. The staff will justify all changes in the football program. Certainly, if you are the one being criticized while others around you are not, you are going to feel bad about it. However, I want you to know that it is not you, personally, that is being criticized. Rather, it will be your performance that is the object of the criticism with the objective, as I said before, of correcting that performance to make it the best possible. Realize that everyone receives criticism, and you are never the only one singled out.

You can expect a positive attitude from our coaching staff. You are going to see us angry. You may see us frustrated. But you will never see us down in any situation, and you will never see us give up. We will always be out to win, and we will always be out to improve the team. We sincerely hope that this attitude will be contagious and infect each and every one of you, because, if it does, we will have a team headed for victory.

You can also expect confidence from our coaching staff that will be shown to all players. In fact, one of our main goals is to instill justifiable confidence in each and every one of you; not false pride, mind you, but confidence based on a knowledge of who you are and what you have to offer. Basically, gentlemen, we want to make you a better ballplayer than anyone else.

In summation, we, the coaching staff, believe that success in football is tied in with the elements of pride, desire, sacrifice, a willingness to cooperate, and a willingness to accept criticism. We believe that an individual can be successful in football and in life itself by abiding with and pursuing these five elements.

We also believe that this is part of our objective—to help you accomplish those goals for yourself. We will be here when you need us; we will *not* give up on you; we will do everything in our power to help you become the finest player and person that you are capable of becoming. That is a promise that we intend to keep.

Now, let's hit the field!

SPECIAL DATA: *Time of speech: about six to seven minutes. While this speech is obviously one given to a football team, the standard philosophy that is offered by the coaching staff applies equally well to all team sports. It would be relatively easy, therefore, to alter the speech for baseball, soccer, and so forth. Moreover, by deleting the reference to a specific sport and changing the "you" to "all players," this could become an explanatory speech to parents on the value of the coaching staff or even part of a sports night program at a school. As we said, the philosophy applies across the board, and there is nothing wrong with the organization of it. Change it to suit your needs, and you will have an informative and entertaining speech.*

$$\boxed{59}$$

TOPIC: *Visualization as a Practice Tool.*

AUDIENCE: *Colleagues, Sports Professionals, and Athletes.*

As coaches, we have a number of tools to help us help our athletes. We have tackling dummies, batting cages, exercise equipment, weight training equipment, and the like. These are tools that, as coaches, we know intimately. We also know that they cost money, need to be repaired, and are generally limited as to the time in which they can be used.

There is, however, one tool which is available to all coaches that costs nothing, that can be used at any time and virtually anywhere, and that never has to be repaired or replaced. It is a tool that can improve the game of each and every athlete. It is a tool that, if I told you about it fifty years ago, you would have laughed me off the stage, but that, with growth and enlightenment, is as real and palpable today as a goalpost or a base.

The tool I am talking about is the mind of each athlete under your care and instruction. It is within your power to add a very valuable training tool to your arsenal by teaching your athletes to use their minds to practice and enhance their games through the use of something called visualization.

This is not voodoo, this is not illusion and stage magic, it is, rather, a scientifically proven, psychological method that athletes can use to improve their playing skills and their performance on the field.

Let's look at it together.

We'll begin with the basic theory that all actions start with thoughts. This is hardly revolutionary, as it is common experience that we think of something before we do it. Before I go to the tap and draw a glass of water, the thought has entered my mind that I am thirsty and want a drink.

The action of getting the drink had to be learned somewhere along the line. Although it seems elementary, I had to learn to hold the glass under the tap, with the mouth of the glass upward, while I turned on the tap and then shut it off once the glass was filled. Of course, this learning took place so early in our lives that we have forgotten the times we held the glass upside down or merely placed it under the tap, expecting the water to flow on its own.

This took place when we were small children. Gradually, we learned that the glass had to be upright, that the tap had to be turned, that it had to be shut off. We learned this through trying, making mistakes, and then correcting those mistakes to get the results we wanted. Once we had learned it successfully, we remembered it for future use and promptly forgot all our failures.

This process applies to all we do. Basically, we learn by trial and error, and once the correct or successful response is learned, it is remembered for future use and all our failures are forgotten.

If we can accept this as true, which our own experience verifies, let's put it aside for a moment, and examine another truth. It is this: before we can be, we must become, and before we can become, we must be able to visualize our goals. Let's look at this a bit closer.

Assume for a moment that I am a teenaged boy in his final year of high school. Considering my physical appearance, that's a difficult assumption, even for me, but let's try. My high school days are drawing rapidly to a close, and very soon I must go out into the world and make a living. What am I going to do with my life?

I decide that I want to be a coach. At this moment, I am not a coach, and in my mind, I realize that before I can be a coach, I must become a coach—I must study, train, receive certification, and the like. Therefore, I enroll in a college and take those courses that will lead toward my goal of becoming a coach.

I could not have done any of these things, however, unless I was first able to visualize my goal of becoming a coach. By visualizing my goal, I discovered what was needed to become a coach, and I pursued that path in order that I might be one. In other words, before we can be, we must become, and before we can become, we must be able to visualize our goals.

Put another way, we first established a goal or target (becoming a coach), then we set out on a course oriented to that end result (we went to school and took the right courses), then we made mistakes along the way (failed a test or fell a dozen times before we learned a correct posture), and through trial and error we learned the skills and we became coaches.

So, we have seen that all actions start with thoughts, and we learn by trial and error until a successful response is learned whereupon it is remembered for future use. We have also seen that before we can become anything, it is first necessary to visualize our goal in order to set a course to become whatever it is that we wish to be. There remains only one more basic theory before we can apply what we know to our athletes and their training.

It is that the mind cannot distinguish between real and imagined experience. This may take a little more explanation.

Hypnosis is no longer the province of magicians or con men. Rather, it is a scientific tool which is used in treating people with certain illnesses, in police work to help eyewitnesses remember what they saw, and throughout psychiatry as both a diagnostic and a remedial aid. In short, it is a serious and indisputable aid.

Most of us realize that a person under hypnosis is susceptible to all sorts of suggestion. For example, if you tell a person under hypnosis that he is standing in the middle of a blizzard and is getting colder by the second, that person's mind accepts the suggestion, he begins to shiver and shake, and he manifests all the symptoms of someone who is very cold indeed. It does not matter that he is sitting in a room where the temperature is 72 degrees; that person is cold. Because the person was susceptible to the suggestion, his mind could not distinguish between reality (a comfortably warm room) and the imagined experience (standing in the middle of a blizzard).

All right, what does all this have to do with swinging a bat correctly, blocking on the line, or being a successful soccer goalie?

Just this: once those, or any skills have been successfully learned on the practice field, the athlete may practice them not only physically, but mentally as well, and this mental practice will help to improve his skill and his results on the actual playing field.

That's a mouthful, to be sure. Let's take a closer look and see it in action.

First, the skill must be learned correctly. We all realize that if we do something incorrectly and do it over and over, all we will be doing is reinforcing a bad habit that may eventually become too ingrained to correct. Therefore, our first task as coaches is to make certain that the skill is correctly learned and can be accomplished successfully by the athlete.

Once the skill is learned correctly, however, it can be practiced not only on the field, but by each individual player through the use of visualization. All that it entails is vividly picturing yourself performing the skill successfully. You must achieve a mental picture of yourself performing the skill as close to actual performance as possible.

Let's give it a try. I am certain that each and every one of you has acquired many skills in sports over the years. I'd like each of you to think of just one of those skills right now. I know that selecting just one may be difficult, as there are many from which to choose, but give it a try. I'm going to use the skill of swinging a baseball bat, but it could be anything from that skill to diving to serving the ball in tennis. Does everyone have just one skill in mind? Good, then let's begin.

You don't have to close your eyes, but it might help if you did this first time. In your mind, see yourself getting ready to perform the skill. Try to make it real. Visualize it; see it; get the mental picture; try to think in pictures. I see myself for example, standing in the batting cage, about to lift my bat.

Now, perform your skill in slow motion in your mind. With each step that you take, try to let yourself experience what it feels like as well as what it looks like. I can feel my grip on the bat; I feel the weight of it; I feel the way I am standing; I feel the bat in the air rather than resting on my shoulder. For you, it may be the way you are standing; the grip and feel of the tennis racket; the breathing and position of your arms and legs. Whatever it is, feel it and see it.

Now, see yourself and feel yourself performing the skill. Here comes the ball; I take a step into it; I feel my weight extended through my arms; I feel the contact; I feel and watch myself follow through with my swing.

Whatever the skill you are practicing in your mind, follow through with it now. See it happening; feel it happening.

Now, relax. Open your eyes, but remember what it was that you just saw and felt. What has been accomplished is that we have just practiced a skill. We all know that practicing skills successfully allows us to perform them successfully on the field. Through visualization, you have just accomplished that objective.

If we believe that the mind cannot tell the difference between real and imagined experience, then we have discovered a very valuable practice tool for our athletes. We know that if we repeat something successfully over a long period of time, it becomes habit. Well, if you practice something successfully in your mind, it is almost like actually doing it. The more you can see and feel the correct way to perform a skill, the more that habit of success becomes ingrained, and the more that successful habit is carried over into actual play.

For you and your athletes, visualization is an easy tool that could give you an extra advantage. Since it requires no effort, only concentration of mind, it can be done anytime—on rising in the morning; while having lunch; just before you fall asleep at night. Moreover, if you visualize something enough, then when you actually do it, you will have the feeling of having done it before successfully. This is the goal of all practice, and visualization is a method which will help you and your players achieve that goal.

If you are going to use visualization with your athletes, however, there is a caution which you must pass on to them. Before they visualize, they must have learned the skill successfully and performed it successfully a number of times. On this, they must seek your guidance. Next, they must realize that visualization does not in any way replace practice or on-the-field technique. Visualization is only a learning aid. It can give them an extra edge only when it is used in conjunction with actual physical practice. Finally, you might caution them that it will not be easy to do at first. The mind has a tendency to wander, and proper visualization requires concentration. They must work at it in order to develop the habit of visualizing.

If they work at it, however, they will find that it will do its task. We all know that sports are played with the mind as well as the body, and the stereotype of the hulking brute of an athlete who cannot spell his own name is a fiction and should be left to the comedians. It follows, therefore, that by using their minds to visualize successful skills, your athletes will be building habits of success which will serve them each individually and the team as a whole.

Remember, no one is doing his best who can do better. Using visualization as a learning aid combined with your training and practice on the field, can give an athlete an extra edge in actual performance.

Just think, ladies and gentlemen, that if each individual did only two percent better than his usual, average job, the results for the team could improve a hundred-fold!

That, like visualization itself, is something worth thinking about!

SPECIAL DATA: *Time of speech: 17–18 minutes. This is the type of speech in which the coach is trying to teach something to his audience. Notice that it is filled with facts. A foundation is given first, then the technique is explained, and the audience gets to participate in trying out what they are learning. Notice, too, that it is not presented as something revolutionary, but as something valuable that one coach wishes to share with his colleagues. Moreover, since the speech is for sports professionals, it presupposes a great deal of knowledge on the part of the audience. This could well be a guide for any lecture you might have to give explaining a new technique, policy, rule, to colleagues. With appropriate changes, of course, it might also be used to explain the technique itself to a group of athletes or team members.*

$$\boxed{60}$$

TOPIC: *What Coaches Expect from Players.*

AUDIENCE: *Suitable for an audience of colleagues or sports professionals.*

(*NOTE: The following speech could be applied to any sport and works equally well with boys' sports or girls' sports. The values are sound for whoever plays and whatever they are playing.*)

Much has been said about what you can expect as a member of this team. That is, you have heard and been told what you can expect from the entire coaching staff. Indeed, I think that it is fitting that you know what the staff can give to you and what to expect from them. There is, however, another side to the picture.

Just as for each right you enjoy as a citizen, you share an equal responsibility, so, too, the area of coaching involves not only what the coaches can give you, but what we expect from you as well.

Let's start with conduct. We expect that you will show proper conduct on the field, of course, but we also expect that you will show this same conduct at home and in school. Great players have a great deal of self-respect, but you cannot begin to respect yourself unless you can show respect to others, and that includes your parents and your teachers as well as your coaches.

Next, we expect that you will be responsible for all equipment. You understand if you fail to return any equipment or if you misuse any equipment and break it, you will be expected to pay for that particular item. While you are paying for it and it is being replaced, however, it cannot be used, and that results in someone losing time in practice. That is something we cannot afford. Take proper care of your equipment, and the problem will never come up.

We expect you to get into and stay in good physical condition. Right now, that means obeying our training rules concerning smoking, drinking, and curfew hours. Further, however, it means that you must stay active after the season is over. To be in good condition, you must implement your own program for physical fitness. Certainly, we can tell you how to go about it, but, in the final analysis, *you* must do it.

We also expect that you will be on time for practices, and that you will practice the same way you will play—giving it the most that you can. If you cannot make a practice, you must contact a coach first. Actually, we expect that you will begin to make it a habit to be on time for school as well, and, speaking of school, we expect that you will be spending time doing homework, school assignments, and studying. If you are doing poorly in school, notify the coaching staff. We will not fix anything for you, but we will see to it that you get the help you need so that you can succeed. Remember, sports have become complicated, and you must be sharp and alert to play.

We expect that you will accept the criticism of the coaching staff in the spirit in which it is offered—constructive advice aimed at improving your abilities as a player and, by projection, the performance of the team as a whole. We do not expect that there is anyone out there who believes that he is perfect and cannot improve. We expect that you will want to improve and will accept criticism with that goal in mind.

Finally, we expect that you will show good sportsmanship, and that you will be proud to be a member of this team. This means that you will help each other both in practice and on the field, and you will show respect to your opponents. Understand that you will beat them, but you will show them respect as well. You will always remember that being a member of this team is something special in your lives. Throughout this season and, I am certain, throughout the years of your adult lives, you will know that you were a valuable member of a vital and dynamic team. You will remember and you will be proud.

This is what we, the coaching staff, expect of you, the players. If you take this message to heart, realize the necessity of your cooperation, and give that cooperation freely and completely, I can promise you that we will have a team in which each individual is a star; a team of well-trained, tough, aggressive players; a team that will not be stopped until victory is theirs.

In the final analysis it will be up to you, to each and every one of you, to give of yourself to the team. I have not the slightest doubt that you will do your best and that we will all become what we want to be—winners!

SPECIAL DATA: *Time of speech: approximately five and one-half minutes. The expectations of the coaching staff as outlined here, are reasonable and proper. You should feel free, however, to add whatever requirements your staff may have for your sport, team, and/or leel. This speech might be used alone, as presented here, or it might be incorporated into a longer speech such as the one on what players may expect from the coaching staff given earlier in this section. In this way, players would have a complete overview of what they must give and what they will receive. With appropriate changes, this even makes a good speech for parents or a similar "non-sports" audience.*

$$\boxed{61}$$

TOPIC: *What Makes a Successful Team?*

AUDIENCE: *Suitable for colleagues and sports professionals.*

When people ask me for the secret of a successful football team, I tell them the story of the man who was walking the streets in New York. He was carrying a violin case, and he wanted to get to Carnegie Hall in order to audition for a symphony orchestra. He was lost, so he stopped a man on the street. "Excuse me," he said. "How can I get to Carnegie Hall?"

The other fellow looked at the man and at his violin case and said, "Practice, man, practice!"

Certainly, practice plays an important part in all that we do both in sports and the other aspects of life. Practice alone, however, is not the complete answer as to what makes a successful football team. It begins with the individual player.

Really, there is no secret to individual success, just as there are no shortcuts to it. Success comes from four elements—desire, hard work, patience, and the ability to bounce back. Basically, a player becomes as good as he wants to become. The more effort he puts into a game, the better are his chances of succeeding. This is a philosophy that can be used from sandlot to professional football, and it is part of the successful coach's strategy to inspire his players.

Success does not come overnight except in bad movies. It takes time and patience to succeed. As coaches, we must see to it that during this period of time, our players develop their skills and gain experience, while also gaining faith in themselves and the others they work with. The players must be made to understand that if they strive they will succeed, and in their individual success will lie the success of the team as well.

Let's discuss offensive play for a moment. Let's say we have a multiple set offense; we run the same basic plays from various sets. On offense, obviously, we must not fumble or turn the ball over close to our goal line, and we must run more plays than our opponents. We also realize that the least amount of mistakes by any offense will spell success.

There are also certain objectives that are common to the offense. The offense must:

1. Control the line of scrimmage.
2. Establish a solid and versatile running attack.
3. Be able to attack each area.
4. Exploit the weaknesses of the opposition or the areas they give you.
5. Possess a strong passing game.
6. Strive for ball control and elimination of turnovers.
7. Execute the kicking game exceptionally well.

The offense is based on movement. The offense must always strive to gain yardage. The offensive unit must be well disciplined, execute each play properly, and remain well-poised on the field. Each man must complete his assignment properly for the offense to move. There must not be a mental breakdown on offense.

Now, look at these objectives for a moment, and ask yourself which is the most important. I think that the most important one is that each man complete his assignment properly. Just as the whole is made up of the sum of the parts, so a successful offense is made up of individual players, each absolutely convinced that he is vital to offense and equally as convinced that he must succeed; that he must do the job assigned him.

If this can be accomplished; if each person on the offense will do his job to the best of his ability with the certain knowledge that without his effort, the team cannot win, then you will have an offensive unit that is disciplined, executes with precision, and remains poised under any circumstances.

A group of eleven individuals, each one committed to achieving each of the seven offensive objectives I mentioned earlier by doing his job in each situation, means a cohesive unit whose mistakes will be few and far between and that will be able to bounce back quickly from those mistakes they do make. Altogether, this can only spell success.

It may be a cliche that on every offensive play, eleven men have an assignment to carry out, but I have found it to be true and it is the backbone of a team's success.

The same philosophy of the individual can be used equally well and, perhaps to even more advantage, on defense.

In order for a team's defense to be successful, each individual player must believe in the defense. Each individual must have confidence in himself. Each player must be saying, "I, personally, will not let the ball cross the goal line!"

Obviously, there is training involved here as well. Defense involves sighting, moving, and hitting, and the players must be drilled in these skills. Proper pursuit and gang tackling are also part of successful defense. We know that it is difficult for the ball carrier to get loose when five or six players are each trying to get a piece of him. We know that constant pressure and pursuit can help demoralize the ball carrier to the point where he may hesitate and make a mistake that will be beneficial to our team. Certainly, these techniques are all part of the training and practice that we give our teams.

However, there is an individual defensive philosophy in which we must train every defensive player as well. Chief among these is aggressiveness. This is a factor which must be maintained by every player on every play. I will not let them pass; I will stop them; I will go after them and stop them. It is up to me.

Consequently, I will stop that third down play. I shall not let that team get inside our ten-yard line. They will not score!

If each individual player is in top physical condition, carries a mental attitude such as the one described, and carries out his assignment as he was trained to do, then you have a defensive unit that operates at peak efficiency and that STOPS the opposing team.

A successful team is one in which each player's ATTITUDE is extremely important. Each player must want to do it and must be willing to pay the price. Each player must believe that his individual success is measured in terms of what the team accomplishes. They must know that victory will go to the team that is more aggressive, and they must want victory for themselves and for their team. They must know that they have to carry out their assignments at all costs and must want to win.

It has been said that football is a game of hardy characters—for men who are tough in *body* and in *spirit*. We all know the truth of that statement. We should also know, however, that we, as coaches, can help create that spirit, that desire, that belief in the individual. We should know that a team composed of individuals, each with the knowledge of what to do, the willingness to do it, and the desire and commitment to play to their fullest for each and every minute of the game, will be a team that seeks success with a passion. That team will strive for success like a well-oiled machine, each part functioning to its fullest capacity. It will be a group of individuals that may truly be called a team.

And, it will be a team that succeeds.

As coaches, we know that we can train players to improve their skills. As coaches, we owe it to our players to train them in desire, courage, dedication, and aggressiveness as well. If we do this, the rewards of our labors will be successful seasons, to be sure, but also successful men who will leave us and carry our training into their lives, and, perhaps, be the better for it.

As coaches, we can do no less than try.

SPECIAL DATA: *Time of speech: nine to ten minutes. There is some very good, sound, and basic philosophy in this speech that, although here it is related to football, could well be applied to any team sport, and most of it could be* *applied to individual sports as well. You might want to use it as is, or you might want to use parts of it when discussing the importance of mental attitude in sports. With alterations, this might also be used as a speech to your players to convince them of the importance of each individual to a winning team.*

62

TOPIC: *What Is a Competitor?*

AUDIENCE: *Suitable for all professional audiences.*

When we speak of sports, we speak of competition, for competition is the heart and soul of the sportsman. Those who engage in sports are competitors by nature, they play because they like the competition of the game.

Because I deal so closely with so many athletes, perhaps it is natural that I am often asked what makes a great competitor; not merely someone who plays at a sport, but a true competitor who stands out from the rest. I have given that some thought, and I am convinced that the definition of a great competitor lies in what other players say about him.

"This guy never gives up. He plays as if every play meant the championship!" I've heard players talk about one of their teammates in that manner, and, to me, that means that the player of whom they spoke is a true competitor. He is someone to whom the game is important; every game, whether it is a scrimmage or the title championship. Everything he does in a game, he does all-out. Each play is important, and he gives his all on each and every play.

I've heard people say, "He doesn't get discouraged when he makes a mistake. He just comes back harder on the next play." A true competitor handles his mistakes; he does not let his mistakes handle him. When he errs, he does not see the error as something to brood about; as something for which to condemn himself; as an embarrassment that will mar his life. No, rather, he sees it as a learning tool. He uses his error to help him correct what he has been doing wrong, files it away for future reference, and comes back to the next play with an even greater degree of enthusiasm, commitment, and drive. He bounces back. He gets up stronger than when he went down.

I've heard people say, "This guy is really consistent. He does his job play after play." For the true competitor, there is no relaxing on the job, and you had better not relax against him. Consistency is his trademark. Time and time again, you will find him doing his job in the same, efficient manner. Never once will he think that what he does is not important, so he can take it easy and wait until the next play. Rather, he will be doing his job even when all others have stopped. He plays from the beginning to the end of each and every play and achieves a consistency of performance that makes him invaluable on any team.

People say of him, "He makes things happen." He is a catalyst. The other members of the team catch fire from him. Because of his enthusiasm and dedication, other players begin to emulate him, and the team as a whole is infected with his spirit. He is a doer. He is the one who rallys the team when everything looks hopeless and turns defeat into victory. He is the spark which ignites the roaring fire, and others cannot help but be warmed by his flame.

They say of him, "He doesn't play cautiously. He's always aggressive; always on the attack." This doesn't mean that he is reckless, doing foolhardy things for the fleeting glory of the moment. Just the opposite. He knows what has to be done, and he does it. When he moves it will be forward; if he falls, it will be forward. He attacks rather than standing back and defending himself. When he sees an opportunity, he takes it. He hits clean, but he hits hard. His physical conditioning and his training serve him well as he pushes ever forward.

They say, "We don't understand this fellow. He's the best player we have, but he never seems to be satisfied with his performance!" What they are observing is the brand of the great competitors. They know that anyone who can do better is not doing his best. They realize that even the best of players can stand improvement. They are never smug and complacent, assuming that they have reached the top and can get no better. Rather, the true competitor is the one whom you will see on the practice field, in the weight room, or in the gym working as hard as possible, even after others have stopped for the day, to add an extra edge, however slim, to his performance. He wants to be the best; he realizes that this comes through hard, relentless training and practice; and he goes after his goal. He refuses, absolutely refuses, to allow a complacent attitude to hold him down.

Finally, they say of him, "He just won't stop. He's more interested in winning than in anything else." For the competitor, a team's loss is his loss. The team's victory is his victory. Winning is important to him. It's not just something; for him it is the only thing that makes his competition worthwhile. He plays sports, and, quite frankly, he cannot understand people who play *at* sports. When he takes the field, he takes it to win; he expects to win; he plays, play after play after play, to win. When he is out there, he has one goal in mind—victory. He sees what must be done to achieve that goal; he counts the cost of the victory in terms of what he must do and sacrifice in order to achieve it, and he is willing to pay the price. He starts, and he doesn't stop until that victory is his. Should he lose, he merely determines to try again with even more fervor until that win is his for all time.

All true competitors pay a price. They pay in terms of hours and hours of practice and hard work; they pay in terms of hundreds of scrapes, bruises, minor injuries; they pay in terms of emotion, because while the victory is twice as sweet, for the competitor, the loss is twice as hard to take.

Yet, for the true competitor, this is a coin that he pays gladly. It is a price that he counts as worthwhile in his life. He expects to be hit, because he is a hitter; he expects his opponents to be tough, because he is tough; he expects to give his effort and become tired, because he knows that it will not be easy to win even under the best of conditions.

Even so, the competitor lives for the competition. It is his pain and his joy; it is his frustration and his fulfillment; it is his slavery and his freedom. Long after the game; long after the stands have emptied, the locker room has cleared, the fans and players have gone on to other aspects of their lives, the competitor carries the lessons of competition inside himself; the lessons that he will apply to life as he did to his game; the lessons that will serve him throughout his life.

SPECIAL DATA: *Time of speech: about eight minutes. Most sports professionals that we know recognize the implicit truth in this speech. As with most truths, however, we don't take them out and look at them nearly often enough. Consequently, a speech of this nature might be ideal as a preseason speech to players; as a speech to coaches on your staff about what to look for or aim for in training; or, as an inspirational speech to a civic group, since its message of doing your best consistently has a great appeal. Naturally, you could add any other aspects of competition or the competitive factor that you deem necessary, or even add anecdotes from your own experience that might enhance the basic ideas.*

Afterthoughts

As we indicated in the introduction to this section, these speeches are aimed at your colleagues or that group of people who are involved in or knowledgeable about sports. They involve sports, and many times they refer to situations and aspects of playing that only coaches or players can fully appreciate. This does not mean, however, that someone with little knowledge of sports might not enjoy them as well.

The speeches on what players may expect from the coaching staff and what the staff expects from players, for instance, may be enjoyable and eye-opening to a group of parents of players. It might engender a very productive discussion, and might even lead to increased parental support of the coach and the team. Certainly, it never hurts if parents know exactly what is required and what will be given during training and the season itself.

Therefore, while these are primarily aimed at your colleagues and other sports professionals, you may find that some parts or even an entire speech is suited to your needs for an entirely different audience.

Use them, and may you find satisfaction and success in their use.

SECTION 6

Touchdown—
Speeches That Inspire

Take an informal poll of your friends who are coaches. Ask them why they chose sports as a profession rather than something else. We would be willing to wager that a good percentage of them will say that they became coaches because, during the period when they were growing up and playing sports, they met someone or had a coach whose example so inspired them that they knew they had to enter the field.

The quality of inspiration cannot be taken lightly. How many acts of heroism and valor have occurred because one person has inspired another? We will never know, of course, but we can recognize that inspiration is a noble and powerful force when used for good and wholesome purposes.

Giving a speech that inspires, however, can be quite difficult. What works for one will not, necessarily, work for another. There are, however, certain basics that are part of all inspirational speaking.

First and foremost, the speaker must be sincere. He must believe in what he is saying, and he must project that belief to the audience. Next, the speaker must believe that he is helping the audience. His sincere desire to communicate valuable insights and information to the audience will be communicated and cannot help but be assimilated by the listeners. Finally, the speaker must be enthusiastic. Actually, this is an outgrowth of the first two, because if you are sincere and you really believe that you can help, then you will be enthusiastic about what you are saying. You will approach the audience and the speech with a certain inner fire that will warm them. Enthusiasm is catching. If the speaker possesses it, the audience will react and react positively.

Within this section, you will find a variety of speeches, both entire speeches and beginnings and closes of speeches, that are inspirational. If you find one that suits your purposes, if you can fully believe in its contents, if you are anxious to communicate it to your next audience, then you will have the enthusiasm to deliver a truly inspirational speech.

$$\boxed{63}$$

TOPIC: *A Classic Pep Talk.*

AUDIENCE: *Team players, coaches, possibly some parents and the press.*

There is something that I am not going to tell you.

I am not going to say that it doesn't matter if we win or if we lose. If I said that, I doubt that anyone here would believe me anyway. We know that winning is better, far better, than losing. We know the joy and exhilaration that come with success on the field, and we know the pain and hurt that come with losing. So, I am not going to tell you that it doesn't matter who wins. We want to win. We will do our best to win. I know that it is the fervent hope of everyone here that we will win.

We have practiced; we have disciplined ourselves; we have worked for this day. We all know what it has entailed. We know the endless hours, the sore muscles, the fatigue, and we know the courage it took to keep on trying when everything within us told us to quit. Yes, we have worked for this day, and now it is ours.

We will go out there and work as a team, as one body, to bring victory to our side. In my heart, I know that it will be ours.

But, while I have not told you that it doesn't matter whether we win or lose, I *will* tell you that it matters more than anything else how we play that game. We will win today, but we will win because we are the better team. We will win because we will make less mistakes than they will. We will win because we have worked harder, practiced longer, and have sacrificed more.

We will go out there and we will play a hard and an aggressive game. We will hold nothing back; we will give it everything we have. But, we will also play a clean game. We will learn to respect our opponents. We will learn to match our strength against theirs, to pit our knowledge against theirs, to try our cunning in the face of theirs. We will come to respect them for what they are, just as we know that they will come to respect us for the team that we are.

Because of this, if we fall, we will work harder to get up and go on. If things look bleak, we will not despair, but we will try harder. If we are on the bottom, then we will know that the only way we can go is upward, and we will scramble and climb harder.

141

I also know that if one of their players falls, our players will be the first to offer their hands to help him to rise.

This is what makes us great. This is what gives us the determination to strive. This is what will give us the determination we need to win.

We are ready. We are willing. We are able.

Now—let's go out there and win!

SPECIAL DATA: *Time of speech: about two or three minutes, depending on audience reaction. This speech could be used effectively in a number of situations. It could be used at a pep rally before the "big" game. It might be used at an athletic banquet held toward the end of the season. It might be used in the locker room before any game. You will notice that this speech encourages players to dedicate themselves to giving the best they have to offer while making certain that they play cleanly and with respect for their opponents. This is generally understood and appreciated by parents and/or members of the press who hear it. This speech also builds naturally to its climax, and, with the last words, you will have the audience standing and cheering, and the team will be inspired to do their best.*

$$\boxed{64}$$

TOPIC: *Inspirational Opening for a Speech.*

AUDIENCE: *Suitable for all audiences.*

Good evening, ladies and gentlemen.

We are here this evening to discover. For a brief moment, bring your minds back to the first time you ever discovered something on your very own. Perhaps it was when you were very young and entailed something as simple as discovering that an object could float in water. Perhaps it was later in life as you struggled with the multiplication tables until that magic moment when you suddenly discovered the reason behind it, and it all became clear. Whatever the occasion was for you, try to think back to that time and try to remember what you felt.

Whatever it was, there was a joy and an exhilaration in that discovery.

Your mind rejoiced in its new knowledge, and something that had been incomprehensible suddenly became clear. It was the joy of learning, and, for that moment, it brightened your life. I know that was how it was for me, and I'd wager that your experience was similar.

Tonight, we are on the brink of discovery again. Through the ideas and insights that will be offered this evening, we will be able to open our minds to new avenues that will lead us to discover a new aspect of knowledge and understanding. It is an opportunity to be cherished.

That is what we offer: not answers, but opportunities. Opportunities to open our minds; opportunities to expand our perspectives; opportunities to exchange our ideas and in that exchange to come to new understandings and appreciations.

It has been said that man, unique among the animals, has the ability to think. Of all the powers with which we have been endowed, surely this is the greatest. The ability to think and to reason has lifted mankind from the mud and sent him to the stars. We here tonight have the wondrous opportunity to use our minds to discover each other and to share in the unique exchange of ideas that brings about the fulfillment of knowledge.

With open minds, hungry for ideas, let us begin our journey to discovery . . .

SPECIAL DATA: *Time of opening: about two minutes. This opening is particularly suited for the beginning of a program or panel discussion on a "hot" or controversial topic, which was how it was originally used. It might also be used effectively to introduce a very dynamic speaker or even a speech of your own that contains some material that the audience might find objectionable. This opening exhorts the audience to view what follows with an open mind. As we are all aware, when presenting something of a controversial nature, this is the best for which we can hope. Try it and see.*

65

TOPIC: *All-purpose Inspirational Closing for a Speech.*

AUDIENCE: *Suitable for all audiences.*

(NOTE: The following anecdote is particularly applicable to any speech in which you are urging your audience to do something, to try something new, or to deal with an existing condition. Further suggestions follow the anecdote.)

. . . Finally, I would like to tell you a story. It's about a wise man who lived long ago and very far away. This wise man was very kind and loving and was, consequently, much beloved by the people of this ancient land.

In this same land, there was a nobleman, a prince, who hated this wise man. He thought that the wise man was taking the love of the people away from him. The people listened to the wise man, not the prince, and that angered the prince very much.

One day, the prince said to his followers, "I have a plan to discredit the wise man; a way that I can make him appear to be a fool.

"Each day the wise man goes to the marketplace where he speaks to the people and gives them advice. Tomorrow, when the people gather, I will go to the square disguised as a peasant. In my hand I will hold a white dove. When the crowd has gathered, I will raise my voice above the crowd and say, 'Wise man! I have a simple question for you. This dove that I hold in my hand—is it alive or dead?'

"Now, while this appears a simple question, it is not, for if he says it is dead, I will open my hand and let the bird fly away. If he says it is alive, however, I will crush the bird in my hand and let it fall dead to the ground. Either way, he will be mistaken; either way, he will appear to have made a mistake; either way, it will appear that he cannot even tell the difference between a living and a dead bird. Thus he will be discredited in the eyes of the people and will lose their love."

The next day came, and, true to his word, the prince disguised himself as a peasant, and he went to the marketplace carrying a white dove. There he waited until the crowd had gathered and the wise man had appeared. He made his way to the front of the crowd and raised his voice.

"Wise man!" he shouted. "I would ask you a simple question. This dove that I hold in my hand—is it alive or is it dead?"

The crowd grew quiet, and all eyes turned toward the wise man. The wise man paused, looked at the prince in a manner filled with compassion, and said, "My son, do you not understand? That which you hold in your hand—it is what you make of it."

It is what you make of it. A wise answer from a wise man. Whether the dove that the prince held was alive or dead depended on the prince and what *he* did with what *he* had.

Tonight, I have told you about a new idea, a new concept, and now I leave it in your hands. What will we do with it? Will it be alive to soar and grow and flourish, or will it fall to the ground dead and unused?

To paraphrase the words of the wise man, It will be what *we* make of it.

SPECIAL DATA: *Time of anecdote: approximately three minutes. We think you can see the value of this anecdote when used as the conclusion of a speech. You have given your audience some insights or a plan or a program, and now you place it in their hands. From this point on, it will be up to them. Working together, you can see to it that the plan succeeds or fails, but it is really up to you. It is what you make of it. Used in this manner, this inspirational ending of a speech has a tremendous impact on any audience.*

66

TOPIC: *A Small Collection of Inspirational Thought Starters.*

AUDIENCE: *Suitable for any audience.*

(NOTE: Obviously, the following are not speeches, and we thought for some time before including them here. They are, however, excellent starters for any inspirational speech. Several suggestions follow.)

It is amazing how much can be accomplished if no one cares who gets the credit.

* * * * * * *

Success is a journey, not a destination.

* * * * * * *

Success requires more backbone than wishbone.

* * * * * * *

Determination is the difference between victory and defeat.

* * * * * * *

It's not the size of the man in the fight, but the size of the fight in the man that counts.

* * * * * * *

An alibi is like a crutch, it is only meant for the lame and the weak.

* * * * * * *

Victory is sweet, but you can't have it without sweat.

* * * * * * *

If it comes easy, question it; if it comes hard, work for it; if it comes at all, enjoy it, because it is yours!

* * * * * * *

Easy Street is always a road to defeat.

* * * * * * *

Luck is what happens when preparation meets opportunity.

* * * * * * *

Enter the game a gentleman . . . leave the same way.

* * * * * * *

When you are completely satisfied that you have played your best game, you probably haven't.

SPECIAL DATA: *Time of each saying: a few seconds. While the sayings are relatively short, the message each contains is huge. Any one of these sayings could be applied to a full-length inspirational speech. They apply equally to any sport and, by projection, to life itself. Consequently, a coach's pep talk or inspirational address at a formal function might begin with one of these sayings and proceed to elaborate upon it. We even know of one coach who has these sayings on placards on the wall of the locker room. Periodically, he will start an instructional period by asking one or more players to read one of the sayings and explain to the team what he feels the meaning to be. In this way, our friend believes, coaches can get the players to internalize the meaning of each saying, thus enriching their playing and their lives.*

67

TOPIC: *What Is a Winner?*

AUDIENCE: *Designed for a sports-minded audience, but really suitable for any group.*

Without a doubt, everyone here tonight has heard the old adage which goes, "It doesn't matter whether you win or lose; it's how you play the game that counts."

I know that I have often heard that expression, and it has often set me to thinking, because my own experience, as well as the experience of many whom I know, seems to contradict the wisdom expressed.

If you ask any athlete, any person who engages in competitive sports, anyone who has ever entered a competition of any kind, or even anyone who plays bridge or checkers—that person will tell you that winning and losing *do* matter. In fact, they matter a great deal.

Winning is better, far better, than losing. It feels better emotionally to win. The rewards, of either money or prestige, go to the winner. The winner gets the accolades. It is better to win than to lose.

However, "how you play the game" is also important. As a nation, America and Americans have always been on the side of the underdog. We like to root for the little guy; for the smaller opponent; for the team that's behind. This is not a "win-at-any-price" situation, however, for we enjoy seeing the result of determination, skill, and dedication, and we despise victories that are achieved through underhanded methods.

Therefore, perhaps the adage should be rewritten to state that "Winning is better than losing, but it is very important how you play the game in either case."

Let us now take this idea one step further. If it is good to win, then it is good to be a winner. If it is important that we play the game in a good and fair manner, then perhaps the way we play will determine whether we are winners or losers.

I speak here, of course, of the athletic field of competition, but this extends into other fields as well. There is victory on the basketball court, the football field, the baseball diamond, of course, but we all know that there are winners and losers in life as well, and that is, perhaps, the biggest game of all.

What is a winner? Certainly we've met them. They are not only those who have won contests of skill, endurance, and determination on a field, whether singly or with a team, but also people in our community whom we know stand out from the rest of us. They are people to whom others go for advice, for counsel, for guidance; people who have achieved something worthwhile and inspire others to do the same. I think it is safe to say that we have all met winners.

What are the traits that distinguish one person from another in this area? What makes one person a winner and another a loser? I honestly believe that the big difference is in how the person thinks; the attitude that governs his or her actions, whether on the field of athletic competition or in the competition of life itself.

For example, how many times in life does something come up that is new; that we must face for the first time; that involves challenges never before met against odds never before encountered? This might be starting a new job, facing a team with an unbeaten record, beginning a new business of our own. Whatever it is, the loser will see the work ahead and become convinced that the challenge is impossible. The loser will quit then and there. The winner will see it as a challenge. Certainly, the winner will have doubts, but he will refuse to quit until it is proven that he cannot do it. In short, a winner is always ready to tackle something new, while a loser is prone to believe that it simply cannot be done.

I really think that this is because a winner is challenged by a new problem, while a loser just doesn't want to face it. Both individuals see the problem, but the winner starts to think of ways to solve the problem even as he views it. The loser sees only the problem, large and looming, and it is so overwhelming that retreat is his only answer. A winner welcomes the opportunity to use his mind and his skills. Maybe he won't win, but he'll give it the best he's got. The loser won't even try.

You see, a winner isn't afraid of competition. Of course, as with all competition, there is a chance that he will lose. The winner, however, is willing to take that chance. He will pit himself against the others; he will play fairly; he will give it all he has. If he wins, he will be thrilled, but, if he loses there will be no excuses needed or given, for he will know that he has done his best. Just as inevitably, the loser excuses himself with the idea that the competition is too stiff and will beat him out.

Of course winners make mistakes. But a winner knows that he is sometimes wrong and is willing to admit his mistakes. When he doesn't win a winner looks at himself and his actions as objectively as possible; finds out where he went wrong or what he did that stopped him from winning; learns from that mistake; and then does all in his power to correct the mistake so that it won't be a drawback next time. The winner does this freely and without reservation while the loser is sitting back somewhere finding someone else to blame for his failure.

A key factor in all of this is the fact that a winner is decisive. Winners make commitments. They analyze a problem, decide on a course of action, and make a decision on which they act with a total commitment of themselves. The loser frustrates himself, and usually everyone around him, with indecision. Maybe it won't work out . . . what if I fail . . . what will others think? Winners consciously decide to accept the challenge.

The greatest difference, however, between a winner and a loser is not in the doing as much as in the approach. You see, I have never met a winner who wasn't positive; I have never met a loser who wasn't negative. A winner thinks positively, acts positively, and lives positively. A loser usually has a negative attitude and a negative approach to everything.

You meet a person on the street, and you ask him how things are going. He responds that the world is lousy. People are rotten, with each person out to get what he can for himself and to the devil with anyone else. No, he isn't doing too well, but that's only because his boss was jealous of him, and so he got fired. Some day he'll show them all and open his own store, but he thinks he'd better wait, because the other stores in town would probably gang up on him and force him out of business. Who have you met: a winner or a loser? I think you know the answer.

You meet another person, and you ask him the same question. He tells you that he is really excited. His job is filled with challenges, but he likes that, and each challenge renews his vigor and determination. Oh, yes, in a few months, he'll be opening his own office. It's going to be touch and go for a while, he is certain, but he really believes that with hard work, he'll be able to make a go of it. He is looking forward to it. He has to go now, because he has a meeting of a group that is interested in trying to help the city's youth. Is this a winner or a loser? You know the answer here as well.

If you want to be a winner, you must assume the characteristics of a winner. You must be ready to try new things and new projects; you must face each new problem as a challenge to be overcome; you must welcome competition with respect rather than fear; if you make mistakes, you must admit them and use them as foundation stones on which to build success; you must be decisive, and your decisions must be backed by your personal commitment; and, finally, you must be positive at all times, especially when the going gets rough. You must think positively, act positively, and live positively.

Do you want to be a winner? Fine, then be one. Think like a winner and act like a winner, and sooner than you think, you will *be* a winner. Being a winner is something that no one can ever take away from you, whether on the grass of the playing field or throughout your entire life.

SPECIAL DATA: *Time of speech: about ten minutes. This speech applies the philosophy of winning to the life experience from the perspective of the athlete. It is, therefore, suited to any audience. The characteristics of a winner that are* *summarized in the next to last paragraph, might also be applied to any team sport while excluding their relevance to life situations. In this way, you might develop an inspirational speech on winning in a specific sport.*

$$\boxed{68}$$

TOPIC: *Ingredients That Make a True Athlete.*

AUDIENCE: *Team members, colleagues, sports-minded individuals.*

In my career as a coach, I have taken charge of hundreds, possibly thousands, of young people who called themselves athletes. Of that number, all of them played at the game, but not all of them, in my opinion, were true athletes. That title I have reserved for those who were special.

You see, in my coaching philosophy there are three ingredients that are necessary for an individual to become a true athlete. I believe that these three elements are desire, character, and cohesiveness. When they act in combination, I know that I have a true athlete on my hands.

Let's talk about desire first. I believe that each player should have the inner desire to be a winner. He should look forward to good competition and the enjoyment of facing the challenge that is before him. This true athlete should set his goals and objectives, and then work to reach them. The true athlete should always know where he is going, and, specifically, how he is going to get there. By this, I do not mean complacency—rather, the true athlete should make every effort to improve the poor areas of his performance. Indeed, the athlete must continually readjust goals for continued improvement. This is all part of desire, and in order for an athlete to give 100 percent desire, his mind must say, "I can," and his heart must respond with, "I will."

Equally important in the true athlete is character, and that is something that I look for in every person I coach. Basically, character is the *real* you. It is what you are at the base of all your dealings and doings. I have never met a true athlete who did not possess a good and positive character. This is extremely important.

Consider, if you will, that every athlete is a spectacle. Because an athlete has very special talents, many people view him as they would a character in a play or a theatrical presentation. Therefore, the athlete has the same power as theater and the media to move us. If the athlete does something that contributes to society in a positive way, there are people waiting to emulate him and follow his example. On the other hand, if the athlete does something contrary to the laws of society, there are people waiting to stumble into his pitfall as well. Therefore, the true athlete has a good and positive character that allows him to be a positive role model to others. Character is like the foundation of a house; it is below the surface, but everything rests upon it. A good foundation will stand up to all onslaughts, while a poor foundation will crumble under assault. A good character is a necessity for the true athlete.

Finally, I believe that the true athlete possesses cohesiveness. As a coach, I prefer no one-man shows; no self-centered super stars. I like to have a team made up of a number of players with a cohesive spirit. Each player should have only one goal in mind—to perform within the team structure for the best possible end result. "No chain is stronger than its weakest link," and, likewise, no team is stronger than its weakest player. Team credit should definitely come first and individual credit second. There is no place on the team or within the individual athlete for jealousy, selfishness, and self-pride.

I want a team of individuals who have no fear of their opponents; a team that plays hard, plays fair, and plays to win. Prior to each game, I want to see a team that unites in the belief that they will not lose; a team committed to playing as one in achieving that goal. Even if the opposing team is taller, faster, and has more ability, there is no reason for any team not being number one in team desire and team cohesiveness.

Desire, character, cohesiveness—these are the ingredients that make a true athlete. Do you have the desire to be a winner along with the willingness to work for it? Do you have the foundation of good character that will allow you to overcome the obstacles rather than crumbling under the stress? Can you achieve the cohesiveness necessary to being an effective team player—one who gives his all for the team's victory rather than for individual glory? These are questions that each of us must answer separately and alone. But, if your answer is yes; if you feel that you have within you these traits and characteristics, then you stand the best chance of all of being a true athlete; a person who is a winner and will continue to be a winner both on the playing field and throughout his entire life.

SPECIAL DATA: *Time of speech: approximately five minutes. This is the type of inspirational speech that a coach might give to his team during preseason, at the beginning of practice, or before the start of the regular season. It can fire up* *the players, and it definitely gives them something to think about. This speech might also be used to express your views to a coaching staff, group of parents, board of education, group of journalists, and the like. Remember, if you really believe what is being expressed, the enthusiasm you add to the words will make this an inspirational speech that will be remembered. If you catch fire, that fire will spread to whatever group you are addressing.*

69

TOPIC: *Interest Versus Commitment: The Signs of Greatness.*

AUDIENCE: *Suitable for any sports-minded audience.*

Recently, my son attended a birthday party where a magician entertained the children. When my son came home, he was bursting with enthusiasm over what the magician had done, and he regaled me with an account of how the magician had made balls, coins, cards, and rabbits appear and disappear, change places, and do all sorts of wonderful things. In fact, my son told me he was so impressed that he wanted to be a magician when he grew up.

Shortly thereafter, I happened to be in a bookstore, and I purchased a book on sleight of hand and magic as a hobby, and I gave it to my son. He embraced it gleefully and ran off to his room, presumably to delve into the realm of magic.

That's about as far as it went. He did one card trick for his mother and me, as I recall, and the book was relegated to a shelf where it gathered dust. He never mentioned wanting to be a professional magician again.

Then it happened that I had lunch with a friend of mine who had enjoyed magic as a hobby since he was my son's age and had made extra money all through college giving magic shows wherever he could. I told him about my son, and my friend answered that he wasn't at all surprised.

"You see," he said, "anybody can do a card trick, but to do this . . ." and he reached up with a bare hand and produced the Ace of Spades from thin air ". . . requires hours and hours of practice in the techniques of sleight of hand. It's not easy, it takes a lot of time and effort. It requires a real commitment."

Of course, that was it. My son had been intrigued by what he had seen. This inspired in him an interest in it. When he learned what was involved, however, he simply would not commit himself to the long and tedious work that was necessary to master the art. Consequently, magic as a hobby slipped down on his list of priorities.

That makes me wonder if the same thing could be said about people who engage in sports. What is the difference between a Saturday golfer and Arnold Palmer? What is the difference between a playground basketball player and Julius Irving? What is the difference between the guy who plays sandlot football with a group of friends and Roger Staubach? Isn't the difference the same one that existed between my son and Harry Houdini?

Certainly, many people are interested in sports. The popularity of all sports has grown over the past years, and today, recreational sports define a multimillion dollar industry in our country. Racket clubs, health spas, and gyms of every kind are doing very well, as more and more people find enjoyment, relaxation, and exhilaration on tennis courts, golf links, and athletic fields of every kind.

People have become better for it. They have gained health and vitality, self-confidence and poise, along with enjoying the comradeship that comes from friendly competition. They like what they are doing, and it is good for them. What better combination could there be.

Yet, we all realize that however much fun it may be, there is a substantial difference between John Doe swinging his racket and John McEnroe serving for game, set, and match. There is a substantial difference between Nancy Doe with her brand new golf clubs and Nancy Lopez coming in at twelve under par.

The major difference is the degree of commitment of the player. To paraphrase my magician friend, anyone can bounce a ball, hit a ball, throw a ball, but it takes a real commitment to become a Kareem Abdul Jabar, a Reggie Jackson, a Joe Namath.

What is commitment? It is a voice within the individual that says, "I have the interest in the sport, but I know that I am not all that I can be in it; I know that I can become better; I *will* become better. Nothing will stand in the way of my perfecting my skill and talent. I will do whatever has to be done in order to grow. This is a personal promise on my part that cannot be broken."

This is commitment. It is a dedication that states emphatically that the individual *will* improve, *will* become the best player in his or her particular sport that he or she can be, *will* allow nothing to stand in the way of that goal. Commitment is going the extra inches when everything in you is screaming at you to quit. Commitment is getting up when the rest of the world is snugly asleep in its bed in order to run or exercise or work on a particular problem related to the sport. Commitment is working at it each and every day. Commitment is never letting go, never giving up, never stopping, even when you are tired, disgusted, and discouraged, and you want nothing more than to crawl into a corner and sleep.

Without commitment, you will still enjoy your sport, and you may even become good at it, but you will never be great at it; never become a name recorded in the annals of sport. Since its inception, hundreds of millions of people have played baseball, but there is only one Babe Ruth, one Mickey Mantle, one Jackie Robinson. There are millions with the interest, but there are relatively few with the commitment that will single them out for greatness.

Of course, with commitment comes a price tag that is paid by the individual athlete. Nothing worthwhile comes without effort. As the current wisdom goes, "No pain; no gain." The price of commitment comes in terms of sore muscles, cuts, scrapes and bruises, delicious foods that must be passed by, rearranged schedules, fatigue, and disappointment. Commitment is not easy, it carries with it no guarantees or assurances, the only thing it promises you is pain and hard work. Yet, if you want to achieve greatness, it is the only path to take.

Yet, I believe that *every* commitment brings success. Commitment gives you the chance of becoming great at your sport, but in the very act of committing yourself, you achieve a victory of spirit. It gives you the knowledge that you *can* plan a goal for yourself, *can* work for something worthwhile and good, *can* overcome your doubts, fears, and sense of limitation. Commitment brings with it a self-assurance and a self-confidence that manifests itself in *all* aspects of your life and stands you in good stead for coping with the pressures that life itself inevitably brings. There is a spirit within the committed person that says, "Whatever comes, I can tackle it unafraid. I *can* do it."

Now, please don't misunderstand me—interest alone is fine. Remember that it was interest that brought you to sports in the first place. Interest in sports will enrich your life, revitalize your health, and provide you with lifelong enjoyment. Interest alone is fine.

If, however, you look within yourself and find there a desire to excel; a desire to be more than merely good; a desire to be the best that you can be; a desire to be great, the only way that you are going to turn that desire into reality is by making a commitment to the sport. This commitment will cost you time and pain, but it will give you the chance at greatness that you so earnestly want. As certainly as I am speaking to you now, it is only through commitment that greatness is achieved.

Therefore, the question is, "Am I ready to make that commitment?" This is a question that I cannot answer for you. Nor can it be answered by parents, friends, advisers, or even by fortune tellers. Rather, it is a question only you can answer.

Do I believe that I can be great? Do I believe that through dedication and effort far above and beyond that which other participants in the sport will give, I can rise above the others in my proficiency and skills? Do I know that I will pay a price for my efforts, and it will not always be a pleasant or easily affordable price? Am I willing to pay that price in order for the chance at greatness? Will I have the will power to do what must be done?

If your answers to these questions are that *yes*, you want greatness; *yes*, you can achieve it; *yes*, you will pay a price; *yes*, it is worth the price and you are willing to pay it; and, *yes*, you can do it—then, by all means, *make that commitment!* Do what has to be done. Achieve greatness.

As with everything in life, it is up to you. You must make the choice; you must do the work; and, if there is greatness at the end of the path, that will be yours as well.

If you can't make the commitment, then don't make it—there is nothing wrong with that. If, however, you feel that you can make it; that you *must* make it, then be yourself, be all that it is possible for you to be.

Be great!

SPECIAL DATA: *Time of speech: slightly over ten minutes. It occurs to us that you might conclude this inspirational speech with the story we gave you in entry 65. This would place the choice directly into the hands of the audience. It is, however, perfectly fine just the way it is. You could add to the speech by giving examples (and there are hundreds of them) of real-life athletes who overcame handicaps through commitment and dedication. That would lengthen the speech, of course, and it is sufficiently tight the way it is now. As always, however, you should make whatever changes suit your style and your audience.*

$$\boxed{70}$$

TOPIC: *The Role of the Coach in the Inspirational Process.*

AUDIENCE: *Adults; fellow coaches.*

"A teacher affects eternity; he can never tell where his influence stops . . ."

With these words, written in his autobiography, Henry Adams honored *all* educators. As coaches, that is primarily what we are—teachers. We exist to teach and train the players who come under our leadership, and the thought expressed in this quotation that what we do on the field, in the locker rooms, and in instructional classrooms may have implications weeks, months, and even years later in the lives of our players is a very sobering one, indeed. It places a real and a very heavy responsibility on the shoulders of each and every one of us.

Yet, I know of very few coaches—very few teachers—who do not accept this responsibility willingly and gladly. Indeed, coaches constantly work toward inspiring their players—their "students" if you will—and exerting an influence that will, as Henry Adams stated, "affect eternity."

How do we inspire? How do we fire up our "students" to do their best and achieve all of which they are capable? Well, there is one way. There is one key element in all inspiration that is available to all of us— enthusiasm.

Indeed, enthusiasm is the key factor in all inspiration. If we are enthusiastic about something—anything—our enthusiasm is communicated to those around us. If you have ever been with someone who is "hot" about something, then you will know what I mean. There is something catching about enthusiasm. It is as if the enthusiastic person is on fire— we cannot help but feel the heat.

How do you become enthusiastic? I feel that it is a three-part process.

First, you learn it. Know your subject matter. Understand the game and all its complexities. Look for examples of the application of what you teach in practice rather than theory. Show them sidelights and insights they had not dreamed of before. Know all you can.

Second, you love it. Become convinced of the value and necessity of what you are teaching your players. See it as a joy rather than a task. Look on it as something about which you want to know more and which you want others to know more about.

Finally, you live it. Bring your enthusiasm out on the field. Enjoy your teaching and your team. Share your personal joy in your subject with those you instruct. Want to make them see the game as you do and work toward that goal. Be happy about being able to teach others what you know.

Nor is this process limited to subject matter. A human being can learn, love, and live such qualities as honesty, equality, brotherhood, and truth. Enthusiasm for these and other qualities that are the hallmarks of mankind at its best will also be communicated to those we instruct if we learn them, love them, and live them.

In 1973, when the New York Mets won the National League pennant, a story came out that one of the players, Tug McGraw, coined a phrase that was adopted first by the rest of the team and finally by all the fans. That phrase was, "You gotta believe!" With that motto and the enthusiasm of the players, undoubtedly helped along by the enthusiasm of the fans, the team went from the bottom of the league all the way to the final game of the World Series.

That story has a direct relationship to our roles as coaches—as teachers who are hoping to inspire our students. If you want to inspire, "You gotta believe!" "You gotta believe" that what you are doing is important and that your players will benefit from what you are teaching them. "You gotta believe" that you can reach them and make a difference in their lives. "You gotta believe" that your "students" will love it as much as you do and will work because of the love that you have communicated.

If you learn it, love it, and live it; if you believe these things; if you act on them; if you carry your personal enthusiasm into your dealings with your students; then you cannot help but communicate your enthusiasm to them and they cannot help but be affected by it.

If that isn't inspiration; I don't know what is!

SPECIAL DATA: *Time of speech: about five minutes. This is an inspirational speech about inspiration. The principles on which it is based are sound, and the actions it suggests are firmly rooted in good educational practices. This is the type of speech that might be given to fellow coaches, by a coach to the coaching staff, or, with modifications, to players who will be helping other players with less experience. Although short, this is an extremely powerful and effective presentation.*

$$\boxed{71}$$

TOPIC: *You Can Make the Difference.*

AUDIENCE: *Suitable for almost any audience (See SPECIAL DATA).*

When my son came home from his first day in the first grade, I asked him how things had gone.

"Terrible," he announced.

Naturally, I tried to get to the bottom of his difficulty, and finally the truth came out.

Looking up at me, he blurted, "There's three boys and ten million girls!"

That was then, of course, and this is now, and I'm certain that today my son would relish those odds. Naturally, he exaggerated, but at that stage of his life he literally felt overwhelmed by numbers.

That's an easy state to get into, incidentally. Just get stuck in any rush-hour traffic jam, and you can very easily feel overwhelmed by numbers.

Once we begin feeling that way, it's fairly easy to take the next step and begin feeling insignificant. I'm only one car among all those other cars on the highway. What can I do? I'm only one citizen among all the citizens of this country. What can I do? I'm only one human being among all the human beings on this planet. What can I do?

Yes, it's easy to feel that way. When we perceive ourselves as tiny and unimportant; when we perceive ourselves as not mattering in the scheme of things; when we begin to look at what we do as incidental and insignificant in a cold and unfeeling world; it's easy to adopt an attitude of "Why bother? It doesn't matter anyhow."

Of course, we all feel that way from time to time—we wouldn't be human if we didn't. It is important, however, that we recognize this for what it is: a momentary setback; a time when the pressures of the world have gotten to us; a time when we are momentarily overwhelmed by the demands of the day-to-day world.

We are important, each and every one of us, and what we do does make a difference. It makes a difference now, tomorrow, and the day after.

Why should I vote in elections, for example? My vote is only a single mark among many. If I didn't vote, it wouldn't change anything. I'm only one person.

What is one vote? I'll tell you. Thomas Jefferson was elected president by one vote in the electoral college. So was John Quincy Adams. Rutherford B. Hayes was elected president by one vote. His election was contested and referred to an electoral commission where the matter was again decided by a single vote. The man who cast the deciding vote for President Hayes was himself elected to Congress by a margin of one vote. California, Washington, Idaho, Texas, and Oregon gained statehood by one vote. The War of 1812 was brought about by a series of events based on one vote. The successor to Abraham Lincoln, President Andrew Johnson, was saved from impeachment by—you guessed it—one vote.

We do make a difference, each and every one of us. If we give up; if we feel that we cannot make a difference, then the difference we make will be a negative one. If, however, we know that what we do will have an effect tomorrow and tomorrow and tomorrow, then we will do our best at all times, and that best will make a positive and a glowing contribution to the world.

If we believe this, then we won't try to be interesting; we will be interested. We won't expect to be pleased; we will be pleasing. We won't wait to be entertained; we will be entertaining. We won't wait to be loved; we will be loving. We won't wait to be asked to help; we will be helpful.

That will make all the difference.

It has been said that to get anywhere in this world, you have to know someone important. I think that's true. You do have to know someone important—you have to know yourself.

Knowing yourself; knowing what you can and cannot do; trying to do your best in each and every situation; believing that what you do today is important and will affect tomorrow; striving, with this in mind, to do what you can when you can will make this world a better place for everyone in it.

Just imagine a world filled with people who know that what they do will make a difference, and who strive consciously to make that difference a positive good for everyone.

That world is a reality within our grasp.

You *do* make a difference, and that difference is *you*.

SPECIAL DATA: *Time of speech: about three minutes. This is an all-purpose inspirational speech that may be used for a variety of purposes and audiences. The speech itself suggests a positive philosophy that, if internalized, cannot help but bring about positive results. The idea that* *what an individual does is important and has influence on the lives of others is one that might be used with colleagues very effectively as well as with team members, support staffs, parent groups, or with any group that needs an uplifting and positive message. Deliver it with conviction.*

$$\boxed{72}$$

TOPIC: *Inspirational, Sports-oriented Poem.*

AUDIENCE: *Suitable for all audiences.*

He showed up one day before practice,
    A kid wearing tee shirt and jeans.
One look would have told you he wasn't
    At all like the kids on the team.

He wasn't as tall as the others;
    The toes of his feet pointed in;
And his knees and his elbows were awkward;
    His arms and his legs were too thin.

But, he said to me, "Coach, it's no secret
    That I'm small and a kinda thin guy,
But just give me a chance, and I promise
    That I will do nothing but try."

It was maybe the way that he said it
    Or the look that was fixed in his eye,
But somehow I knew I believed him,
    And I said, "O.K., kid, you can try,

"But I'll tell you it won't be so easy,
    And I'm not gonna give you a break;
You'll work just as hard as the others,
    And you'll earn the position you make."

Well, the kid started in with a smile,
    'Though he knew he was in for some pain,

For he traveled a road that was rocky;
        He fought for each inch that he gained.
The other kids often would tease him—
        Call him names and play tricks on him, too.
They'd trip him and tackle him harder
        Than anyone needed to do.

But the kid would just smile as he lay there,
        Then pick himself up with a grin
And brush off the pain and get ready
        To go back and try it again.

He tried twice as hard as the others,
        And when practice was over I found
He would work and he'd labor for hours
        All alone, with no others around.

Then the jokes and the name-calling ended
        As I guessed that someday it must,
And they treated the kid as an equal,
        For they knew he was someone to trust.

That kid made the squad 'cause he earned it—
        The smallest of all on the team,
But he played with a courage that made him
        Far greater than many I'd seen.

Now, often when my life is troubled,
        And problems mount up to the sky,
I think of the kid who came to me
        With only the promise to try.

And I think how in trying, he made it,
        In spite of the strife and the pain;
In spite of the odds stacked against him;
        When everyone thought it in vain.

And it gives me the spirit I've needed
        To allow me to cope and get by,
When I think of the kid who succeeded,
        'Cause he had the courage to try.

SPECIAL DATA: *Time of poem: about two minutes. There are a number of uses for a poem such as this. It is easily incorporated into any inspirational speech. It is a powerful ending* *for any spech that details a new project or the start of something. Printed up and placed on a wall or as part of the literature given to players, it is a constant reminder and inspiration to try one's hardest.*

Afterthoughts

We cannot overemphasize the importance of delivering a speech that is meant to be inspirational with enthusiasm. You can have the best material in the world, containing true gems of wisdom, but it will go unheeded if it is delivered in a dull and flat tone as if someone were reading a telephone book.

If, however, the speaker will first become enthusiastic about his topic and then prepare and deliver his speech or one of the speeches in this section, when he delivers the speech that enthusiasm, that joy, that concern will be communicated to the audience. The audience cannot help but respond and be inspired.

SECTION 7

A Collection
of Effective Speeches
for Retirements
and Testimonials

Coaches, we have found, are very frequently called on to speak at retirement dinners and testimonials. Whether the occasion be for a fellow coach, a player, an alumnus, or someone even obliquely connected with sports, his friends and associates have gone to some trouble to prepare this honor. Therefore, if you have been invited to speak, it is because of some special relationship you bear to the honoree. Perhaps it is one of your coaches when you played, or perhaps a lad whom you coached, or perhaps a colleague with whom you have worked for many years. Whatever the case, you know the honored individual, and you are expected to deliver a speech based on that knowledge.

Unless it is specifically stated otherwise, you may safely assume that you will be one of a number of speakers. Consequently, retirement speeches and testimonials should be kept relatively short. As a general rule, these speeches should rarely exceed five minutes. If, however, you are specifically designated as the principal or only speaker, then your speech should lengthen accordingly.

Humor is always appreciated in these speeches, provided, of course, that the humor is warm and personal. If at all possible, the humor should be based on some personal experience with the honoree. It goes without saying that the humor must never embarrass the honored person or make him uncomfortable. It is always wise, furthermore, to place the humor at the beginning of the speech and close with genuine and heartfelt praise or good wishes for the individual.

The following pages contain a number of examples of speeches that are appropriate for a variety of circumstances and relationships. Furthermore, the Special Data *sections following each speech contain many hints and suggestions for their effective delivery. May you deliver them in good health, and may the retiree or honored guest find pleasure and enjoyment in them.*

RETIREMENT SPEECHES

$$\boxed{73}$$

TOPIC: *Retirement of a Coach.*

AUDIENCE: *Adults; mixed audience of relatives, friends, and colleagues.*

Someone once defined the term "mixed emotions" as watching your mother-in-law drive over a cliff—in your brand new Cadillac!

I don't know about that, and I am certain that mothers-in-law as a group are undeservedly maligned. I do, however, appreciate the term "mixed emotions" in its fullest sense this evening, for, as I watch Bill Howard sit here, and I realize that in a few short weeks Bill will be retiring from coaching, I am at once the happiest and the saddest of people.

I am happy, because Bill Hoard will finally be getting the relaxation he deserves after all these years. I am happy that Bill will, as he has told me, get to travel and visit for a while with his children. I am happy that he and Betty, his charming wife of almost 43 years, will get to have some time together and take those vacations they always planned but somehow never got around to. For all the good things that this retirement means for Bill, his wife, and his family, I am overjoyed.

I am saddened, however, because his retirement means that we who are left after him will not see him as frequently as we would like. I am saddened because he won't be there to go to for advice, counsel, insight into problems, or just the friendly smile and kind word that Bill was never without and that made your day a little brighter. I am saddened, because there will be new athletes and new teams who will never know Bill's coaching, his guidance, his expertise, and his care. I am saddened, because it will be so difficult for us to live up to that record of greatness and gentility, skill and perseverance, courage and spirit that Bill leaves as his legacy. Because he will touch our lives less often, I am deeply saddened.

Bill, I know that I speak for everyone present this evening when I tell you that you will be sorely missed. We have learned from you over the years, and we take our consolation in the fact that what you have taught us, both by practice on the field and by example in your life, will continue to be our guide in dealing with the generations of athletes yet to come.

Bill, we love you, and may your retirement be filled with the riches you deserve.

SPECIAL DATA: *Time of speech: about three minutes. This is the short type of speech we spoke about in the introduction to this section. Notice that it is rather general and could almost apply to any coach who retires after many years of service. The next speech is an example of one that is a bit more specific in its content.*

$$\boxed{74}$$

TOPIC: *Retirement of a Coach, II.*

AUDIENCE: *Suitable for any audience.*

I want to set a rumor to rest this evening. Yes, Bill Howard and I go back a long time, but there is absolutely no truth to the story that Bill used to paint dinosaur eggs brown and use them for footballs.

Actually, I have known Bill for over twenty-five years, and in that span of years, you get to know a fellow pretty well. I think that tonight I am going to take a chance at ending that friendship by telling you some of Bill's hidden secrets—things which he has told no one, and that I know only because I either saw them happen or was involved in some way. Bill wouldn't want me to be telling you some of this, but a retirement is a very special occasion, and I believe you have a right to know what kind of a man we are honoring tonight.

What kind of man is Bill Howard? If a kid had the desire, Bill had the time for him. I've known Bill to stay hours after the rest of us went home working with a player who had a problem. I've known him to give up his evenings, his Sundays, his vacation time, to help a player improve. He never told anyone about this.

What kind of man is Bill Howard? I have known kids—too many to count—who had personal problems at home; who were flirting with drugs and danger; who were close to dropping out of school and life; who had real problems with parents, teachers, girlfriends, and life in general. I have seen these kids literally turned around in their lives by Bill's counseling. Never in public, but alone, where no one could see, Bill would talk, cajole, threaten, plead if he had to, but he would show them a better way, a way to surmount their difficulties; and he stood behind them every minute while they began to take positive charge of their lives. I know of kids who could have ended up in the worst possible condition and who are today responsible workers, parents, and citizens, all because Bill Howard took the time to care. Bill never told anyone about this.

What kind of man is Bill Howard? I have seen Bill reach into his own pocket to see to it that a kid got enough to eat or wasn't left out of an activity because he could not afford it. Bill was rarely repaid in money, and he never asked for it. When I asked him about that once, Bill simply told me that he got repaid in other ways. Perhaps you know what he meant. Again, this is something Bill never told anyone.

What kind of man is Bill Howard? I have seen him agonize for hours over plays and players. Yes, he had a team, but to Bill that team was composed of individuals, each with special talents, special needs, and special handling requirements. Bill designed his strategies in order to get the best from each player and to put each player in the situation that was best for *his* individual talents and growth. That was no easy task, and the time that Bill put into it is beyond measure. Yet, Bill Howard never told anyone about this.

Yes, we know Bill's outstanding record as a coach, but these are the hidden qualities, the special actions that no one saw except Bill and the kid that he happened to be helping at the time. Bill never told anyone about the quiet good that he did. For Bill, it was enough that he had done it.

What kind of man is Bill Howard? You must judge that for yourself. As far as I am concerned, he is a man who is now retiring after a brilliant and spotless career as an outstanding coach and an outstanding human being. He is a man to whom I wish the best that can be in the years to come. He is a man who has earned whatever good will come to him in his retirement years.

He is a man for the rest of us to emulate; a man for us to respect; a man for us to honor; and, most important to me, he is a man whom I am proud to call my friend.

SPECIAL DATA: *Time of speech: about five minutes. Not only is this a slightly longer speech than the first one, but notice how much more specific it is, drawing for its material from the speaker's personal relationship to and knowledge of the retiree. It is also clear that the speaker is a very*

close personal friend and is qualified to know the sub-
ject's personality in special ways. Therefore, he is al-
lowed to get personal. Don't use a glowing and highly
personal speech such as this if the subject of your speech
is only a casual acquaintance or someone you only know
from the job. In that case, stick to the records and use
general terms. If, however, you are a close friend and
can spread some personal insight into the positive na-
ture of the subject, then a speech patterned after this
one is dramatic, dynamic, and certain to move any
audience.

75

TOPIC: *Retirement of a Coach, III.*

AUDIENCE: *Suitable for any audience.*

I think you all know about Bill Howard's habit of never sitting down
during a game but pacing back and forth until the final whistle. Well, now
that he is retiring, the truth may at last be told. You know how Bill always
wore that coaching outfit in our team's colors? Well, every year, I would
order it one size too small, and Bill never wanted to sit down and possibly
embarrass himself before a stadium full of fans.

Of course that's a joke, as anyone who knows this man's outstanding
physical condition will tell you. Actually, I believe that Bill's pacing was
an example of his fantastic surplus of energy—energy that he put into
whatever he did both on and off the field; energy that not only made Bill
a good coach, but a great one.

As Athletic Director, I have known Bill Howard both personally and
professionally for several years. It is without qualification that I tell you
that I know of no finer human being and no finer coach than the man who
sits here and whom we are honoring tonight on the occasion of his retirement.

I just spoke of Bill's energy, and I have witnessed it in action during
practice and games. I could also speak of his skill and expertise—skill in
turning disorganized crews of would-be athletes into precise, functioning

teams that have led us to more than one state championship, and expertise at getting the best out of each athlete and designing strategies that worked under the most trying conditions.

I could also speak of his humanity. I could tell you of how he was always willing to go out on a limb for one of his players who needed help. I could tell you of how he inspired his athletes by personal example and personal enthusiasm rather than rhetoric and speeches. I could tell you how, as a friend, he was always there when you needed him, always ready to give that helping hand.

I could also speak of the respect that Bill Howard commands from his players, his fellow coaches, and the coaches and players on our rival teams. I could tell you how this respect is not given gratuitously, but has been earned over the years by what this man has accomplished in his own life and in the lives of others. I could, I am certain, fill hours and hours reading the congratulatory messages and messages of praise that this man has received since word of this retirement dinner was spread.

I could tell you all of this.

However, there is no need for me to tell you these things. Bill Howard's life as we know it speaks more eloquently of this man than any words it might be my privilege to say about him. His life has been a living speech showing his dignity, his ability, and his humanity—a living speech of which it has been our honor to be a part.

In the years to come, we wish Bill all that he has earned over the years—happiness, joy, rest, respect.

Bill, I know that you are the one to be honored tonight, but in a real sense, it is not you who is honored—it is we. We are honored to be allowed to share this occasion with you. We are honored to have been a part of such an exemplary life. We are honored to have known a man such as you.

May all the best come your way, Bill. If anyone deserves it—you do.

SPECIAL DATA: *Time of speech: about four minutes. Although this speech is filled with praise (as most retirement speeches are— can you think of one you've heard that wasn't?), it does not delve as deeply into the subject's personality as the one before it, nor is it as general as the first one in this section. The person giving the speech was the subject's job superior (boss). Knowing this, the audience realizes that the speaker was in the position to know of the subject's record of performance which, you'll notice, was incorporated into this speech.*

$$\boxed{76}$$

TOPIC: *Retirement of an Athletic Director.*

AUDIENCE: *Suitable for any audience.*

Let's speak for a moment about pressure. With any job there comes a certain amount of pressure, but let that job involve handling people and the pressure is increased tenfold. Make those people coaches, administrators, officials, and teams, and the pressure index pops off the top of the scale and keeps right on going.

That, ladies and gentlemen, is precisely why I have so much respect for Tom Masterson. For over twenty years, Tom has taken the pressure and handled it like the champion that he is. As Athletic Director, he has dealt with all sorts of crises from shipments not arriving on time to irate coaches such as myself. In all of these situations he has remained the one fixed point in a sea of confusion; the rational voice in a babel of despair; the cool head in a room filled with heads so hot the steam escaped through the ears.

Indeed, it has been my privilege to work with Tom for so long. I got to see him in action, and, to my everlasting gratitude, I got to know him. The same qualities of concern, calmness under pressure, caring about people, and willingness to give of himself that made him such an outstanding athletic director have also made him the most outstanding and the most trusted of friends. I cherish that relationship, and I know that it will continue long after Tom is no longer in his official position and I can't yell at him any more.

No one can deny that Tom Masterson has earned his retirement. Over the years, Tom's contributions to organized sports, to the players and coaches, and to the general public have enriched us all. Tom's work has provided us with enjoyment, personal accomplishment, and a sense of pride. The largest part of that pride is our pride that we have known a man of his caliber, a man of his dedication, a man of his integrity.

Therefore, Tom, it is the wish of everyone here that your retirement be filled with at least as much happiness as you have given to us over the years. If that wish is even partially granted, you will be smiling, indeed, and that will add to our happiness as well.

Congratulations, Tom Masterson, on a brilliant career. As you have given so generously to others, may your retirement give to you the very best that life can offer.

SPECIAL DATA: *Time of speech: about three and one-half minutes. Here is a retirement speech where the subject is defined through the work that he has done. This is another good approach. Although general in nature, this speech parallels what the subject has accomplished in his career with the feelings of the audience for a good retirement. Although this speech was aimed at an Athletic Director, there is no reason why the same general approach could not be used for a retiring coach.*

$$\boxed{77}$$

TOPIC: *Retirement of a Sports Official.*

AUDIENCE: *Suitable for any audience.*

Ed Perry, it's about time you relaxed. You've been an official for over thirty years, Ed. You've officiated at countless games. You must have made hundreds of thousands of calls; handed out thousands and thousands of penalties; called hundreds and hundreds of really close calls. All that had to produce some tension, Ed, so it really is time that you relaxed.

Therefore, if somebody will remove Ed's dark glasses and bring in his seeing-eye dog, we'll get him comfortable and I can begin.

Actually I want you to know that Ed doesn't mind that little joke, and gave me permission to kid him a bit. We are actually very good friends as you know. After all, you can't spend years standing nose to nose with a person and calling him a myopic idiot without becoming very close.

You know, that was a joke, but it has a ring of truth to it, because the first time I met Ed Perry was when I was a coach, and Ed had called a penalty against my team. I remember that my arms were flailing about and my voice was at least a thousand decibels strong. Then, I came face to face with Ed Perry and those steel-blue eyes, firm jaw, and will of iron. Naturally, I lost, and the penalty stood. We have been friends since that day.

We all know that without order, organized sports would very quickly become organized confusion. Yes, officials keep us honest, but they do more than that. They are the ones who see to it that the games keep moving, that both sides are treated fairly in the contest, that athletes and teams have the chance to be the best that they are capable of being. Quite frankly, without them there would be no sports and no sportsmanship.

Ed Perry represents those ideals at their best. Here is a man who is honest, impartial, and almost painstakingly fair. As a real tribute to him, I can think of no finer honor than the fact that, in over thirty years, I have heard coaches, players, and fans disagree with this or that particular call, but I have never—*never*—heard anyone doubt the integrity of this man.

Thank you, Ed Perry, for the thirty years that you have devoted to us. Thank you for the hours and hours of caring and concern from which we all benefited. Thank you for being strong when the rest of us grew almost irrational in the heat of the contest. Thank you for caring about sports and the young people in our charge. Thank you for *all* the calls, *all* the arguments, *all* the moments of greatness that it has been our honor to participate in with you. For all the generations of players, coaches, and fans who have been fortunate enough to have had you in their lives—thank you for a life well-lived and a job well-done.

May your future be as golden as your past, and may you take with you good memories, our wishes for the best that life can give, and—most important—our love.

SPECIAL DATA: *Time of speech: about four minutes. Officials really are important, no matter what we may think of an individual call. It is fitting, therefore, that a retiring official be honored in the manner shown in this speech. Notice that it starts with some humor at the expense of the subject. This is fine provided the audience realizes that you are not serious and are only joking, and that you have first asked permission of the subject and informed him of what you intend to say. Remember, you must never take the chance that the subject will be embarrassed, even unintentionally, by what you say. Note how, in this speech, the audience was informed that the subject had given permission for the good-natured ribbing. Note also, that the kidding quickly changed to sincere praise.*

$$\boxed{78}$$

TOPIC: *Retirement of a "Friend to Sports."*

AUDIENCE: *Suitable for any audience.*

I am very pleased, indeed, to have this opportunity to say a few words on the occasion of John Heggers' retirement. As many of you know, I serve as head coach at (name of institution). As most of you also know, John Heggers has had a life-long love affair with sports. I am, therefore, in a fine position to tell you about an aspect of this man which has enriched the lives of hundreds if not thousands of people, adults and youngsters alike.

John Heggers started out as a player of sports in both high school and college, and by all reports did his usual exemplary job. When he left college and began his career in business, however, he did not leave sports behind. In his personal life he has continued to engage in sports activities and physical fitness, and, I understand, those who have faced him on the tennis court and golf links have faced a formidable opponent. Besides engaging in sports, however, he has also devoted considerable time, energy, and funds to making sports enjoyable for countless others.

As chairman of our booster club, he has constantly striven for ways to help our young people engaged in organized sports. He has conducted fund-raisers, organized committees, spent many thankless hours, sold hot dogs, gained community support, and, in general, made himself invaluable to our sports program. Thanks to John Heggers, we have a new stadium. Thanks to his constant and unselfish work on our behalf, we have the lights for night games. Thanks to his unselfishness and dedication, the coaches and players know that if there is a problem, he will always be there to help; if there is a need, he will step in to fill it; if there is something to be done that will help our players and our team, he is never too busy, never too tired, never without the personal integrity and resources to see the problem and reduce it to solvable proportions.

In short, John Heggers has proven himself to be a friend to sports. He is, however, much more than that title implies. He is a friend to every youth who had a chance because John was there to help. He is a friend to every coach who knew that he had the support of a man of John's character. He is a friend to every fan who finds enjoyment and fulfillment in the sports program of which John Heggers is so vitally a part. Yes, he is a friend to sports, but more important, he is first and foremost a friend, and we are honored to call him so.

John, may your retirement provide you with continued good health and happiness. On behalf of the silent voices of the thousands of athletes, coaches, and fans who have been so deeply touched by your contributions over the years, may I say a sincere thank you, and may God bless you throughout your life to come.

SPECIAL DATA: *Time of speech: about three minutes. We can never underestimate the good that has been done for us and our players, as well as sports in general, by someone who dedicates himself or herself to helping our team or sports program. It is altogether fitting, therefore, that the person receive the acknowledgment he or she deserves. A speech such as this, therefore, helps accomplish that purpose.*

79

TOPIC: *All-purpose Poem for Retirement Speeches.*

AUDIENCE: *Suitable for all audiences.*

(*SPECIAL NOTE: The following poem could be used alone, or it could be an effective conclusion for a speech for a retiring individual. If you honestly mean everything that is in it and deliver it with sincerity, we have found it to be extremely dynamic and dramatic.*)

It seems it's been forever
      Since the first time that we met;
We've shared some days together
      That we just cannot forget.
There was work and there was laughter;
      There were tears and triumphs, too;
Successes and disasters,
      But somehow we came through.
Yes, we worked to make things last,

And yes, we had to strive;
But, God, our blood ran hot and fast,
And, God, we felt alive!
It's those moments we'll rely on;
They bespeak the way we feel,
For we started out as iron,
But we ended up as steel.
And now in days that yet will dawn,
Although we'll be apart,
Those memories, we know, will spawn
A smile in our hearts.
Now take our wishes with you
For Blessings from Above;
For happiness in all you do;
But most of all—for Love.

SPECIAL DATA: *Time of poem: approximately one minute. If you think that this poem is a bit sentimental, consider that at a retirement affair, the mood is undoubtedly just as sentimental. Believe us, the effect on the audience and the retiree will be substantial. If you use this poem as the conclusion of your speech, be certain not to add any comments after it. It is strong enough to stand on its own, creates a mood in the audience, and its impact would be lost by further commentary.*

Afterthoughts

No matter who is retiring or what you relationship may be to that person, your speech will be effective and appropriate if you do two things: mean what you say and say it from your heart.

If you feel a special affection for the retiring person, then you don't need inflated words or grand rhetoric. Simply saying what is in your heart will be far more eloquent than any wealth of words.

Practice your speech and try to deliver it without papers or note cards. Speak plainly and incorporate the retiree's name in your address. Say what is in your heart.

Follow these rules, and you will give a meaningful retirement speech that will be appreciated by everyone.

TESTIMONIAL SPEECHES

$$\boxed{80}$$

TOPIC: *A Poem Suitable for All Testimonial Speeches.*

AUDIENCE: *Suitable for all audiences.*

> If your life were an open book,
> > The pages would be tinged with gold,
> And we would read a story there
> > To be remembered and retold.
>
> For we would read of how you gave
> > To each and every one you met
> The fullness that your heart could give;
> > The love that no one could forget.
>
> And you would take a special place
> > Within our minds and our hearts, too;
> A place we'd often come to dream
> > And there, with love, remember you.

SPECIAL NOTE: *Time of poem: less than a minute. Admittedly, this is a sort of all-purpose poem that could be used to advantage in a variety of speeches. It works particularly well, however, in a testimonial-type speech. It expresses a feeling of warmth toward someone who is admired, and it conveys a great deal of feeling in a relatively few words. It also has a very favorable impact on any audience.*

$$\boxed{81}$$

TOPIC: *Testimonial for a Coach.*

AUDIENCE: *Adults mostly; colleagues, players, officials and others.*

There has been quite a bit of talk in medical circles about the dangers of something called "stress" recently. Stress occurs throughout life, and, according to medical findings, it can have some devastating results. Doctors now tell us that stress can cause everything from headaches to acne to ulcers to heart attacks.

Of course, I do not dispute their findings. I will say, however, that if what they tell us about stress is true, then this man, sitting to my right, should be the world's first walking and talking ulcer. I can think of few jobs as filled with constant stress as the one that Coach Ron Harris does each and every day.

Coaching is a roller-coaster job at best. When a team is winning games, the coach becomes a cross between Superman and a saint. When the team loses, it seems that everybody has a piece of advice to give, and most of it is far from complimentary. There are schedules to contend with, medical problems to deal with, and a group of eager youngsters to train into a cohesive unit. There is strategy to be planned and implemented. There are a thousand little details that mount into one gigantic headache. All of this must be dealt with knowing that when the team takes the field, it is the coach who is two short hours away from being a hero or an object of scorn.

That's enough stress for anyone, and we cannot help but have respect for someone who handles that situation day in and day out and not only manages to stay perfectly healthy, but does the job in an exemplary and extraordinary manner.

It is just such a man that we are here to honor this evening.

Coach Ronald Harris is a man who works with tension yet remains calm. He is a man who takes chaos and creates order. He is a man who deals with hundreds of kids with varying backgrounds and temperaments and produces a team that functions as a single body on the field. He is a man who works hard, gives of himself, never gives up, and, in the process, manages to uplift and inspire any boy lucky enough to have him as a coach.

Now, we must ask ourselves, how can he do this? How can he be such an integral part of these stress-producing situations and emerge as a pillar of strength and concern? How can he work and work and work, see a player or a team fall, and resolve only to work harder for the next time? How can he spend those long, extra hours working with each and every player to try to shape that player into the best person he is capable of becoming?

How? The answer is simple. It is as simple and as wonderful and as courageous as the fine athletes he produces. It is this . . . Coach Harris cares.

Yes, he cares. He cares about each and every boy on that field. He cares about the morality and personal growth of the individual boys more than the mere winning or losing of the game. He cares that each boy gives his best. He cares that his team strives for excellence while keeping its honor. What other definition do we need—that is love, and that love is returned by his boys and manifests itself in the drive and vitality that has been evidenced in the superlative record of the season just finished.

Therefore, it is fitting and proper that we have gathered together this evening to tell this man a thing or two. We want to tell him that he has earned our respect; that he has earned our admiration; that he has been judged in the heart of everyone here and found to be the worthiest of men.

For your years of concern and toil, for your never-ending dedication to the goals of your profession, for your tireless efforts on behalf of the youth of this community, we honor you this evening.

But, know this, Coach, and know it well—it is really you who honor us by being here tonight, by being on the field with our boys, and by being the kind of person that we know you are.

For everyone here I thank you, Coach Harris, from the bottom of my heart.

SPECIAL DATA: *Time of speech: about five minutes. Coaches who have been around for some time usually acquire quite a following in the community, particularly if they are good, such as the subject of the speech above. Therefore, it is quite often the speaker's duty to reflect that community feeling, particularly when the coach is to be honored in some way. The only additions you might want to make would be to go into detail about the season or the record, if it is appropriate to do so.*

| 82 |

TOPIC: *Testimonial for a Coach, II*

AUDIENCE: *Adults mostly; colleagues, officials, players, friends.*

This is not the first time that I have had some words to say about Coach Ron Harris. Indeed, as the coach of a rival team, I have faced Coach Harris many times across a playing field, and, believe me, he has given me more than one occasion to say a few well-chosen words about him and his ability.

Yet, the words I will say here will be no different than those I have chosen to use so many times before when we have faced each other as rival coaches. Whether my team has beaten his, or his team has emerged victorious, my opinion of Coach Harris has remained the same. Over the years, whether in victory or in defeat, Ron Harris, in my opinion, has been and continues to be a professional of the highest caliber, a man of honor, and a gentleman.

When you play against Coach Harris' team, you know three things: You will be facing a well-trained, cohesive unit; you will be facing a team that is fired-up with enthusiasm and the will to win; and, you will be facing a team that plays hard, but plays with fairness, integrity, and sportsmanship. These are the characteristics of any team that Ron Harris coaches, and they are the marks of the man himself.

Ron Harris knows what he is doing. This past season's record has proven that to the chagrin of myself and my fellow rival coaches. As a coach, he is an expert both in training and in strategy. He has the ability to pull a team together into a functioning unit which is very hard to stop. For this ability alone, he is respected and admired throughout the league.

Ron Harris can inspire. Ron lives his sport with a fire and enthusiasm that communicates itself to his players. They, in turn, become just as enthusiastic, just as ready and willing to give their all, just as fired-up and inspired as their coach. Often, this has been the winning edge which Ron has given to his team.

Ron Harris is a man of honor. When he wins, Ron is the first person to shake the hand of the losing coach, and when he loses, he is also the first to congratulate the winner. When Coach Harris gives his word, you know that it is done, and no one has any doubt but that he will keep his promise. If a player should fall, it is Coach Harris and his staff who will be out there to give aid, whether the player be one of theirs or one of ours. In short, the entire league knows that he is an honorable, caring individual who means what he says and can be trusted. He communicates this quality to his players, and it is evident in their behavior both on and off the playing field.

Therefore, we, his rival coaches, are overjoyed that you have chosen to honor Coach Harris this evening. Indeed, we welcome the opportunity to tell the general public what we have been saying about him for years among ourselves. We are extremely pleased that you see him as we have come to know him—as a man of integrity, honor, and expertise whom we are proud to have as one of our number and privileged to call our colleague and our friend.

May you enjoy this evening, Ron, which everyone here present knows you so richly deserve.

SPECIAL DATA: *Time of speech: about four minutes. Here is a testimonial for a coach as given by the coach of a rival team. As such, it is highly effective. If you should ever be asked to do something similar, remember that whatever your personal opinion may be, the audience is there to honor the subject, and it is your task to find what you honestly admire about the person and tell the crowd about that. Respect and integrity should be your guides in this situation.*

83

TOPIC: *Testimonial for an Athletic Director.*

AUDIENCE: *Adults; colleagues, friends, officials.*

Ladies and gentlemen.

We are here this evening to honor our athletic director, Mr. Martin Bell; Marty to his friends. On this occasion, I have just one question to ask—why him?

I mean, just because he has served as athletic director for the past twelve years and in that time has built our athletic program from a loose collection of people playing with a ball into a solid group of teams and organized sports activities, is that any reason to honor this man?

Simply because he has treated his position not as a job but as a vocation, putting in hours and hours beyond those required to make certain that our youth had the best facilities, the best training, the best chances for improvement that it was possible to have, is that any reason to honor this man?

Just because he is always available to the coaches, the players, and the administration; is always able to make the heaviest of burdens a little lighter; is always there with sound advice and support in times of crisis; and always brightens the days of those about him despite the problems his position may be offering him personally—is *that* any reason to honor this man?

I'm asking you—do the qualities of personal integrity, loyalty, honesty, competence, grace under fire, compassion, concern, and the ability to work beyond what others expect in order to serve our young people mean so much to us that we should honor this man?

What's that? Did I hear someone say that these were, indeed, reasons enough to honor a man of Marty Bell's character? Did I hear someone say that everyone who is privileged enough to know him knows first hand of his abilities, his involvement, and his personal commitment to the athletic program and our youth? Did I hear someone say that it is about time that everyone knew of the high regard we all have for this man and his selfless dedication to us?

Come to think of it, I did hear someone say those things. I said them to myself, to my wife, to anyone who would listen when I heard that this honor was to be bestowed on Marty. Over the years, I have come to know Marty, and I have come to understand what an inspired, dedicated, and highly competent person he is and how we are indeed privileged to have him as our athletic director.

Why him? I'll tell you why. Because of the years he has spent thinking of the good of others rather than himself; because of the hours he spent when no one could see, working for the best that it was possible to provide for our youth; because he has been and is the best of friends, the best of champions, the best of workers for the good of others—that's why, and that's why it is we who are honored to have a man of Marty Bell's abilities and character work and live among us.

Congratulations, Marty, for an honor that we all know that you have earned over the years. With you in charge, we look forward to a bright future filled with the promise that you provide us each and every day.

SPECIAL DATA: *Time of speech: between three and one-half and four minutes. This is an effective testimonial speech. After reading it, you understand that the speaker is not questioning the honoring of the subject, but using a device to dramatically point out the basis for the honor. When delivering it, you must make certain that the audience understands this as well. We suggest that you overact* *the first paragraph, with mock concern and wide gestures. This will let the audience know that you are not seriously questioning the honor. From the second paragraph on, they will understand the point of the message and will get the full impact of the speech.*

$$\boxed{84}$$

TOPIC: *Testimonial for a Team Physician.*

AUDIENCE: *Adults; coaches, professionals, friends, general public.*

A few weeks ago, I went to a doctor, and I said to him, "Doc, it hurts when I do this. *(Arm out at right angle to body; drop forearm and hand; swing forearm back and forth with elbow as fulcrum.)* What should I do?" The doctor said, "Simple, don't do this." *(Repeat action; wait for laughs to die down before continuing.)*

Maybe I should have gone to see Dr. Carl Simkins, who, for the past fifteen years, has served as our team physician. The reason I should have gone to him is that the words "No," "Can't," and "Don't" are simply not in his vocabulary. Rather, as a physician and as a human being, his speech is filled with "Yes," and "I will," and "You *can* do it."

Certainly, I could speak to you of his knowledge and his skill as a doctor. I could tell you stories about people who are walking around and healthy today whose futures would have been far less fortunate had "Doc" not been there with his marvelous mind and consummate skill. I could tell you about near tragedies that never happened because Doc was able to prevent them through his knowledge and expertise. I, and the hundreds upon hundreds of people whom he has tended and mended over the years, could speak eloquently of his powers as a physician, but that is not what I want to recall for you this evening.

Rather, I would like to speak to you about Carl Simkins, the man.

I would like to speak to you about a man who gave of himself to others far beyond what was expected of him. I would like to speak to you about a man who is highly respected not because of his title or position, but because he has earned the respect of the entire community over the years. I would like to speak to you about a man to whom others go for counsel and advice for their lives as well as their bodies, because they know that Doctor Carl always has the time for them; always is interested in them; always is willing to help. This is the person about whom I would like to speak. This is Dr. Carl Simkins.

As a coach, I can tell you that I have personally seen this man mend spirits as well as broken arms and legs. I have been a first-hand witness to his concern for the youth of this community. I have seen him provide for our boys what no money in the world could have provided—love, care, concern, and help in time of trouble.

If you need Doc Simkins, he is there. It doesn't matter when it is or where it is—if he knows that he is needed, he will be there. He will be there to advise, to treat, to help out in whatever way he can, to inspire, and to be a friend. I, personally, have never known a person who gives more or expects less in return. Give him the chance to help, and for Doc Simkins, that is payment enough.

I am delighted that Doctor Carl is receiving the honors that we, his friends, feel he has deserved for years. I can think of no one more deserving of your praise and acknowledgment.

I know that I speak for all of my colleagues on the coaching staff; for all of the players you have helped over the years; for all of their parents; and for the silent voices of the people whom you will help in the years to come when I say, thank you, Doc. From the bottom of our hearts, thank you for caring; thank you for being there; and, most important, thank you for being the warm and wonderful person you are.

Well done, Doc, well done!

SPECIAL DATA: *Time of speech: about four and one-half minutes. An outstanding team physician is an invaluable asset, as all coaches know. If such a person were to be honored, a speech such as this would fit the bill. On such an occasion, you might want to add to this speech by recounting a particular incident in which the doctor was particularly valuable, acted prudently, was sensitive to the athletes' needs, and so on. Just retell the incident as you recall it. A good place for it would be just after the seventh paragraph and before you begin the wrap-up of the speech. Just say what you feel about the physician, and you will do fine.*

$$\boxed{85}$$

TOPIC: *Testimonial for an Athlete/Alumnus.*

AUDIENCE: *Mostly adults; possibly team players, coaches, friends, etc.*

It is inevitable, when speaking of someone who has achieved something great in his life, that people will say, "I knew it from the moment I first saw him. I looked at him, and I said to myself, 'That person is headed for greatness.' "

I wish I could say that about our guest of honor tonight, but, in all honesty, the first time I laid eyes on Brad Hopkins, he was standing on the field with a hundred kids who looked more or less just like him, and I didn't even notice him.

I don't remember, quite frankly, what I told that assembled group on that afternoon, but I think it was something about having to earn a position on the team. Obviously, Brad was paying attention, because practice began immediately, and Brad Hopkins began to earn his position, as he soon earned my attention and that of the coaching staff, his fellow players, the fans, the media, and the community.

If you ask Brad, he'll tell you that he's "nothing special," because that's the kind of young man he is. However, if you ask me, and the people on our staff who coached him through his years with us, we will tell you quite a different story.

We will tell you of a young man to whom football is more than a game—it's a commitment. We will tell you of a person who gives 100 percent of himself at all times, whether on the practice field or the playing field. We will tell you of someone who has outstanding individual talents; who stands out above the others; who shines as a brilliant star, who is, nevertheless, a team player; who puts the good of the team above any individual record he might achieve; who is never too busy or too tired to help the other members of the team.

I will tell you of the long, extra hours when practice was over and the other players were home with supper and family and a chance to relax that found Brad working alone to perfect his technique, to develop and strengthen his body, to go that extra inch, to, in the words of that great coach, Vince Lombardi, "be all that he was capable of being." I will tell you of the hundred lonely, silent ways in which Brad worked alone, not because I or the other coaches required it, but because he, within his own mind and spirit, wanted to improve; wanted to test the limits of that of which he was capable; knew he was capable of growth and went at it with a desire and a fervor unmatched in my experience as a coach.

I could, of course, detail Brad Hopkins' brilliant record. I could speak of his academic standing as an honor student. I could tell you of his contributions to charitable work in our community and elsewhere, notably through the Big Brother program. I could tell you of the high regard in which he is held by the faculty and administration, by the students, by the members of the team, and by everyone who has come into contact with him. Yes, I could tell you of all of this, but I think that everyone in this audience tonight knows those facts only too well.

Therefore, I will speak to Brad Hopkins himself, who, I am certain, is sitting here wondering what all the fuss is about, because a sense of humility is also a part of his makeup. I will say to you, Brad, that it has been *my* privilege to have been your coach. I am overjoyed to have had a player during my career who responded as you did; who was as good as you; who was someone whom I knew I would remember for years and years with fondness, affection, and with some sense of awe and wonder.

There are many people who would view this evening as a culmination or end result of what you have accomplished. I am not one of them. Rather, knowing you and knowing that of which you are capable, I look on tonight as a ship's launching; as the countdown to the rocket's flight. Your future lies before you, Brad; it is in your hands; and, knowing you, it can be nothing but bright.

With your success, I have no doubt that the world will be made a little better and a little brighter for us all.

SPECIAL DATA: *Time of speech: about four and one-half minutes. Again, this effective speech could be made even more so by adding a personal reminiscence of some incident in which the speaker was involved with the subject which shows the subject's character or skill or any combination thereof. If you decide to do this, a good place to include it would be after the third paragraph. Also, again, remember that sincerity and enthusiasm are your keys to success, whatever you say.*

Afterthoughts

There are certain characteristics that testimonials and retirement speeches have in common. They are both meant to honor some individual, and they must both be warm expressions of good feelings toward the subject. Since they will undoubtedly be delivered before an audience, they must be pleasing and understandable to that audience as well.

Therefore, keep in mind that, when composing a speech for a testimonial or retirement, you should avoid inside jokes that might not be understood by the audience; you must never tell an anecdote (even if it's true) that embarrasses the subject; you should use humor only with a subject who is a personal friend; if you use humor, it should always be at the beginning of the speech; and, you should honestly mean everything that you say.

If you follow these suggestions and speak what is in your heart with clarity and conviction, you will give a retirement or testimonial speech that will be remembered by everyone, particularly by the subject of the speech for whose benefit it was given in the first place.

SECTION 8

Dignified and Meaningful Eulogies and Memorials

Delivering a eulogy is probably one of the most painful tasks that a coach can undertake. Whether it is a student athlete, someone connected with the sports program, or a fellow coach who dies, if you are asked to speak at the services and deliver the eulogy, you can assume that the situation will be loaded with emotion, and it will be a difficult task for you. Yet, as we all realize, none of us would ever turn down such a request, for if the family has turned to you at this trying time, you cannot do less than respond.

A memorial service is hardly pleasant, either, but memorials are at least blessed with the distance of time. Memorials can be held weeks, months, and even years after the passing of the individual, and time, that greatest of all healers, has had the opportunity to work. Nevertheless, as much care must be taken with the memorial speech as with the eulogy, for you are still dealing with an emotional situation.

There are some general rules regarding eulogies and memorials that, if they cannot make them pleasant, will at least make them fitting and appropriate.

Obviously, under no circumstances must humor enter into a eulogy. It doesn't matter how well you knew the person—keep humor out of it. Humor should also be kept out of memorials except under very special circumstances *which will be detailed later in this section. Keep the eulogy and memorial short, under five minutes. Speak about the person and the accomplishments of the person. Keep it positive and never speak about how much he or she suffered. If at all possible, try to end it on a note of hope or with a look toward the future. These general rules will go a long way toward helping with any eulogy or memorial.*

Your biggest aid in any eulogy or memorial will be your sincerity. If you had a genuine affection for the person, and you speak of what is in your heart clearly and simply, you will deliver a better eulogy or memorial than if you used volumes of inflated prose. Let your heart be your guide, and you will not go wrong.

The following pages contain several examples of effective eulogies and memorials. We have selected them, because we feel that they are both dignified and simple, and do the best in a trying situation. It is our hope that you will never have to use them, but, if you do, we know that you will be able to find something appropriate.

EULOGIES

$$\boxed{86}$$

TOPIC: *Eulogy for Deceased Classmates/Teammates at a Class/Team Reunion.*

AUDIENCE: *Adults; members of a particular class/team.*

(SPECIAL NOTE: Coaches are often invited to attend class and/or team reunions. They may be asked to speak on many subjects related to the class or team, including delivering a eulogy for the members of the class or team who have died since graduation. Our friend, Dr. Chester B. Ralph, has been kind enough to share with us the following eulogy, which is highly dramatic and appropriate for the situation.)

Ladies and gentlemen . . .

It has been a little more than _____ years since we last met as a class (team) at _____ on the occasion of our graduation. It is inevitable, in that span of years, that many of our friends and classmates (teammates) will have been taken from us.

It is, therefore, altogether fitting and proper that we should pause in this hour of levity and reflect in our own lives the memory of those who have died.

I ask that we now bow our heads in silent meditation, and each of us, in his own way, pay tribute to the memory of those who do not answer when their names are called.

(SPECIAL NOTE: When all heads are bowed, the speaker recites the following poem.)

Now the hour of reunion has arrived,
> In this room of mirth and cheer;
And silence descends as if from heaven,
> Upon the group assembled here.
Slowly die the fire's last embers,
> As the night grows still and serene,
And we toast our absent classmates (teammates)
> Who have passed beyond the screen.

We behold with eyes grown older,
      With eyes that have a magic scope,
Life's abandoned fires that smolder
      On the distant trail of hope;
And our memories are beguiling
      When the lights are soft and low,
For we see our classmates (teammates) smiling
      As they smiled long ago.
So to you, our absent classmates (teammates),
      With our hearts and hands held high,
We drink a toast to your sweet memory
      That will never, never die.

SPECIAL DATA: *Time of eulogy: about three minutes. On a personal note, we were out of high school less than a year when three of our classmates died from various causes. It is sad, but it does happen. Therefore, it is best to be prepared for it. If you are ever in the situation where you use the eulogy above, be prepared for its impact. It is extremely dramatic, and its dynamics are added to by the very nature of the gathering. There will be no applause, and we have personally witnessed occasions where several adults had to leave the room to compose themselves following its delivery. It is a highly dramatic tribute to deceased classmates or teammates, and should be delivered simply, without any attempt to embellish it with vocal dramatics.*

$$\boxed{87}$$

TOPIC: *Eulogy for a Coach.*

AUDIENCE: *Mixed audience; family members, colleagues, friends.*

Mrs. Hartnett, Tom and Mary *(deceased coach's children)*, members of the Hartnett family, ladies and gentlemen . . .

When the news of Ben's passing reached us, his fellow coaches, it hit us with a tremendous impact. We were saddened, and his death has left us with a void that can never be entirely filled. All the members of the team, the other coaches, and I cannot help but sense this to our abiding and everlasting sorrow.

In this time of sorrow, our only consolation is the knowledge that we were privileged to know and work with Ben over the years. During that time, we came to know him as a person of intelligence and integrity, always willing to help, whose life and career were, indeed, an inspiration to us all.

We also take comfort in the fact that a part of Ben will continue to live, reflected in the lives of the young people whom he coached, guided, and inspired over the years. Ben was a man who gave unselfishly of himself, perhaps the greatest gift of all, and those student athletes who were fortunate enough to fall under his care will carry the ideals, knowledge, and moral principles he instilled in them into the world at large. The world will be a better place because of it.

Our hearts and our prayers are with you at this most difficult of times.

SPECIAL DATA: *Time of eulogy: about two minutes. Note the address at the beginning of the eulogy. The first person addressed is the surviving spouse, then the children of the deceased, then any special person of note who might be attending such as a mayor or congressman, and finally the members in attendance, addressed as "ladies and gentlemen." Note also that this is short and simple, detailing the deceased's contributions and the affection of those with whom he worked. It is also dignified, adding dignity to an already exemplary life. Remember, there is never any applause or audience reaction following a eulogy or memorial, only silence. Therefore, deliver your speech, acknowledge the family with a nod, walk over to them and say a few personal words, and retire to your seat.*

88

TOPIC: *Eulogy for a Coach, II.*

AUDIENCE: *Mixed audience; family members, colleagues, friends.*

Mrs. Billings, Angela, Mayor Smith, ladies and gentlemen . . .

I stand here, and I feel very inadequate, for I realize with a frightening clarity that whatever I say, mere words can never express what I feel at the passing of Jim Billings, our head coach and my personal friend.

I was doubly honored in my relationship with Jim, for I worked with him for many years as a colleague as well as counting him as one of my closest and dearest friends. I came to know Jim pretty well, and I was able to witness, first hand, his exceptional talents. I knew him as a man of warmth and wisdom, universally liked and admired by his fellow coaches, adored by the athletes he coached, and respected deeply by everyone with whom he came into contact.

Jim Billings was a man who, once you met him, you could not forget. He will continue to live in the memories and in hearts of those whom he has left behind.

His memory is one we will cherish, and I think that somehow he knows that we will carry on in the manner that he taught us each and every day, by sterling personal example, throughout an exemplary life.

SPECIAL DATA: *Time of eulogy; about two minutes. Here is another very short eulogy, but it is to the point, personal, and warm. You could, of course, detail the deceased's accomplishments in life if you wish, but it is just as effective in this shorter and more direct format.*

89

TOPIC: *Eulogy for a Student Athlete.*

AUDIENCE: *Mixed audience; family members, friends.*

Mr. and Mrs. Kendall, Bobby and Jean, members of the Kendall family, ladies and gentlemen . . .

I speak with the voice of many, for I know I represent all the coaches and the coaching staff; every player on every team; and, I believe, the entire community, when I express the grief and shock we feel over the untimely passing of Thomas Kendall. He was known to us as Tommy, and we knew him as someone very special, indeed; as someone whom we were proud to have as a player, as a friend, as a member of our team.

Coaches and players alike, as well as many people who merely had the privilege of seeing Tommy play, have asked me to convey to you their sorrow and their deep sense of loss. I do this, and I add my own sympathies. We will all miss Tommy.

We all know that the loss of a child is one of the greatest tragedies that life can bring. When we speak of someone as popular and talented as Tommy Kendall, it is a tragedy that affects us all.

Mr. and Mrs. Kendall, we know that words seem meaningless at a time like this, but please know that we join you in your grief.

Our sincere sympathy and our fervent prayers are with you at this time of loss and sorrow.

SPECIAL DATA: *Time of eulogy: less than two minutes. While no one is happy about the idea of a loved one dying, at least they are somewhat prepared for the death of an adult, especially if the person is of advanced years. Nothing and no one is ever prepared for the death of a child. On a personal note, our careers have brought us to too many funeral homes to visit the families of children who have died. We'll tell you honestly—it is never easy, and the words are never right. If you must deliver a eulogy for a student athlete, therefore, it is essential that it be short, to the point, and sincere.*

$$\boxed{90}$$

TOPIC: *Eulogy for an Athlete.*

AUDIENCE: *Mixed audience; family members, friends.*

Mrs. Hopewell, members of the Hopewell family, ladies and gentlemen . . .

It is inevitable, at times such as these, that our minds turn inward and we reflect on our friend as we knew him. When I do this, I am flooded with memories, all of which fill my soul with an appreciation for the man we all knew as John Hopewell; memories which make his passing more painful and the sense of loss greater.

And, I do remember. I recall vividly the first time I saw John. He was a high school student then, trying out for the team I coached. I remember his enthusiasm, his drive, and the way he would respond to criticism, striving, always striving, to perfect himself and his technique. I remember the selflessness of his commitment; the humility that always put the good of the team first; the help he gave to other players, never seeking to be rewarded, content with what he could give to others.

We all remember his brilliant record on the playing field. Indeed, John Hopewell did not remain a "face in the crowd" for very long. His talent and skill, driven by his personal dedication to excellence; his outstanding sportsmanship; and his desire to win cried out with an eloquence that could not help but be recognized his fellow players, the press, and the fans who loved him.

He was not a high school hero whose glory faded on graduation day. Throughout college he continued to grow, continued to be an inspiration to others and a leader among his fellow athletes, continued building a brilliant career and earning the admiration and adulation of the thousands who saw him play. All of this, mind you, while holding an academic average that, of itself, would have compelled our respect.

It was only natural, therefore, that he should make the transition to professional sports and begin on a path that, as none of us who knew him ever doubted, would lead to the outstanding success he so well deserved.

Now, too soon, that path has ended.

We have no words adequate to state what we feel in our hearts. We know there is an emptiness that refuses to be filled. We know that we will miss him and that his absence leaves an ache that cannot be soothed.

Yet, we have our memories. In our minds, we continue to see him smile. In our hearts, we recall with warmth and affection his wit, his kindness, his tenderness, his open and giving nature. We remember him— what he was; what he said; what he accomplished in his short time with us—and we cannot help but be inspired by that memory.

We who will carry on realize, I think, that during our lives we were privileged to have been touched by the life of someone truly great, truly fine, truly an example of the finest that humanity can become.

We have had the honor to know him, and we are better for it.

SPECIAL DATA: *Time of eulogy: about five minutes. This is slightly longer than the previous eulogies, and also details the deceased's career a bit more fully. Indeed, if the deceased has had a career in which there have been major* *accomplishments, it is always acceptable to detail those accomplishments during a eulogy.*

$$\boxed{91}$$

TOPIC: *Eulogy for a Coach Who Met with an Untimely Death.*

AUDIENCE: *Mixed audience; team members, colleagues, family members, sports officials, possibly sports dignitaries, friends.*

(SPECIAL NOTE: When someone who is relatively young and healthy passes away unexpectedly, it is a particularly sad occasion and emotions will run high. If you should ever be faced with delivering a eulogy under such circumstances, we highly recommend the following, which we believe is one of the finest we have ever heard for such an occasion.)

Mrs. Adler, Mr. Adler *(the deceased's father)*, Elizabeth, Mayor Langly, dear friends . . .

Adlai Stevenson was once asked to comment about a man who had met with an untimely death. He said, "It is not the years in a life that count; it is the life in the years."

Joseph Adler has been taken from us. This thought brings us abiding sorrow. While death is never welcome, we are, at least, prepared for it in a person of advanced years or someone who has fallen victim to illness. Therefore, we are doubly devastated when it happens to someone of Joe's years and someone of his amazing vitality.

However, I would not like to speak to you of death today. Rather, I choose to speak of the vitality that I just mentioned. I would like to tell you of a man who, to paraphrase Mr. Stevenson, filled his years with life, even if his life was not filled with years.

I would like to tell you of the Joseph Adler I knew. He was a man who was comfortable wherever he went and with whomever he was sharing his time. On the practice field with a group of rookies or addressing a seasoned team during half time; while talking to a community group, a board of education, a gathering of sports officials, or a single kid who needed some comfort or advice; whatever the circumstance, whoever the people, Joseph Adler met the situation and the people with enthusiasm, concern, and energy. His positive attitude could not help but affect those he was with; could not help but influence the situation and aid in bringing out the best in everyone. When Joe Adler set his hand, mind, and will to some task, he did it with a vitality that made you realize that he was not going to let go until the job was finished. It inspired in you, meanwhile, a confidence that, indeed, it *could* be done; that it was worthy of being done; that *you* could have a hand in its completion.

I think that perhaps one of the best indicators of that vitality and drive is the fact that while there were people who disagreed with Joseph Adler, Joseph Adler had no enemies. They might disagree with Joe, but they respected him, and his opinion as well. Indeed, Joe Adler was respected as a man of honor and integrity. He was someone you *knew* you could trust; he was someone to whom you could always go and find a willing listener with a receptive ear; he was someone who could be counted on to offer help in each and every case.

This is the life of which I am speaking; *this* is the vitality; *this* is Joseph Adler.

Now—too soon—he is gone. I don't think we can fully comprehend it yet. But, we shall—oh, we shall. Our lives will be emptier for his absence, because they were made fuller by his presence.

Therefore, we honor his memory; a memory that each of us carries inscribed in his mind and heart; a memory in which Joseph Adler yet lives—the vital, intelligent, warm and humane person we all knew and loved so well.

We resolve, therefore, here and now, to cherish that memory and to nourish it; to keep the spirit of Joseph Adler alive and use it as a guide to spread those principles of honor and morality in which Joseph Adler believed; to spread them throughout our own lives. In so doing, we will remember and we will know that once we had the honor of knowing someone like Joseph Adler, and that has made us better people and the world a better place to be.

SPECIAL DATA: *Time of eulogy: a little over five minutes. We feel that this is a particularly good and very powerful eulogy. You will notice that it doesn't skirt issues. It acknowledges the untimeliness of the death in direct and simple terms, but still it manages to pay a strong and highly dynamic tribute to the deceased. This is the type of eulogy that will be deeply appreciated by the family and will be remembered for years.*

$$\boxed{92}$$

TOPIC: *Eulogy for a Sportsman (all purpose)*

AUDIENCE: *Mixed; family members, possibly colleagues, friends.*

Mrs. Jones, members of the Jones family, associates, colleagues, and friends . . .

We are the slaves of words. All too often, they are all we have to express those wordless feelings that so fill our minds and hearts. Yes, words are all we have, and yet, at times such as this, they are simply not enough.

We use, for example, a word like "sorrow," but what does it mean? We are each faced with a personal loss now. Each of us will feel it and carry it and live with it, because someone we cherished so much has been removed from our lives. Yet, all we have to express what we are feeling is a word like "sorrow."

We try to describe what we felt for our friend and colleague, and, once again, we are limited to words. We use a word like "honor," but what does it really mean? We all stand as living proof of the greatness of our friend. We saw his dedication; we were witness to his care and concern; we stood in awe of his great wit, intelligence, efficiency, and tact; we whispered prayers of thanks that we were privileged enough to be associated with a person of his worth. We *lived* our friend's "honor," yet all we have is the word, and it seems grossly inadequate to do him justice.

To sum up what he was and what he did, we use a word like "love," but what can that possibly convey? We saw our friend pour forth love on a daily basis. We knew of his care and concern for those who came into his life. We saw the gentleness, warmth, and compassion with which he handled every situation. We were privy to the hours and hours of work he put into perfecting his skills so that he might be the best he could be, to help those who needed his help. Our hearts swell with the memories of how he lived that word—the word, "love."

There are other words that we might use—words like dedication, intelligence, efficiency, morality. All of these and more would fit him, but a lexicon of superlatives would not be enough, for he was a man who personified the finest definition of each term.

Yes, we are the slave of words, but let us be heartened, today, by the fact that rather than mere words, we will use our memories to keep a part of him alive within us. We will use those images that are inscribed within our hearts to cherish the legacy that he has left for us all—that legacy of love and honor which he lived every day, which was his life, and which, in truth, can never, never die.

SPECIAL DATA: *Time of eulogy: about three minutes. This is a different type of eulogy that establishes a theme (in this case, the inadequacy of words) and carries the theme throughout the speech. This can be an effective technique. You will notice that nowhere in the speech is the deceased's name mentioned. Rather, he is referred to as a "friend." Some speakers believe that this is the best approach as, they claim, everyone is only too aware of the subject. Others claim that this makes the eulogy seem rather formal, and that frequent mention of the subject's name makes for a warmer and more personal eulogy. It is, of course, up to you.*

93

TOPIC: *Concluding Poem for a Eulogy.*

AUDIENCE: *Suitable for all audiences.*

The time has come to close the book
       And set it on the shelf,
And yet the message lingers on—
       In memory of itself.

We've read what has been written there,
       The story of a life;
A story filled with care and love
       That overcame the strife.

A story of integrity,
       Of courage, love, and pride,
That touched us deep within our souls;
       That stirred us deep inside.

Now, 'though the book be shut and set
       In honored place apart,
The inspiration of its tale

Lights hope within our hearts.
For we will use what we have read
    To overcome the pain,
In honor of the life we saw
    That was not lived in vain.

SPECIAL DATA: *Time of poem: about forty seconds. Of course, this poem could be used by itself, but we feel that it would make a very effective ending to a eulogy for someone whose life has been an inspiration. The central image of the person's life as a book whose story has inspired all who have read it will be readily understood and appreciated by any audience.*

Afterthoughts

The greatest eulogy ever written might be in a speaker's hands, but if it is delivered insincerely; if the speaker does not believe what is being said; if it is "tossed off" as "just another speech," then it will be as empty and meaningless as reading the back of a cereal box.

Conviction in a speaker's voice, and genuine sorrow and concern in his heart, on the other hand, will mean more than any finely wrought words. It will mean a warm and genuine eulogy that will be remembered.

Whether you choose from the eulogies we have just presented or use them as models to write your own, if you say what is in your heart and keep in mind the feelings of the family of the deceased, you will do just fine.

MEMORIALS

94

TOPIC: *All-purpose Memorial Poem.*

AUDIENCE: *Suitable for all audiences.*

So many days have passed, and yet
    The memory remains.

And still of soft and silent nights
    You come to us again.

We see you as we knew you once;
    You seem to smile, and then
We see ourselves there at your side
    As often it had been.

And we return the smile you give
    And cherish in our hearts
The thought that we had days to share
    Before we had to part.

And we find that time has not erased,
    Nor has its passage paled,
That warmth we held for you in life;
    That love that has not failed.

And so, dear friend, we keep you close,
    Although we are apart,
And visit with you daily in
    The visions of our hearts.

SPECIAL DATA: *Time of poem: less than a minute. This poem would fit well into any memorial speech. It is reflective of a wide variety of emotions about the person being remembered. As it does not specify a particular individual, it can be effectively used for anyone. If necessary, it could easily be changed to first person address. Just be sure to make the necessary pronoun changes throughout the poem. Whatever you choose, please make certain that it is delivered with sincerity, warmth, and understanding.*

95

TOPIC: *Benediction for a Memorial Service.*

AUDIENCE: *Suitable for all audiences.*

My dear friends . . .
I suppose that it takes an occasion such as this to remind us of the

highly fragile nature of our bodies. Yet, that reflection often brings with it the sense that there must be something beyond flesh, blood, sinew, and muscle; something that continues; something that gives meaning to the time we have spent in this place.

Within that very thought, there is something eternal; something in us that reaches for life beyond our physical existence.

Today especially, as we turn our minds and our hearts to the memory of our friend, we sense that feeling of eternity, for we realize that he continues to live within each of us. We cherish that memory, and within us we feel that somewhere, somehow, a spirit of his magnitude must continue glow with the brilliance he shared with us during our brief time together.

We are vividly aware that his presence honored us who knew and loved him. Let us, therefore, remember him and honor him within our minds and hearts.

SPECIAL DATA: *Time of memorial benediction: just over a minute. This particular benediction might be called a "nonsectarian" version of a benediction. You will notice that while it does allude to immortality in an oblique manner, it does not mention the Almighty at all. In certain situations where you are speaking before people of highly divergent beliefs, you might find that a benediction such as this which phrases things in humanistic terms might be highly fitting.*

96

TOPIC: *Benediction for a Memorial Service, II*

AUDIENCE: *Suitable for almost every audience.*

Dear friends . . .

Let us bow our heads, and each in his own way remember the subject of our gathering today.

Dear God, please hear us now. Humbly, we ask Your blessing upon this gathering today. We have come together to remember and pay tribute to our friend, Philip Golden. We know that it was Your will that he was taken from us, and we understand that we must accept that and take comfort in the thought that he is with You even now and is at rest.

Oh, Lord, grant that we may carry on the work that he pursued while he was among us. As Philip's life of service and unselfish giving of himself to others was pleasing in Your sight, grant that what we may do, inspired by the example provided for us by our association with Philip Golden, be equally pleasing to and blessed by You.

Grant, dear Lord, that the soul of Philip Golden rest in Your eternal love and peace.

Amen.

SPECIAL DATA: *Time of memorial benediction: a little less than a minute. This second version of a benediction for a memorial service mentions God directly and has pronounced religious overtones. It is more appropriate for a clergyman to deliver than for a coach or layman, but we thought we would provide you with this version as well. You will be in a position to know your audience, and only you will be able to judge what would be best for them. If you do choose this one, you will find it to be simple but effective.*

$$\boxed{97}$$

TOPIC: *Memorial to a Coach.*

AUDIENCE: *Suitable for all audiences, but geared towards adults.*

Dear friends . . .

Tonight, we have gathered together to pay tribute to someone we all knew very well; to someone who was our friend, our colleague, our teacher, and our inspiration.

It was one year ago today that Coach Donald Bender was taken from us.

When I think of Don Bender, my mind is flooded with a vast number of images. I see Don on the practice field, his whistle around his neck, moving, always moving as he supervised the drills; instructing; encouraging; and reprimanding where it was necessary. I see him during a game, his hands on his hips, pacing the sidelines. I see his intensity showing on his face, and I know that in his mind he is out on that field running each and every play. I see him after a losing game place his arm around a dejected player. I see him being carried off the field on the shoulders of his players when his team won the state championship. I see him, and he is laughing, laughing.

I see these things when I think of Don Bender, and I see even more.

I see him fighting for an athlete who was in trouble. I see him standing up for the principles in which he believed against all odds. I see him working on committees to help improve our sports program. I see him speaking up for his kids in the face of budget cuts.

I see these things when I think of Don Bender, and I see even more.

I see him working long, extra hours to help the athletes and the team. I see him speaking quietly to a player; helping that person overcome a problem; counseling; offering his advice; and standing by it. I see and I feel the deep concern that he felt for each and every player on the team. I see him in the quiet times, away from the din of the crowd, still giving of himself, happy and content to be of service.

Yes, I see these things when I think of Don Bender, and I smile. I remember his vitality and his ready wit that could change the gloomiest of days into one filled with sunshine; and all at once, he is back with me again. I remember his commitment to our student athletes; to the highest principles of morality; to sportsmanship and honor which, to Don, were not words, but the building blocks of his life. I remember this and I am proud to have known a man of his caliber.

Then I realize, to my sorrow, that Don Bender exists now only in my memory.

However, that isn't true, for Don is alive. He is still a part of our lives. I see him in the players he coached who still carry with them the high moral principles that he instilled in them. I see him in my own actions when I do something that was inspired by his example; his concern; his courage. I see him in you, who carry on his dedication and involvement. I see him in all of us who have had our lives changed forever and for the better because we knew this outstanding example of humanity at its best. I see him, and I know that he continues to live.

Donald Bender lived a life of service and of giving. He has given us so much. Now, it is our turn to give.

Let each of us give to Donald Bender our solemn pledge that as he gave to help others, so will we give; as he fought for what was right, decent, and best for his kids, so we will fight; as he worked to be the best person he could be, so we will strive. He has left us an outstanding model on which to shape our lives.

If we give Don Bender this pledge, we cannot help but nurture the learning and growth of all those we touch throughout our lives; we cannot help but make the world better; we cannot help but deal from love and courage and selflessness.

That, ladies and gentlemen, is a memorial Don would have loved!

SPECIAL DATA: *Time of memorial: about four minutes. This is an exceptional memorial that should be used to honor an exceptional coach. It expresses a very deep sentiment about someone who gave a lifetime of service to sports and young people, and affirms his contribution in positive terms and in terms of the present rather than the past. As a tribute, it is outstanding. As a definition of the finest in coaching and dedication, it is also unparalleled.*

$$\boxed{98}$$

TOPIC: *Memorial for a Group Tragedy.*

AUDIENCE: *Suitable for all audiences.*

(*SPECIAL NOTE: As history affirms, the sports scene is not immune to tragedy. It does happen that several players from a team, players and coaches, et cetera, may meet with tragedy at the same time. The following memorial was originally written about a tragedy that occurred in an elementary school, but it could apply equally well to any similar situation. It is so powerful, that we have decided to present it as it was first written. As you read it, think in terms of what you would say if a similar tragedy struck your team or coaching staff.*)

Dear friends . . .

We gather together today on the anniversary of one of the greatest tragedies ever to befall our school system and our community.

It was a year ago today that a bus filled with fifty eager, excited, and happy students set out from our school for a day that was to be filled with learning and fun. As we are all aware, the bus never reached its destination.

The chaperones and twenty-eight of the students ended up in a hospital, some with extremely serious injuries that affect their lives even today.

Twenty-two students never returned.

At first, the magnitude of the loss did not register. It was simply too great a tragedy to be comprehended. It was as if the shock of the news was so great that we were numb in the face of the onslaught. I remember the silence in the school when we first heard; a shocked, deadly silence that was more devastating than the loudest and most piercing of screams.

Then, with time, the full impact hit us head on, and a sorrow beyond words—a grief that could never be adequately expressed—settled on us. And we came to understand the true meaning of the loss we had suffered and the emptiness that it left behind.

Then came the question; the inevitable question that mankind has surely asked from time immemorial; the cry that erupts from the depths of sorrow—Why? Why had this happened? Why had our children been taken from us? We knew the mechanics of what had happened, but our question went deeper than that. It struck at the reason behind it all; it asked for the cosmic rationale for twenty-two of our children to be denied life.

While that may be a universal question, the anwer to it has always been extremely personal in nature.

No one person can say why it happened, but each of us, in his own heart, must come to terms with it and find an answer in his own way. For some, it is slow in coming; for others, it never arrives. If it ever does, it will come in the sanctity of the individual heart that loved, that cherished, and that so deeply felt the loss. It is there and there alone that we will find peace, and it is there that each of us must seek an answer.

So, we come, at last, to this day. Time has passed, and day has followed day. The seasons change as before; spring follows winter. Yet, it is not the same for our children are not here to smell the crispness of the winter's air or to marvel at the beauty of the spring flowers. *That* has made all the difference.

We pause now, in the day-to-day operation of our lives, to remember them as they were—the vital and laughing children we all knew. There is still sorrow for their passing, and we know that time will never fully erase the pain nor fill the void, but there is also joy that we had them for a while, and our lives were made fuller by that association.

We will resolve, therefore, that they will not have died in vain; that we will keep them alive in our hearts and cherish their memories; that our love for those around us will be made stronger by the special bond that we will always have with them, our children.

We know this in our hearts, and to them we say, sleep our children until that time when we may awaken with you to face a new and a brighter day.

Sleep . . . with our love.

SPECIAL DATA: *Time of memorial: close to five minutes. The memorial above is extremely powerful and touching, and we know that we, personally, would have a difficult time delivering it in anything that even approximated the circumstances described. It would, however, be extremely effective and dynamic for everyone in the audience. It is our hope that you never have occasion to use this as a model for a similar memorial.*

99

TOPIC: *Memorial for an Athlete.*

AUDIENCE: *Mixed audience; players, friends, family, dignitaries.*

Mr. and Mrs. Benson, members of the Benson family, honored guests, friends of James Benson . . .

Jim Benson was a student at our school, but he was much more than that. As a player on the basketball team, he was an outstanding example of a student athlete, dedicated and hard working, always giving 100 percent of himself for the team. As his coach, I found him a delight to work with; as a human being, I was enriched to think that this was the type of young man that would be a part of our future. Not only on the playing court, but in his work with the student council and the school's honor society, he showed himself to be a rare individual endowed with intelligence, warmth, common sense, and an intense desire to give of himself for others. He made us all proud to know him.

It made it all the harder, therefore, to learn of the tragic accident which took him from us. There was no one on the team, the coaching staff, or the school who was not deeply affected.

Therefore, we have gathered today to pay tribute to his memory and to express what we have felt all along in our hearts.

One of Jim's closest friends was . . .

(You now introduce a few people who speak about the deceased student athlete. The speakers should be few in number and a mixture of both players/students and adults who knew him. Their speeches, particularly the ones of his fellow students/athletes should be discreetly screened for appropriateness. When all the speeches are given, you step forward once more.)

Now, I would like to show you this plaque, commissioned by the student council of this school and financed by voluntary contributions from students, athletes, coaches, faculty, and staff. On it is inscribed the name "James P. Benson" along with the inscription, "Honor in studies; honor in athletics; honor in life . . . we shall not forget." This plaque will have a prominent place at the entrance to our gymnasium so that those who come after may know of the high regard that we all had for Jim. Mr. and Mrs. Benson, you would do us a great honor if you would please accept this in Jim's memory and with our deepest sympathies and love.

(At this point, you go to Mr. and Mrs. Benson, present them with the plaque, and shake hands with them. If, and only if, it has been arranged beforehand that Mr. or Mrs. Benson or both wish to speak to the assembly, then you gently lead them to the microphone, discreetly step back, and allow them to speak. If they indicated that they did not wish to speak at all, then after handing them the plaque and shaking hands, you would step back to the microphone alone. Whatever the case, there will be applause when you go to the parents. When you have given them the plaque, join in the applause. Whether the parents speak or not, when you return to the microphone, you conclude the ceremony.)

Jim Benson was a credit to his parents; to our school; to the team who so loved and admired him; and to himself. Those of us who knew him understood that we were very fortunate, indeed, to be associated with someone so fine. Today, we honor his memory with this plaque, but, as we leave here to resume our own lives, let us also resolve to honor Jim's memory in our daily lives and to cherish his memory in our hearts, that he may continue to live among us throughout all the days to come.

Thank you, and good afternoon.

SPECIAL DATA: *Time of presentation: variable, depending on the length and number of speeches given. The preceding is an example of a complete memorial program at which you might be asked to officiate because of your special relationship to the deceased. This material also attempts to guide you through the actions and procedures nec-*

essary for such an event. As with most activities, the keynote of its success will be planning. The parents should be notified well ahead of time. If they have objections to it, the matter should not be pressed. Nor should they be forced into speaking if they do not wish to do so. Also, they should be informed of exactly what will happen. For example, suppose they were not aware that a plaque was to be presented, and this got them so emotionally upset that they fainted or had to be escorted off stage. This would not be good for anyone concerned. If, however, they know what to expect, and exact plans for the progression of the memorial assembly are made and noted in advance, it can provide a very fitting memorial and an appropriate vehicle for all who knew the deceased to express their feelings to the parents.

100

TOPIC: *A Coach's Introduction to a Memorial Ceremony.*

AUDIENCE: *Suitable for all audiences.*

Good evening, ladies and gentlemen . . .

Every day in my duties as a coach, I am witness to the human drama. I see young people working toward a goal and striving to be the best that they are capable of becoming. Yet, even as I watch, help, counsel, and advise, I am aware that while we may all share a common humanity, our individual lives vary greatly in quality. From the mass, a few people are singled out in our minds as being exemplary. These are people who live their lives with such dignity, such morality, and such honor, that we realize at once that we are associating with someone who is very special. Not only on the playing field, but in life as well, this is a truth that our experience affirms. When such a person is taken from us, we know in our hearts that it is fitting and proper to stand up and proclaim for all to hear that this was a life so well-lived that it is worthy of note, worthy of respect, worthy of honor.

When a life shines forth as a bright beacon of what can be accomplished in this imperfect world we know that we must extoll its virtues and hold it up as a role model for those who will come after. When a life is that outstanding, mankind is shaken by its loss.

That is why we have gathered together this evening. Our dear friend, Bill McGuire, has left us, but we who are left remember what his life entailed and what it meant to us and to all with whom he came into contact. We know what he gave, what he did, what he was. We remember, and this evening we gather to express our sorrow that he is gone and, more important, to express our thanks and our appreciation for the legacy of honor, selflessness, dedication, commitment, and service that he left us.

SPECIAL DATA: *Time of introduction: about two minutes. Quite often, especially if there was some special bond between the coach and the deceased, you may be asked to act as moderator of a memorial ceremony. You would be expected to give a memorial speech, but you would also be expected to introduce other speakers, get the ceremony started, and keep it moving throughout. The preceding speech would be an appropriate introduction to such an affair. Following it, you would introduce the other speakers, saving your speech for last. Following your speech, there would either be a benediction, or you would be expected to close the program. You would then sum up the evening's activities and bid everyone a good evening. The next speech gives a good example of what you might say.*

$$\boxed{101}$$

TOPIC: *A Coach's Closing of a Memorial Ceremony.*

AUDIENCE: *Suitable for all audiences.*

Thank you, ladies and gentlemen, and a special thanks to all of you who spoke this evening about our friend, Bill McGuire.

This memorial program now draws to an end, but our memories of Bill will continue long after we leave this room. In life, he gave to us of himself, and that was a magnificent gift which enriched us all. In death, his memory and the inspiration of his life continue to make our lives better for having known him. Bill McGuire was a warm, wonderful, and gentle man. We shall not forget him.

Thank you for coming.

Good evening.

SPECIAL DATA: *Time of closing: less than thirty seconds. When all the speeches and the ceremonies have been concluded, the emotional atmosphere of the gathering is typically highly charged. It is best, therefore, to end the proceedings as simply and straightforwardly as possible. The short ending above is particularly appropriate, because it sums up the general feeling about the deceased, leaves the audience with something to think about, and puts a definite end to the ceremonies.*

Afterthoughts

If we could leave you with one idea about memorials firmly established in your mind, it would be this: Do your homework. By that we mean that anyone who speaks at a memorial should take the time to work out or adapt a speech so that it will be personal and reflective of the person being honored. Certainly, you can use one of the speeches in this section, but be certain to adapt or alter it so that the personal and individual qualities of the subject come forward.

You must also do particular homework if you are in charge of the entire memorial program. If everything is well-planned in advance, it will run smoothly. Just make certain that you have seen to every detail such as whether or not a relative of the deceased will speak, where the speakers will sit, where the microphone will be, and so forth. Planning guarantees efficiency.

Finally, as we have told you many times before, if you merely say what is in your heart, there is no one who can possibly fault your efforts. That is the final secret of all successful eulogies and memorials—sincerity. With it, all tasks, even something as draining as a speech of this type, are possible.

SECTION 9

A Coach's Playbook
of Special Speeches
for Special Events

There will be times when you will be asked to speak at an occasion that does not necessarily fit into one of the headings in this book. That is the reason for this section, in which we investigate some special speeches for special occasions.

For example, there will come the time when you retire, and you become the object of the retirement speeches of others. You will be expected to say something after all the other well-wishers have finished. It may happen that you will be the guest of honor at a testimonial, and, once again, you will be in the same position. Suppose your team has had a winning (or a losing) season. You will be expected to say something about that to the press or some assembled group. Moreover, coaches are quite often asked to officiate at Sports Night banquets and are expected to speak. Each and every one of these special events, and more, require that you be prepared to speak and say something meaningful and fitting.

Therefore, within the pages of this section you will find speeches on everything from statements to the media on winning and losing seasons to a highly effective speech about a life in coaching which might be used to advantage at your own retirement dinner or at a testimonial given in your honor. As with the other speeches in this book, they are all ready to go, and they have been proven effective time and again under rigorous conditions.

The key to the effective use of any or all of these special speeches is, of course, personalizing them for your presentation. Change the names of people and places to fit your specifications; add personal anecdotes and stories where you find it appropriate to do so; deliver them from your point of view and in your personal style and you will have a speech that will be remembered.

Good luck, and remember—have fun!

TOPIC: *Speech for a Winning Season.*

AUDIENCE: *Press, team members, parents, general adult community.*

Let's start by acknowledging something we all know—it's good to win!

The season has ended, and our record stands for everyone to see. We have every reason to be proud of it. We worked for it. We fought for it. We sweated for it. It is ours!

Perhaps we should just accept it for what it is, an outstanding tribute to the dedication, diligence, and hard work of a superb group of young athletes. Certainly, this is what our record shows. We see reflected in it countless hours on the practice field, sore muscles, infinite patience, and a fierce determination on the part of each of our players to be the best he is capable of being.

Perhaps, also, we should take a closer look at our record and see in it something else. Perhaps we can also see the untiring efforts of everyone who supported those athletes, from the cheerleaders who spurred them on to victory to the young man who collected the towels after the games. All—and I mean this sincerely—all of them have played a vital and necessary part.

No machine works well if even a single part has broken down. Let one belt break in the motor of your car and see how well it runs. So it is with us. Without the complete and total support of everyone who contributes to our team, it will not—it cannot—be the excellent, functioning, winning team that we have been privileged to see this past season. So, to these, our support personnel, this victory, this record, is really your record as well.

Perhaps, also, we can take a closer look at our record and see in it something else. Yes, our players are vitally important. Yes, our support people are vitally important. But, there is one other group, just as important, just as vital, and just as necessary to the total victory. It is to them that I would speak now.

I am speaking of you, our fans, our parents, the people who sat on the sun-baked bleachers and huddled inside blankets in the freezing cold; who shouted with us in the joy of triumph; who had the faith in us when things looked bad; who willed us to win; who lifted our hearts, strengthened our resolve, and gave every ounce of your energy to filling our souls with support, determination, and love. Without you, defeats would have been crushing and victories would have been but hollow shells.

This is your victory also. Yours is the record of which we are so proud. Yours is the honor of our team as well. We are grateful to you, and, in all honesty, we could not have done it without you.

Let us take a closer look at our record and see in it our victory, the victory of everyone who is a part of this team. Players, coaches, team workers, cheerleaders, the people who took tickets at the home games, our fans, our parents, our friends—this is *our* record.

We have been victorious. We have had a winning season. We have worked; We have striven; We have won.

We may all be justly proud of it.

Thank you . . . and, wait 'til next year!

SPECIAL DATA: *Time of speech: about four and one-half minutes. At the beginning of this speech, remember to wait for the cheers and applause to die down before you continue. If you wish to elaborate on the season's record, do so after the second paragraph, but leave the ending of this speech alone. It is powerful enough to stand on its own. This speech would be particularly effective for a press conference, awards dinner, or a team post-season dinner where parents and/or members of the faculty and administration were present as well as team members.*

$$\boxed{103}$$

TOPIC: *Speech for a Losing Season.*

AUDIENCE: *Press, team members, parents, general adult community.*

Ladies and gentlemen . . .

Well, the season is over; the equipment is packed and stored for another year. Now it is time to look back at what we have accomplished over the past weeks.

What is a team record? If it is nothing more than a list of games won and lost, then I suppose we would have to agree that this past season was not the best in our history.

I like to think, however, that a team record is something more than what is entered in the win-loss columns, and, for a moment, I'd like to explore that aspect of it.

When I look at that record sheet, there is something I don't see. I don't see those kids who came out for the team not certain that they could make a lap around the track, much less play in a regular game. I don't see their dedication and effort as they worked to strengthen their bodies; as they learned to play with others for the good of the team; as they studied and memorized the plays and the drills until they were part of their basic reactions. I don't see their sweat, their effort, their personal victories as they conquered themselves and their own weaknesses and became team members. The record doesn't show this.

When I look at that record sheet, there is something else I don't see. I don't see the brotherhood and unity that developed until the team became a single unit; each person striving, not for individual glory, but for the best he could do to aid the *team* to victory. I don't see that selflessness, that giving attitude, that devotion. The record doesn't show them.

When I look at that record sheet, there is something else I don't see. I don't see the courage that I was privileged to see every week on the playing field. I don't see the victories over pain and heartbreak, the sportsmanship that allowed them to embrace the opposing team after losing by the narrowest of margins and congratulate them for their efforts; the integrity that allowed them not to curse a bad call or a bad bounce of the ball but merely to make them determined to try all the harder the next time. Again, the record doesn't show this.

No, the record doesn't show this at all, but I see it; I know it; and I feel it and treasure it within my heart.

You know, there is an old test of whether a person is an optimist or a pessimist. You are supposed to show them a glass with water in it up to the mid-point and ask if the glass is half empty or half full. I guess I must be an optimist, because when I look at our record for the past season— our *real* record and not that paper shadow of wins and losses—I see it as completely full; full of personal triumph and growth; full of practice and promise; full of the glory of young people fighting and striving for a goal; full of the vitality of effort directed for the common good.

This is what I see, and I also see a source of pride for everyone connected with the team. I see a **team** made up of individuals with different tastes and talents who pulled together as one, who worked as one, who fought and cried and laughed as one; who gave everything they had individually for the team as a whole. I see this, and it fills my heart with joy.

This is *my* record; this is the record I choose to remember; this is the record that I will carry away from this season. This is a record of which we may all be justifiably proud.

I defy anyone to deny that!

SPECIAL DATA: *Time of speech: about five minutes. This is the type of speech, originally used after a disastrous season, which doesn't concentrate on defeat. Rather, while it acknowledges a losing season, it concentrates on the personal achievements of the individual players who make up the team. After a losing season, there is no need to rehash the record; usually, your audience is all too familiar with it already, and a speech such as this can have a very uplifting effect.*

104

TOPIC: *Coach's Address at a Sports Night Dinner.*

AUDIENCE: *Mixed audience; adults and student athletes, family, friends.*

Ladies, gentlemen, and the athletes of the Blue and Gold . . .

We have had an outstanding dinner, made all the better because we shared it together.

Indeed, it is being together that makes so much of what we do in life worthwhile. I don't have to tell you that, because all of you here are well aware of what is meant by the term "team spirit." During the season, when you get out on that playing field, there is no one who does not recognize the fact that you function as a single unit; as a team. Because of that, and because of the practice, dedication, and hard work that you have put into making that team the best it could be, you have achieved victory after victory. We, here tonight, are proud of you.

But, understand something. We would have been just as proud of you if you had not won a single game. We would have been proud of you, because you learned how to work together for a goal that was bigger than any one person. You learned to cooperate for the good of all, and that has made you the oustanding young men (women) whom we applaud and admire on this night.

Nor am I merely saying words or speaking only for myself. This dinner tonight stands as testimony to what everyone here feels for you.

There is, however, another feeling here tonight; one which you should share with us as well.

Along with the pride and respect we feel, there is the realization that we are all part of a much larger team, a team in which everyone here plays a very important part. The name of that team is humanity.

We are all part of the family of mankind, and, as such, we all have a team position to play. From the teachers and your coaches who instruct you, to the parents who raise you, care for you, and love you, to the members of the opposing team who provide you with a challenge so that you may perfect yourself and your skills, we all play a part in a game called life.

Because we all play our parts, because we all function as members of that team, we can strive to be the best that we are capable of becoming. If we do that, the team—mankind—cannot help but be the better for it.

Therefore, while all of us here assembled applaud your efforts as athletes during the past season, we also applaud your efforts as human beings. We applaud your dedication; your spirit of sacrifice for the good of others; your willingness to work together for that common goal. These qualities that you share are not very common in the world, I am sad to say, and when we find them in people such as yourselves, it is only right that we acknowledge them for what they are.

We are well aware that what you accomplished on the playing field is only the forerunner of what you will do in life. That gives us renewed hope for a bright and a positive future for all of mankind.

So, to the members of the team—to everyone here and elsewhere who had a hand in this night—I say, "Well done, well done, indeed!"

Thank you.

SPECIAL DATA: *Time of speech: about four minutes. Sports Night dinners and banquets at the end of the season are quite common, especially if the coach is affiliated with a school. It seems only natural that the coach is expected to attend and to address the assembly. The preceding speech is one example of an appropriate speech for such a gathering. All speeches of this nature should be upbeat and give credit to the athletes, their parents, and all support personnel.*

$$\boxed{105}$$

TOPIC: *Acceptance of Retirement.*

AUDIENCE: *Adults; colleagues, friends, family.*

(SPECIAL NOTE: The following speech would be one given by the subject of a retirement dinner—you. When all the speeches have been made and the gift or gifts have been given, the audience usually expects the recipient to say a few words.)

I was going to start out by saying, "my friends," but after some of the jokes that have been made at my expense tonight, I think I'd just better say, "ladies and gentlemen."

You know, I was watching closely as these people came up to speak tonight. Most of them I have known for almost all of my adult life. I was absolutely shocked, therefore, when I looked at them tonight and realized how fat and bald they had become.

And, what they said! At one point my wife poked me in the ribs and asked me whom they were talking about. I told her that I didn't know, but if it turned out that they were talking about me, I was going to sue the school system for not giving me a better salary.

Seriously, however, I did have a difficult time listening to those speeches. They paint a picture of a life spent in coaching and physical education, and they are extremely flattering. For all those kinds words, I am grateful, and I thank you. From my heart, for all that love, I thank you.

Yes, I have a professional career of thirty-five years to look back on, and I know that the memories from those years will remain with me in the days ahead. Of course, not all of them were good times, but neither were they all bad. Rather, they were like all of life, a mixture of hills and valleys, ups and downs, that make up a span of years. Yet, as I look back even now, the unpleasant fades into the background, and that which was good and worthwhile remains vivid and clear in my mind.

There was so much that was fine. I have been privileged to watch kids grow and mature; I have seen our athletic program expand and develop; I have seen sports and coaching grow into a powerful and dynamic field. It gives me the greatest pleasure to know that I was a part, however small, of it all, and I am thankful that I was allowed to be there.

Now, I am stepping aside, but I am not stepping down. Sports and coaching have been my life, and I fully intend to keep abreast of all that is happening. I also fully intend to visit from time to time just to keep in touch and, of course, to see to it that all of you keep on your toes.

I do look forward to retirement and to finally having the time to pursue some personal interests and, most important, to be able to spend more time with Arlene, my wife of thirty-seven years whom I love dearly. However, while I do look forward to all of this, I know that I shall also miss my daily contact with you, my colleagues and my friends.

Because—and make no mistake about it—if some of the things that have been said about me this evening are true, it is because I have, in my professional life, been fortunate enough to be surrounded by some of the finest professionals this country has ever produced; people whose dedication, drive, and expertise could not help but rub off on me. I have learned from you all, and I shall be eternally grateful for that tutoring.

For all that has been said this evening, and for all that has been done, you have my deep thanks; for all the toil, care, and concern that you have poured out to those in our charge over the years, you have my respect; and, for all you have been, are tonight, and will be tomorrow, you have my love.

Thank you for everything.

Good evening.

SPECIAL DATA: *Time of speech: about four and one-half minutes. You will notice that this speech started out very humorously. It also contains slight but very warm digs at the speakers who were obviously friends of the subject. This was effective because of the very special relationship that existed between the speaker and the audience. The warmth and the love in the latter part of the speech are evident. This is the type of speech that will have an audience on its feet, applauding wildly, at the end.*

$$\boxed{106}$$

TOPIC: *Speech About an Athlete Who Has Been Seriously Injured.*

AUDIENCE: *Adults; the press, administrators, colleagues, general public*

Ladies and gentlemen, I would like to begin by making a statement. Last Saturday, during a regularly scheduled football game, Douglas

Arnold, a player on our team, was seriously injured during one of the plays. As he carried the ball, Doug was tackled by one of the defensive players on the opposing team. When he failed to rise following the tackle, we were immediately on the field and at his side. It was apparent that Doug was injured far more seriously than merely having the wind knocked out of him. Within seconds, Dr. Farris, our team physician, was at his side along with several trained members of the First Aid Squad. Coach Houten, the coach of the opposing team, immediately asked their team physician, Dr. Lyle, to assist in any way possible. When it was determined that Doug had suffered an injury to his back, the ambulance was brought on to the field, and, using all proper medical techniques, Doug was transported to St. Luke's Hospital.

At present, we know that Doug has suffered a traumatic injury to his spine which has left him incapable of movement from the waist down. The exact extent of Doug's injury and the effect that it will have on him in the future are still being determined by medical testing. I can tell you that I have been assured by several medical authorities that Doug's life is not in jeopardy. As far as his paralysis is concerned, we do not know at this time whether this is a temporary or permanent condition.

Those, ladies and gentlemen, are the bare bones of what happened last Saturday. If I left it at that, however, I would feel remiss in my obligation to Doug's fellow players, our staff, and to Doug himself. Therefore, I am going to ask that you indulge me for a few more moments.

We have had a chance to view the films of the incident. Indeed, Coach Houten and I, with the entire coaching staff, school administrators, and several league officials, have run those films several times. We have studied the incident, talked about it, rerun it in slow motion, backwards and forwards. After hours of study, everyone involved has come to the same conclusion.

Basically, neither of the players involved was at fault. The young man who tackled Doug did so in a legal and proper manner. He was performing his function as part of the team. He performed that function as he and every other athlete in his position had been trained to do. He tackled in the legal, prescribed manner. The films offer clear proof of that and of the fact that there was no, I repeat, no undue violence or evidence of vindictiveness in the action. In other words, this young man tackled Doug the same way that he has tackled dozens of other players throughout all the games in which he has played. There is no doubt in our minds of this.

Nor is there any question that Doug was at fault in any way. Doug was carrying the ball properly, as he had been trained to do. He was running in a normal manner such as we have seen him do on many occasions. His body was in a proper position for running, and there is nothing to indicate that he was doing anything other than what he should have been doing at that time. In short, Doug was performing his task correctly. Doug was in outstanding physical shape. I spoke to him on the day of the game, and he was as bright and alert as ever. Doug's mind was clear and his body was strong. He had been tackled many times the same way that he was tackled on Saturday. There is no doubt in our minds. Doug was completely without fault in this incident.

Yet, it happened. Doug now lies in St. Luke's Hospital paralyzed from the waist down. Tests to be performed shortly will determine whether this is a permanent or a temporary condition. It is the deep and fervent prayer of everyone—coaches; players on both teams; the school faculty and administration; the fans who watched the game; everyone to whom I have spoken—that Doug's injuries may be temporary and that he may soon be back with us. With every ounce of our beings, we pray for this.

I was with Doug on the field after it happened, and I was allowed to see him briefly later that night at the hospital. He had been given a sedative, and he was groggy when I entered his room, but he recognized me. We spoke for a while, and it appeared that he was getting sleepy, so I started to leave. He stopped me, he looked up and said, "Coach, I'm gonna beat this. I'm gonna make it."

I had no words at that time; my emotions were in my throat. I smiled, watched as he drifted into sleep, and I left.

But, I want to tell you now that I believe him. He *is* going to beat this. He *is* going to make it. I have known, trained, and worked with this young man for three years now. I know what a talented, intelligent, determined person he is. I have seen him commit himself to the game and work long, hard, and demanding hours in order to perfect himself. I have seen the sweat that went into it. I know the will that kept him at it until he accomplished his private goals.

If his condition proves, as we all hope and pray, to be a temporary one, then I know that Doug Arnold will win. He will do whatever is necessary in order to come back. He will not be alone. Every coach, every trainer, every physical therapist, every athlete on this team will be at his side. If he needs training and therapy, these people will be there. We will be there when he needs us, whenever he needs us, wherever he needs us. We will take our inspiration from Doug himself. We will not give up; we will never let him down; we will work whatever the cost until we have achieved our goal. Doug taught us this by his example when he was with us, and now it is our turn to apply those principles in his case. No one forces us to offer this; no one forces us to do this. We offer and will do this gladly, willingly, with pride and with joy, because Doug has been, is, and will continue to be a prized and valuable member of this team.

But, if the worst should happen . . . Well, Doug told me personally that he was going to beat this; that he was going to make it. I firmly believe that this will be true no matter what happens. To some, a handicap is a crushing blow from which they never rise. To others, it is a setback to be dealt with and overcome. I know Doug is one of the latter. Whatever happens, Doug will rise above it. It may take him time; it will certainly cost him pain and effort, but it will *not* hold him down; it will not crush him. We all know Doug as a person of intelligence, insight, wit, and ambition. We have no doubt but that his future, whatever his physical condition, will be filled with success. A physical handicap could never keep a person of his caliber from rising in the world.

Doug, Mr. and Mrs. Arnold, we want you to know that you have our deepest sympathies for this tragic accident. We join you in your concern. We also want you to know that we are here for you. You have our support not only in terms of prayers and good wishes, but practically as well. When Doug needs us, you have our promise that we will respond in whatever way we can. You also have our belief in Doug; a belief based on our knowledge of him as a teammate, an outstanding human being, and an inspiration to us all; a belief that *nothing* can beat him, can subdue him, or can tie him down for long.

Working together, there is nothing but hope for whatever the future may hold.

Thank you for listening, ladies and gentlemen. Now, if you have any questions, I will try to answer them . . .

SPECIAL DATA: *Time of speech: about six minutes. The above speech might serve well as the beginning of a press conference that is held after a tragic incident of this nature. While it is the hope of every coach that nothing of this type befall the players, it does happen. If you are required to speak about it, this speech offers a good model as it details what happened, offers a calm and positive appraisal of the situation, and even offers some hope for the future. Just be sincere in whatever you say, don't be afraid to let some emotion out, and you will do fine. Above all, be truthful. This coach could use the boy's*

> *words, because that's what the boy said to him. You*
> *would not, under any circumstances, put words in the*
> *boy's mouth. Speak simply and honestly of what you*
> *know and feel.*

107

TOPIC: *Introduction to a Speech Before a Legislative Body.*

AUDIENCE: *Adults; members of the body you are addressing, press.*

(SPECIAL NOTE: There may come a time when you will be called on to testify before or give an address to a legislative body either for or against some proposed statute, rule, or bill related to sports or physical education. The following is an introduction that you might use effectively on such an occasion.)

Honored members of the State Legislature (*Or, whatever body you happen to be addressing. Check in your local library for the proper form of address, as this may vary from body to body according to that body's particular custom.*)

I welcome the opportunity to address this Legislature, and I wish to thank you for affording me the opportunity to do so.

As human beings, we sometimes get to feeling a bit superior. We make plans, arrange meetings, conduct business, and go on with our lives with the certain knowledge that we are in control. It's just about that time, however, that the hurricane strikes, the blizzard blows, or the river floods, and we find out how easily our plans, our meetings, our business goes by the boards as we find ourselves chastised by the elements. It is as if we had forgotten the basics, and then those basics assert themselves and refuse to be forgotten or ignored.

So, too, when dealing with the important and pressing issues of our times, we tend to forget another basic. We concentrate on one aspect of a problem, one angle of a solution, and we forget that nothing is single-sided; that any one thing is a part of a larger, greater whole. We see sports, for example, as a form of recreation, and we are correct, but that is only one aspect; one angle.

We must also remember that organized sports in our schools and on our playgrounds affects the lives of thousands of our children and, by projection, their families. We must remember that sports teach values—traditional moral values of fairness, equality, sportsmanship, and the basic values of getting along with others in a pluralistic society. We must remember that, for many children, sports offer their only acceptable outlet for frustration and aggression that might otherwise be channeled towards society as a whole. We must remember that sports offer our children physical fitness; a mental attitude that says that the individual can win in spite of handicaps; a knowledge that the individual can succeed without resort to violence, drugs, or anti-social behavior. We must remember that to many of our children organized sports is the difference between success and failure, not only on the field, but in life itself.

Above all, we must remember the basic fact that organized sports is a school. Its classrooms may be the playgrounds and playing fields of our state, but the lessons taught there are as valuable and as real as any taught in a red brick building with a flag flying in front. Here, the lessons we teach are not only in the skills and techniques of the particular sport, but they are lessons in living itself. They are lessons that, as any coach will tell you, have meant the salvation of many a life; lives that are now productive and contributing to the community. These lives might otherwise have led to a dead-ended alley and a burden on society as a whole.

Yes, we must always remember that the lessons of sports are, for our children, the lessons of life.

I am certain that this body recognizes this fact and sees the picture as a whole. I am indeed pleased to testify before you.

SPECIAL DATA: *Time of introduction: close to two minutes. Following this introduction, you would proceed to present your major speech or answer questions as the situation demanded. This introduction, however, gets the audience "back to basics" so to speak and places the responsibility for positive action squarely on their shoulders.*

$$\boxed{108}$$

TOPIC: *Speech Requesting an Increase in the Athletic Budget.*

AUDIENCE: *Adults; those administrators who handle budgets.*

Good evening, ladies and gentlemen. I'd like to thank the board for giving me this opportunity to address them on the subject of the athletic budget for the coming year.

You know, someone once told me that I had a very odd habit. I asked him what it was, and he said, "All right, tell me why you answer every question with a question?"

I said, "Do I do that?"

Perhaps my friend was right, because if someone were to ask me why the athletic budget for next year should go up, my answer would be, "What hasn't gone up?"

Indeed, this is a part of the problem. Those items which cost X amount today, will cost X plus two or three or more tomorrow. Prices do not stand still, and, as everyone knows, there is not a manufacturer in the world who says, "You know, I like you. You can have it at last year's prices."

Yet, the increase in prices is only a contributing factor to the rise in budget that I propose. The most important factor; the factor that cannot be ignored or shaved or ameliorated in any way is the student athlete.

Our athletes are our number one concern. It is for them that we have organized sports. It is for them and for their development and welfare that we have set up programs of training and competition. Indeed, everything we do is done with them in mind.

This is as it should be, for we exist in order to educate our children, and sports and physical training are vital and necessary parts of that education. The ideal of the healthy mind in the healthy body is as real today as it was to the Greek philosophers who first thought of it. Our teams and our programs of organized sports provide that education.

But, as any teacher will tell you, you cannot teach modern history with a book that is 100 years out of date. Much of our equipment is usable and safe, but much of it, as I detailed in a report to this body, needs replacement. We have also added games to the schedules of many of our teams, and the consumable supplies such as tape, first aid supplies, and the like must be increased proportionally. I refuse, as I know that you would refuse, to allow our children to take the field without proper taping and supplies. Yes, we want our children to play, but we want them to play safely, with as much chance of avoiding injury as possible. If a child is scraped or bruised or suffers a minor cut, I, for one, want to know that there are enough antiseptic, band-aids, and gauze pads to take care of it on the spot.

Please do not misunderstand. I realize that this is your desire as well, and I am not implying that leaving the budget the way it is will mean that our children will be injured. What I am saying is that without an increase in the athletic budget for the next year, there will have to be cuts somewhere. Since no one wants to cut supplies, the cuts will have to come elsewhere. That may well mean that we will have to cut games from the schedule in order to conserve the supplies we have. It may mean that we will have to cut some drills or practices because the equipment is not functioning or simply not there. It may mean that, out of necessity, our children, our athletes, will be getting less than the full potential that we could be offering.

In short, if the athletic budget is not raised, then the question arises, where will we cut? Shall we tell our athletes that they will not be playing against this or that school because we can't afford the supplies to keep them safe in the game? Shall we *tell* them about the proper way to block and tackle on the football team but tell them that they will have to think about it rather than practice it because the sled is so old that it poses a threat to them? Shall we tell a group of youngsters that the sport in which they want to play has been cancelled for the year so that the money can go to other teams in sports that are more popular?

I do not want to do this, and I firmly believe that you do not want this either.

The athletic budget comes out of the general school budget, and money, or its lack, is a problem everywhere. No one wants to pay higher taxes, myself included. All of this is understandable. It is also understandable, however, that our children want to engage in organized sports. It is also understandable that sports provide them with a lifetime learning experience, recreation, and physical health and vitality. It is also understandable that the safety and welfare of our children come first, before other considerations.

Consequently, determining the athletic budget is not an easy task. Nor is it easy to have determined one only to have an athletic director come before you and ask for more. However, I ask you to realize that what I ask is not for me; it is not for you; it is for our children, who should have the best possible chance to develop and become the best that they are capable of becoming. It is for them that I request this increase.

It is they and they alone whom you must consider in making your decision.

Thank you for giving me the opportunity to speak to you this evening.

SPECIAL DATA: *Time of speech: about five minutes. Quite often, coaches and athletic directors must plead a case for increased* *funds before a school board, board of directors, or the like. This is one example of what might be said. Notice that nowhere in the speech was the board or body blamed for anything. Rather, several times their problems were appreciated and acknowledged. Remember, it is never a good idea to antagonize those who hold the purse strings, no matter how convinced you are of your cause. A good, solid case, well presented, with a plea that strikes at their responsibility, will accomplish much more than any amount of shouting.*

109

TOPIC: *A Coach's Address to an Alumni Gathering.*

AUDIENCE: *Mostly adults; alumni and possibly their families.*

Welcome, Class of 19**!

It has been a number of years since I saw some of you as athletes, as cheerleaders, as fans in the stands. I'm very happy to see that you have all continued to grow and develop. Of course, in some cases that I see, you have grown right through your hair and developed into a size 60 portly, but you have grown.

Personally, I continue to be the sleek, handsome devil I always was. (*Wait for laughter. If the group is too polite to laugh, say, "Well, if you'll let me get away with that, you've also grown far more polite than I recall!" This* will *get laughter.*)

Seriously, I am delighted to see each and every one of you, and I am overjoyed that you invited me here this evening.

It is inevitable, I suppose, that time shapes our memories, and we begin to remember things as we would have them be rather than as they actually were. However, I do not find myself with that problem this evening. Most of you I recognize instantly, and when I remember the days when our relationship was a bit different than it is now, I do so with joy, with warmth, and with great fondness.

That is not to say that we did not have some difficulties. Indeed, I remember some of you from the football team running lap after lap. I recall your first days of practice, and I only wish now that I had had a camera then. I could have made a fortune selling those photographs at the door this evening. Oh, yes, I remember.

I have many fine memories of this class, but if you were to press me to say what I remembered most clearly and with the greatest affection, I would have to say that it was your enthusiasm. Yes, I remember that you were enthusiastic about sports; enthusiastic about our teams; enthusiastic about our school; enthusiastic about the future; and enthusiastic about each other.

When I spoke to many of you earlier this evening, I was overjoyed to find that the intervening years have not lessened that enthusiasm; have not dampened your fire; have done nothing to lessen your spirit. Indeed, I find you as fresh and exciting this evening as I did when I was your coach and teacher. You were very special then, and you are very special now.

Of course, we have changed, and that is inevitable. Today you ride in your cars rather than on your bikes; you concern yourselves with the future of your families and providing them with a rich and full life instead of letting that book report due on Friday consume your entire attention; you carry your own children rather than carrying books in your arms. All of this is a change; a massive change that we call life.

Yet, what is essential in you—what made you so vital as students and so admirable as adults—has not changed. These are the qualities of honesty, courage, commitment, and purpose which singled you out during your student days and which you have not lost over the years. These are the moral values that make life good, wholesome, and a promise of joy. These are the moral values that you will teach to your children and that will make their futures bright.

This evening, many of you thanked me for coming to this gathering. I tell you now that it is I who thank you for inviting me. In days gone by, you were the hope of the future. Now the future has arrived, and my heart is filled with joy to see that the promise was fulfilled.

Thank you for having me, and may the days of your future be as bright as my memories of you in the past. If this wish comes true, then your footsteps will be lighted forever more.

Thank you and good night.

SPECIAL DATA: *Time of speech: about four minutes. Even if you had the worst experiences of your coaching career with some of the members of a particular class, a gathering of alumni and their families is no place to voice it.*

Inevitably, years have passed, and their memories of you are filled with warmth. It is best to respond in kind. If you are asked to officiate at the proceedings, you might want to add to this speech by delivering the eulogy for a class reunion which we gave in Section Eight if it is appropriate. It would fit nicely into this speech just before the last paragraph.

$$\boxed{110}$$

TOPIC: *My Favorite Half-time Speech (Strictly for Laughs)*

AUDIENCE: *See Special Data section.*

(SPECIAL NOTE: Not one word of what follows is meant to be taken seriously. Rather, this is a comedy special for coaches. More information on when and how it should be delivered is given in the Special Data section immediately following the speech.)

All right, you guys, listen up! No, come to think of it, you'd better listen sitting down—you need the rest.

Well, here it is half-time once again. Now, I don't want any of you guys to get discouraged just because they have a slight lead of forty-six points. Remember, we've been in this position before. Of course, whenever we were in that position before, we always crawled off the field at the end of the game because they beat the heck out of us, but you can't get discouraged; there's always hope.

In fact, there were some very good things that I could say about your playing during this first half. The fact that my mother told me never to lie prevents me from saying them, but I could if I wanted to.

Take Hanrahan, for example. Hanrahan single-handedly blocked their point-after kick just before the half-time whistle. What's more, he did it in the most unique way I have ever witnessed. Just as soon as the doctor removes the ball from Hanrahan's mouth, he'll be in here, and I want you to give him a nice round of applause.

And Carson, I want to congratulate you on making up a brand new defensive play. For those of you who didn't see it because you were still throwing up, Carson got up to that defensive line and took his position as center. He looked across at their six-foot-three-inch, two hundred and forty-five pound noseguard, and on the spot Carson developed what he is calling a "lookout block." The minute the ball was snapped, Carson turned around to face his own men, shouted, "Look out! Here he come again!", and dropped to the ground and covered his head with his hands. That was quick thinking, Carson—lousy football, but quick thinking!

I think the best tackle of the first half has to go to Harris. Harris hit low, he hit hard, he hit clean, and the object of Harris' tackle crumbled away. In fact, the only criticism I have of that tackle is the fact Harris tackled a cheerleader instead of one of the guys on the opposing team. What's that? Yes, Harris, I know—you thought her pom-pom was a football, and we're going to work on that, son, but you should have realized that the people you're supposed to tackle don't wear those little skirts.

While we're on the subject of mistaken identity, I'd like to publicly tell Billings that the lateral he threw was right on the target. I only wish you had thrown it to one of our guys rather than the referee. I mean, the sight of that striped shirt holding the ball with a look of complete surprise on his face as the entire defensive squad descended on him—well, it was just horrible. Incidentally, reports from the hospital say that the ref is doing just fine, and he should be able to walk in about a month. But, in the second half, will you watch that kind of stuff, Billings, please!

Now, let me say a few words about our quarterback. Jones, where are you? Will somebody tell me where Jones is? What? Oh, there you are. Jones? Come on. Jones. Stop that. Jones, I hate to see you curled up in the corner like that. That's it, take your thumb out of your mouth, stop crying, and come over here. What? No, you can't have your Mommie until *after* the game. Just sit here and try to listen.

First of all, Jones, you looked great on that field. You looked proud and fierce and determined. Unfortunately, then they tossed the coin and the game began. After that, you seemed a bit upset if I may say so. I mean, when the ref called that offsides on us just because one of our players happened to be sitting on the defensive guard's chest before the ball was snapped, I thought it was unfair. I didn't like it any more than you did, Jones, but let me give you a little advice. Lying down and kicking your hands and feet and then threatening to hold your breath until you burst is not going to get the ref to change his call. What's more, the fans get upset when they see their quarterback turning blue!

You did, however, make our only score of the first half. It was just beautiful. Jones, when your father set off that half-stick of dynamite on the side lines, the other team was so distracted, you just ran right through them without being touched. Incidentally, Jones, does your father have any plans to replace those bleachers? Oh, that's good, because besides the bleachers, it also took out both rest rooms, and you have no idea of how nasty the fans can get when those aren't available.

Okay, so now it's time to go back for the second half, and I . . . Jones, I asked you to stop crying. Carson, not you too! Harris . . . Jones? Assistant Coach Ferris, will you please pass out the tissues. What's that, Billings? Yes, we have to play the second half! Come on, now! What's the matter with you guys? I know they outweigh us by one hundred pounds per man; I know they are taller by a foot per player; I know they have more speed; they're rougher; they're tougher, but I ask you, are we men or are we mice? Well? Aw, come on, guys, you shouldn't have to think that over— you should know the answer. Hanrahan, stop that squeaking in the back!

All right, forget the question. Let's just get out there and do the best we can. Oh, yes, there is one other thing. Could you *all* please try to remember to get on the *right* bus after the game. It was so embarrassing last week ending up at the Shopping Mall rather than the school.

I have an announcement that I was going to save until after we won this game, so I might as well make it now. I have decided to retire from coaching. All right, you guys, stop applauding and listen for a moment! You see, I've been having some medical problems lately, and my doctor says it is all due to the stress of coaching. There's just too much pressure and stress in this game. So, starting a week from Monday, I am taking a new job with less stress, less frustration, and less pressure—I'll be driving a nitroglycerine truck over twisting mountain roads. That, I know I can handle.

All right, Tigers, let's go!

SPECIAL DATA: *Time of speech: a little over five minutes (possibly longer, depending on audience reaction). This is a very "special" speech, indeed. It is strictly for laughs and, we feel, very good humor. Where could you use it? Well, how about at an athletic awards dinner, a sports night activity, any recreational gathering of your colleagues, lodge or club meetings, an alumni dinner (presenting it as "remembering" the half-time speech you once gave to their team), faculty-student talent shows or fundraisers, or any occasion where it is understood that the purpose of the evening is to have a good time and enjoy each other's company. It is particularly effective if your* *team has just had a winning season. Then, you might substitute the actual names of the players on your team for those in the speech. You will find that they laugh hardest of all. You might also try delivering it wearing a sweat shirt (preferably stained), a whistle around your neck, and a cap on backwards. Rehearse this before you give it, give it with enthusiasm, and you will have a winner on your hands.*

111

TOPIC: *Introductory Speech to Members of the Press.*

AUDIENCE: *Adults; members of the press and media.*

Good afternoon, ladies and gentlemen, and thank you for coming today. As you know, this is our first meeting of the current season, and we have a long road to travel together as our saga unfolds. In this journey, as in every journey, each traveler has his or her own responsibilities and particular tasks to perform.

You, the ladies and gentlemen of the press, must report what you see and hear to the public who, to a large extent, depend on your insights and skills of reporting to gain knowledge of what is happening with and to their team. In this manner, you satisfy the needs of thousands of sports fans throughout the community.

For us, on the coaching staff, our responsibilities lie mainly with our players in conditioning them and training them and allowing them to become the best which they are capable of becoming. That is not, however, where our responsibilities end. We, like you, have a responsibility to our fans and our community to provide them with accurate information regarding this team so that they may be informed, participating spectators and supporters.

If these are our individual responsibilities, then we also share one common responsibility, and that is to provide as accurate, truthful, and meaningful an account of what is happening as is humanly possible.

Toward that goal, I will make you a promise. For myself and for my staff, I promise that we will always be available to you. We will be available for interviews, for information, and for commentary whenever you may require it; when things are going great and when things are not going so great as well. Whatever the situation, I promise that we will answer your questions with honesty, frankness, and openness. I have nothing but optimism for our relationship over this coming season, and I know that I and my entire staff will work to keep that relationship as solid as possible throughout the year.

In return, I ask that you take us up on our promise. I ask that you come to us for information; that you come to us as well when there is a controversy; that you let us help you help your readers by supplying every side to any issue that may arise. Together, we can supply accurate, factual information to our public for their good, for your good, and, perhaps most important, for the good of the players on our team.

Now, shall we begin . . .

SPECIAL DATA: *Time of introduction: about 90 seconds to two minutes. You know, Napoleon once wrote that he would rather face three hostile armies than one hostile newspaper. There is great truth in that statement. What you never need is a local press that is against you in any way. This introduction, therefore, aims at establishing an open, working relationship between the coach and the press. If such a relationship can be established, it is definitely a step in the right direction.*

┌─────────┐
│ **112** │
└─────────┘

TOPIC: *Women's Athletics: Yesterday, Today, and Tomorrow*

AUDIENCE: *Suitable for any audience, but most effective with adults.*

Let's look forward by looking back about 100 years. That would place us in the latter half of the nineteenth century, and, although we would have to look very closely, we could find women actively engaged in sports. Well, that is, sports of a kind.

One of the most popular sports for women at that time was something called eurythmics. You may have seen old photographs of groups of women dressed in those special outfits designed by Amelia Bloomer and named after her. They stood, in one position preferably, and they lifted bowling pins or hoops above their heads and stretched their arms out and back. All this was done in unison, often to piano accompaniment. That's it. Exciting, isn't it? It did have one large advantage, however. It was considered "proper and refined" for young ladies.

Of course, the fact that girls have always played as hard as boys and often joined in boys' athletic activities on the village green or in the farmer's field was largely ignored. They were, after all, children, so they could be forgiven; they didn't know any better. Of course several innovators pointed out that young ladies might require exercise, but the general consensus was that eurythmics and other light exercises were the best suited to the "delicate natures" of women and to the uplifting dignity of "the fair sex."

One extremely funny incident concerning women and sports occurred in 1891 at the International Young Men's Christian Association Training School, later to become Springfield College, in Massachusetts.

A young man named James Naismith, lately out of theological studies and acting as physical education instructor at the school, developed a game that he envisioned would provide exercise and interest for his classes while teaching his boys the values of clean and moral living. The game he came up with became known as basketball, and the rest is history, except for the little-known incident of James Naismith and the first game of women's basketball on record.

You see, basketball really caught on at Springfield, and soon it was being played regularly in Naismith's classes. People from the surrounding area began to drop in to watch this new game. That also included several young ladies from the Buckingham Grade School that was located nearby. Usually, lunch hours would find them "dropping in" to the gymnasium to watch and shout encouragement to one side or another. Naismith himself recorded that these young ladies amazed him by shouting fully as loudly as the male spectators.

Perhaps it was inevitable, but soon, a daring group of these ladies approached Naismith and asked if they might try this new game of basket ball. They must have done some pretty fast talking, because Naismith consented, providing some rules were established first. All spectators were eliminated. The doors of the gym were closed and locked before the game began, as were the windows. The ladies wore long, trailing dresses with mutton-leg sleeves and either street shoes or ladies' lawn tennis shoes. The only man to be allowed in the gym was Naismith, himself, who would officiate.

Mr. Naismith did not have an easy evening. Early in the game he called a foul on one young lady who proceeded to doubt the marital status of Naismith's mother and father. When that happened, Mr. Naismith is reported to have "blushed scarlet," and it was several minutes before he could, or would, continue.

There is no record of who won that game or even what the final score was, but James Naismith later recorded that he would have to think very long and seriously before he ever allowed another group of females to play his game. The ladies were, it seems, far more violent and played in a rougher, more undignified, and more reckless manner than did his "young gentlemen."

One can only speculate at what James Naismith would think if he saw a game of women's basketball today. Perhaps he would repeat that slogan of a few years back, "You've come a long way, Baby!"

Let us be honest—that slogan is true: women's sports have come a long way, a very long way, indeed. From the 1900 Olympic Games where the only women's event was lawn tennis to the olympics of today with full participation by women in almost every area of competition; from school systems that spent small fortunes on boys' sports, and relegated girls to exercises in the gym if it wasn't being used by the boys to schools across the nation recognizing girls' sports as an integral part of the curriculum and providing funding for girls' teams; from media coverage that placed news of women's sports on the "ladies' page" or buried it in the obituaries, to coverage on the sports pages alongside the men's sports and even prime time TV and radio coverage of certain women's sporting activities.

The signs of the development of women's sports are encouraging. Today, a woman jockey is no longer a rarity. Girls, as well as boys, can go to college on athletic scholarships. There are professional women's teams, and talented women athletes are being scouted by them. It is typical rather than atypical for the daughter as well as the son in a family to be engaged in school- or community-sponsored athletics.

Make no mistake about it, however. These changes only came about because many people—men and women alike—fought for them, worked for them, and, in some cases, went to court to gain equality on the athletic field for women. It is to these people as well as the female athletes who have given their strength and their spirit to the games that women of today owe their thanks.

What about the future of women's sports? Will women's sports ever gain the same status as men's sports? Will Madison Square Garden ever be filled to the rafters for a playoff of women's basketball? Will women athletes some day receive the same salaries as their male counterparts?

These questions remain to be answered. I can, however, give you my own opinion.

When I meet a person who tells me that he or she is not prejudiced and then proves the point by referring to his or her many black friends or Jewish friends or Catholic friends or Spanish friends or whatever friends, then I know that that person is, consciously or unconsciously, lying through his or her teeth. Indeed, the only time we have finally left the specter of prejudice behind is when we can like or dislike *that* person rather than that black person or white person or Catholic person. It is only when we see people without labels that we can say that prejudice no longer plays a significant part in our lives.

So it is, I believe, with sports. I hope that there will come a day when we can all sit down to enjoy a game of basketball rather than a game of men's basketball or women's basketball. I hope that we will someday be able to say, "What a fine athlete!" rather than "What a fine female athlete." I hope that there will come a day when people will enjoy, watch, participate in, and be a part of *sports*, without caring whether the sport is being played by male or female teams.

Does this sound like a dream? Stranger things have happened. If, less than 100 years ago, you had told Mr. Naismith what his "gentle game" would turn into, I doubt he would have believed you.

Therefore, let's all make an effort to make speeches such as this one completely unnecessary. Let's lend our support to athletes and sports, whether male or female. Then, perhaps a speaker fifty or so years from now will again be able to say, "you've come a long way, people!"

When that happens, as I believe that someday it will, it will not be men who have benefited, and it will not be women who have benefited— it will be humanity!

SPECIAL DATA: *Time of speech: about eight minutes. If you wish to shorten this speech, you could do so by removing the anecdote about James Naismith. We think, however, that it is very humorous, and audiences react well to it. Women's sports have been the neglected child for many years, and it is important for coaches to speak out for their development. This speech can be used equally as effectively before colleagues and lay audiences. It has also been used, with variations, during the kickoff of a fund-raiser to support girls' teams. We believe that you will find it very effective with a strong and positive audience reaction.*

Afterthoughts

The coach is usually expected to give a speech at a special event involving sports. We hope that, within the previous pages, you have found something that will be of service to you when one of these situations comes about.

Although we have stressed it time and time again, it bears repeating here. The key factor in any speech is the honesty and sincerity of the speaker. It does not matter that the situation may be emotionally charged; it does not matter that the audience may be hostile; it does not even matter if the audience is on your side, as in a speech accepting a testimonial or retirement. Whatever the situation, if you speak honestly about what you feel so that the audience knows that what you are saying is from your heart, the audience will respect you and your presentation.

Whether you choose one of the speeches in this section, adapt one to your particular set of circumstances, or compose your own, if you deliver it with your heart, you won't go wrong. Be sincere, and all else will follow.

SECTION 10

A Seasonal Guide
to Speeches
about Sports

Naturally, as coaches and "workers in the field" so to speak, our attention is consumed with sports for the greater part of our lives. While this may be perfectly natural considering our profession, it is not unwarranted to say that sports take up a great deal of the attention of a vast majority of the American people. Indeed, all one has to do to appreciate the truth of that statement is to be in a city with one of the participating teams during the World Series or the Superbowl. The talk is of almost nothing else, and it is as if the entire town has shifted into high gear. In a like manner, one can experience the high spirits in a school or a small community just before the "big" game. Indeed, whether it is sandlot or professional, whether it is played in the Astrodome or the back field of P.S. 122, people and sports have formed a bond. It is a marriage of minds, and the marriage is alive and well.

It is no wonder, therefore, that people in general like to hear about sports, and especially enjoy hearing about them from the coaches and players of the game. Indeed, the coach is a popular speaker at many functions and with many audiences, clubs, lodges, and organizations. Should the coach ask what his audience would like to hear about, more often than not, the reply is, "Just tell us about your sport."

That is exactly what you will find in this section. The following pages contain speeches about a number of different sports that are played in America today. Because so many sports revolve around schools, and the school year usually starts in the fall, we have arranged the speeches from football to baseball; from fall to summer. Every fact mentioned in these speeches has been verified and is correct, so there is no possibility of anyone finding your research faulty. They are upbeat, positive speeches that concentrate on the history of the sport as well as the emotion that it engenders.

In short, there is something here for every season. A coach called on to speak about his or any other sport will find something of use in the following pages.

TOPIC: *Football*

AUDIENCE: *Suitable for all audiences.*

Some place back in antiquity—perhaps in Rome, perhaps in Greece—the bladder of an animal was inflated, two groups of people formed, and they generally punched, carried, and kicked this object toward a goal. The concept was amazingly simple—the group that got the inflated bladder to their goal the most times won the game.

The playing of this "game," however, was anything but simple or pleasant. At first, there were few, if any, rules, and from all accounts, these early games were extremely violent. In fact, some of the players didn't survive the game. Some of these contests were so violent that it took decrees from kings and minor wars to stop them. At that time, the games were called mellays, or *mêlées* in French. Our modern word "melee" meaning a riot came from this term, so you have some idea of what it must have been like.

During the middle ages the art of shoemaking came into its own, and the animal bladder was replaced by a large leather ball. The violence still continued, but gradually, rules for the game began to evolve. By the time 1800 rolled around, the game varied from place to place, but the one rule that everyone agreed on was that the ball was never to be passed by hand or carried in the direction of the opponent's goal.

Then, at Rugby School in England in 1823, an incident occurred that was to change all that. During a "football" game at the school, a player named William Webb Ellis actually grabbed the ball and ran with it in his hands. He nearly got expelled for his behavior, and it certainly wasn't "cricket," but many of the players and spectators had the odd feeling that it made the game faster and more exciting. This grew, and, eventually, rules were introduced that allowed carrying, passing, and running with the ball. This became the game of "Rugby" or English football, which is the father of our own modern sport. If you visit Rugby today, on one of the walls you'll find a plaque which is inscribed, "This stone commemorates the exploit of William Webb Ellis who with a fine disregard for the rules of football as played in his time first took the ball in his arms and ran with it, thus originating the distinctive feature of the Rugby game."

On the other side of the Atlantic, Americans played a form of English football that they called "Ballown," presumably because the game went to the team that most "owned" the ball during the contest. Accounts of these early games were a little confusing, primarily because rules for its play varied from place to place and school to school. In some places carrying the ball was permitted, while in others it was not. In general, however, goals were only scored by kicking the ball, and a goal had no numerical value—it was merely "a goal." The team with the most goals at the end of the game won the contest. Even in places where carrying the ball was permitted, a run across the goal line (modern football's chief scoring play) counted for nothing, but merely gave that team a free kick at the goal.

Incidentally, the ball used was round and made of rubber, and a goal was scored by kicking this object *under* a crossbar between two upright posts. Under the Princeton rules of 1867, there was no time limit for the game. Rather, the contest ended when one team had scored six goals.

Not to be outdone by Princeton, Harvard developed rules which allowed the carrying of the ball and were more like Rugby. It was known as the "Boston" game, and when the first intercollegiate rules conference was held in 1873, Harvard was not invited because of their unorthodox game.

Football was rapidly gaining popularity during this time, and coaches, players, and the public realized the need for some sort of standardization. Throughout the late 1800s and early 1900s the game underwent some drastic changes.

The round rubber ball became the egg-shaped Rugby ball which, in time, reduced in size. Play went from 25 men on a side to 11. Running the ball across the goal line and "touching it down" became the chief scoring play, and its value changed from no points but a free kick to 2 points, to 4 points, and finally to 6 points. Score by a kick changed from having to go under to having to go over the crossbar and went from counting as "a goal," to 5 points, to 2 points, and to 1 point following a touchdown. While tackling, in one or another form, was always legal, it wasn't until 1888 that tackles below the waist were legalized. Yes, these were years of drastic change for the game of American football, but out of them came the game we know today.

Had you seen a game in 1900 it might have been recognizable as football, but only barely so. Indeed, it took the intervention of the President of the United States to make football what it is today.

The new rules and regulations established during the late 1800s were cumbersome to say the least, and they were also open to interpretation from school to school and conference to conference. Players were being seriously injured, and many fans believed that the game had grown pondersome and slow-moving. Moreover, existing eligibility rules excluded a number of schools from participation. In late 1905, President Teddy Roosevelt asked representatives of Princeton, Harvard, and Yale to come to the White House. There, he charged them with the responsibility for developing a more open and a considerably less brutal game so that football might survive as an "American sport."

These representatives, along with the representatives of 28 other colleges, formed a committee that was the forerunner of the National Collegiate Athletic Association, and, on January 12, 1906, they met with the existing governing body of football. From this conference, football as we know it today was born.

Among other things, they did something that would prove revolutionary in nature. They legalized the forward pass. This was one of the greatest steps in forever separating American football from English Rugby. The forward pass had been recommended by a man named John Heisman of Penn State several years earlier, and was to become one of the mainstays of the game.

The rule changes made between 1906 and 1912 were so far-reaching that all subsequent changes seem minor by comparison. In effect, they elevated the game of football as played in America.

Take, for example, what happened on November 1, 1913. Notre Dame was playing Army at West Point. Thanks to the new rules, two Notre Dame players named Gus Dorais and Knute Rockne were able to use the new forward pass to defeat Army 35-13. From that defeat, Army's coach, Charles Daly, saw just what that pass could do, and allowed two of his players, Vernon Prichard and Louis Merillat, to use it in Army's climactic game with Navy. The result was a 22-9 Army victory, and no team was ever quite the same again.

As the sport of football grew, so did its popularity with the fans. From muddy fields with only the ground for seats, the circumstances of fan attendance mandated the building of stadiums. In 1903, Harvard built a stadium made of concrete that could seat 50,000. Shortly thereafter, Syracuse built its Archbold Stadium which could seat 35,000. Yale followed suit in 1914 with an 80,000 capacity stadium that covered 25 acres. It was described as the most magnificent structure of its time. Today, we need only think of the massive, covered stadiums with interior climate controls and seating in excess of 100,000 to realize that football has maintained its mass appeal over the years, and that appeal continues to grow.

Indeed, we could spend hours talking of famous coaches, outstanding players, remarkable plays, and fantastic games. This has been, and will continue to be, a major part of many fine evenings when friends gather. As we talk, we realize that football is an intrinsic part of American life; that football is more than a game; that football is a relaxation, an energizer, a bone of contention, a refuge and a haven, a vicarious thrill for millions of people, a proving ground for the best athletes America has produced, and as many things to as many people as watch it or participate in it.

Put another way, football is a living entity. It is blood pulsing through the veins and telling us that we are alive and well. It changes, of course, because all living creatures undergo change, and change is what life itself is all about, but it remains a vital and ecstatic part of our lives.

I, for one, am very glad that Mr. William Ellis picked up that Rugby ball and ran with it. How about you?

SPECIAL DATA: *Time of speech: about nine minutes. This is a speech that goes over very well with any group of football players or fans. You should not, however, underestimate its effectiveness with a non-sports audience. We'd be willing to wager that even people who profess to dislike all sports have heard some of the names mentioned here and would be fascinated by some of the facts. You should feel free to use as much or as little of it as you need to add some history of the sport to your next speech.*

$$\boxed{114}$$

TOPIC: *Basketball*

AUDIENCE: *Suitable for any audience.*

If physical education class hadn't been so boring, basketball might never have come about. You see, back in 1891, physical education consisted mainly of calisthenics, working with apparatus, and marching. The students, in general, hated it. That was the problem faced by the young physical education instructor who had recently graduated from the Presbyterian Theological College of Montreal. His boys at the International

Young Men's Christian Association Training School, later to become Springfield College, didn't care for the physical education program, and he was determined to do something about it. What he did became the only major sport that is strictly of American origin. He invented basketball.

His name was James Naismith. He had been born in 1861, and during his schooling at the theological college, he became convinced that he could teach young men about clean and moral living much better through sports than he could by preaching from a pulpit. That was why, in the year following his graduation, he was at Springfield in the physical education department.

But, back to his problem. How could young James Naismith make his classes more interesting to his students? He reports that he meditated and prayed often in those days, and tried to come up with a new game that would keep the attention of his students while providing them with beneficial physical activity. He was encouraged in this pursuit by his department head, Mr. Luther Gulick, who told Naismith that he might try incorporating several existing sports into a new one.

After much agonizing trial and error, James Naismith borrowed, changed, modified, and adapted ideas from football, soccer, hockey, and other outdoor games, and came up with a game for which he had no name but that he felt would fill the bill. Attempts at bringing outdoor games inside to the gymnasium had only resulted in a number of broken windows and several injuries as players met hard wood floors rather than resilient earth. Naismith wanted something where there would be a minimum of injuries, a maximum of movement, and something that was conducive to the indoors.

Naismith came up with five principles for his new game:

1. There must be a large, light ball that is easily handled.
2. Whenever the ball is in play, no man on either side would be restricted from getting it.
3. No one could run with the ball.
4. The goal must be horizontal and above the heads of the players.
5. Although both teams will occupy the same space, there will be no personal contact.

He also drew up 13 rules to go along with these principles, and, one day in December of 1891, he explained the rules to his class of 18 students. They formed two sides of 9 each and the game began—almost. It seems they had forgotten the goals.

Naismith's idea was to nail two square boxes, one at either end of the gymnasium. He sent for them, but the janitor returned word that they had no spare wooden boxes. However, there were two peach baskets in the storeroom. Would those do?

The game began, and, to everyone's amazement, including James Naismith, the students liked it! For the record, they played for the entire period, and, after much running and shooting, a student named William R. Chase threw the ball from mid-court into the peach basket. The first basketball game in history ended with a score of 1-0.

The students enjoyed the game so much, however, that when they went home for Christmas vacation, they told families and friends and their local YMCAs about it. Soon, Naismith was being deluged with letters asking for the rules of this new game where one tossed a ball into a peach basket—you know, the "basket" ball game. The demands became so insistent that on January 15, 1892 Naismith published the rules in the campus paper.

As the popularity of the game spread, some confusion crept in. At first, it was used in physical education classes only, and everyone in the class participated. This meant that the number of players on a side depended on the size of the class, and, in 1892, a coach at Cornell divided his class of 100 students into two sides and let them have at it. That game was a disaster. So, in 1894, teams began to experiment with the number of players on a side and the size of the playing area. By 1895 the number of players was fixed at five by mutual consent and has remained the same ever since.

Back at Springfield, during those early experimental games enthusiasm among the players grew so high that word of the contests soon spread throughout the area. Soon, people from nearby began dropping in to take a look. This included several young ladies who were teachers at the nearby Buckingham Grade School. They would stroll in during lunch hour, and they were soon shouting as loudly as the other spectators. They approached Naismith and asked if they might try it. The first women's game on record took place behind closed doors with spectators strictly forbidden. The ladies wore long, trailing dresses with mutton-leg sleeves, with street shoes or tennis shoes. Naismith himself officiated at this game, and it is reported that he "blushed crimson" when he called a foul on one young lady and she proceeded to doubt the marital status of his mother and father.

Changes in the physical conditions relative to the game occurred rapidly. In 1892, for instance, the peach basket was replaced with an iron hoop with a basket of heavy woven wire. At first, they had to put up a ladder after each goal to retrieve the ball, but someone thought of cutting a hole in the bottom and allowing the ball to fall through. Since it was the official's duty to get back the ball, they loved it.

Fans at this time delighted in sitting behind their opposing team's basket and leaning over the railings to deflect an incoming ball, so it was decided that a screen would be placed behind the basket. This was later replaced by a four by six foot board of wood. This proved effective, and later it was replaced by a glass "back board" so that fans could see better.

Originally, the game was played with a soccer ball. In 1894, however, the Overman Wheel Company marketed the first "basketball." It was larger than the soccer ball and laced like a football. It wasn't until 1937 that the laceless ball came into play, to be replaced in 1949 by the official "molded" ball.

Basketball, although developed in America, quickly spread throughout the world. Canada adopted it immediately, which is hardly surprising as many of James Naismith's original class members were Canadians. In 1893, the game was introduced in France, and the following year, 1894, found it in China and India. In 1894 the game was also demonstrated in London at the 50th anniversary of the founding of the YMCA. In 1900, it was introduced into Japan, and it was played in Iran in 1901. It is even said to have been introduced into South America by missionaries who taught it to the tribes they aided. Today, of course, there is hardly a country in the world where basketball is not played, and it has become an Olympic event.

Whether it is on a hardwood court with a crowd wildly cheering on their favorite college or professional team, or on a playground where two or three kids have gotten together with a ball and a hoop, basketball, that marvelous creation of a man who wanted nothing more than to provide his class with an interesting exercise, provides entertainment and exercise for untold millions of people each year.

Well done, Mr. Naismith—well done, indeed!

SPECIAL DATA: *Time of speech: about eight minutes. Personally, we find the history of basketball to be fascinating. This speech attempts to communicate some of that fascination. We are certain that your audience will like it as well.*

$$\boxed{115}$$

TOPIC: *Wrestling*

AUDIENCE: *Suitable for all audiences.*

We seem to have a fascination with records. We enjoy finding out the strongest, tallest, shortest, fastest in all sorts of activities. If this is true, then I have something which must qualify in that category. That is what I would like to tell you about today—the world's oldest sport. Wrestling.

I can make that claim, because of the discovery of an ancient temple and tomb near the Nile in Egypt called the temple of Beni Hasan. Within its walls were discovered literally hundreds of statues and sculptures depicting wrestling matches. What's more, the intriguing aspect of this discovery is that the sculptures show virtually every wrestling hold and fall known today. The temple dates back to at least 3000 years before Christ, and, as those sculptures tell us, wrestling was already a highly defined sport.

Indeed, there is some speculation that wrestling may have been introduced into Greece from either Asia or Egypt. Certainly, it was an important part of early Greek culture. For instance, in the classic epic of Homer, *The Iliad*, there is a description of a wrestling match between Odysseus and Ajax. That description coordinates almost exactly with the sculptures found in Beni Hasan and later in the ancient city of Nineveh.

Wherever it originated, it was undoubtedly the Greeks who raised it to a fine art. In 704 B.C., it was introduced as a sport in the 18th Olympiad. At that time, contestants wrestled nude. Before the match began, their bodies were rubbed with oil and then dusted with fine sand to afford each contestant a better grip.

Wrestling in Greece took two forms. One was called the *pankration* (which translated to "all-strength") style and the other was called the Upright Style. *Pankration* was a no-holds-barred style that was allowed into the Olympic games. The only things you *couldn't* do were bite your opponent and gouge out his eyes. Virtually everything else, including kicking and strangling, was permitted. Upright Wrestling, on the other hand, was part of the pentathalon. In this style, the allowable holds differed little from those used in modern-day wrestling. The winner was the first contestant to throw his adversary to the ground three times. In contrast, *pankration* style matches ended only when one contestant admitted defeat or was physically unable to continue the match.

Closer to home, wrestling developed very early in English history. The literature of England, indeed, is filled with references to and descriptions of the sport. The styles varied throughout the country in those early days, from starting matches with both contestants already locked in each other's arms to matches where the contestants wore loose-fitting canvas jackets that opponents were allowed to pull and grasp. Even the monarchy was affected. It has been reported from reliable sources that King Henry VIII was a very powerful wrestler who often exhibited his skill to his court, whether they wanted to see it or not.

Today, wrestling is generally divided into two styles. There is the so-called Greco-Roman style and free-style. Greco-Roman is seldom used in the United States, although it does have popularity in Russia and certain Scandinavian countries. Free-style is reminiscent of the Upright Style of the early Olympic games. It is conducted under strict rules with time limits for bouts and the time required for a "pin." Points have also been assigned to various holds, moves, and take-downs. Over 90 percent of all amateur wrestling in the United States is conducted under NCAA rules.

Of course, I would be remiss if I did not tell you about another type of wrestling conducted in this country. That is what has been termed "professional" wrestling. These bouts with their easily defined "good guys" and "bad guys," their reliance on acrobatics, acting ability, and the contestants' skill at whipping an audience into a frenzy may be interesting to watch on TV if nothing else is on, but have no place in the world of athletic competition. Indeed, have you ever noticed that those matches are not even advertised as bouts but as "exhibitions"?

In high school and college gymnasiums across our great land, however, free-style wrestling under sponsored rules continues to be a contest of strength, skill, and thinking ability that is gaining increasing popularity with both participants and spectators. The next time you attend such a match, look closely and consider that these young men are following in an athletic tradition whose roots are lost in time. They might well be performing in the halls of the temple at Beni Hasan or on the fields of Greece. They are following in the footsteps of gods and kings.

It's enough to make you realize that wrestling is anything but just another sport.

SPECIAL DATA: *Time of speech: about five minutes. If what we have seen is any indication, the popularity of wrestling is definitely on the upswing. A speech such as this could be used for the parents of the wrestlers you coach, for the wrestlers themselves, to give them some perspective*

*on their sport, or even to a general audience, as it
contains some rather interesting facts. It would be relatively easy to find more information on the two major
styles of modern wrestling if you wanted the speech to
be longer.*

116

TOPIC: *Track and Field*

AUDIENCE: *Suitable for any audience.*

Let's return to the cave. Let's go back, way back, to the days of
primitive man. In those days, mankind really had only one problem—he
had to survive against enormous odds and under very harsh conditions.
To do this, early man had to depend on his skills. He had to be able to
run fast; his movements had to be lithe and dexterous; he had to be strong;
he had to be able to leap and jump; after he developed spears, he had to
be able to use them with speed and accuracy. All of this was necessary if
he was to avoid danger and hunt down animals for food. It is not an
impossible assumption, therefore, that when not actually engaged in a
struggle for survival, primitive man practiced these skills both alone and
with his fellows.

This may have been the source from which track and field competition
emerged. When you consider that track and field consists of competition
in jumping, running, and throwing various objects such as the javelin, this
theory begins to gain credibility.

We know that track and field events are recorded well before the
current era in such places as Greece, Egypt, and certain Asian civilizations.
Certainly they were an important part of the ancient Olympics and remained so until the games were discontinued in 394 A.D. by the Roman
Emperor Theodosius. Then, in 1154, track and field turned up in London.
"Athletic sports" was the British term for what we call track and field. The
city of London provided fields for their practice in that year. They were
stopped again for a short time by the decree of King Edward III because,
he contended, they interfered with the practice of archery, which was
important for defense. They returned during the following century, however, and rose to prominence and popularity during the reign of King
Henry VIII who, it was said, was fairly good at throwing the hammer.

During the nineteenth century in England, foot races for money became popular. Amateur races began to spring up as part of the athletic programs of various British colleges, and, in 1849, the first regularly organized athletic meeting was held by the Royal Military Academy, Woolwich. Other prestigious schools, such as Oxford and Cambridge, followed suit, and soon "athletic sports" (track and field) were firmly established in Great Britain.

Meanwhile, here in America the New York Athletic Club held the first indoor track and field meet on November 11 in the year of its founding, 1868. Three Civil War veterans, John C. Babcock, Harry E. Buermeyer, and William B. Curtis, had formed the club that started on September 8, 1868 with 14 charter members. On November 11, 1868, the first meet was held under their sponsorship at the Empire Skating Rink. Because the building had no cover, canvas was spread over it. A running track of eight laps to the mile was hastily built, and contestant Bill Curtis became the first man in U.S. history to wear spiked running shoes.

In 1879, the New York Athletic Club gave up its management of these events, and this led to the formation of National Association of Amateur Athletics. Due, however, to a certain laxity in enforcing the amateur rules, control was given over in the year 1888 to the Amateur Athletic Union of the United States.

Today, track and field events are a part of every Olympic competition as well as flourishing on college campuses and in high schools throughout the land. While track and field events involve competition, they are also used to sponsor good physical conditioning and to develop strength and stamina. In fact, the armed services of many countries, our own included, sponsor track and field events and training for their ability to physically condition the athlete. Moreover, track and field events are often occasions for exercises in good will between countries at special international "invitational" meets.

Whether for physical training for for the thrill of sports competition however, track and field events seem as popular today as they ever were. Whether it is the split second of heart-stopping tension as the vaulter reaches for the heavens or the wild cheering excitement as a clustered group of runners speeds toward the finish line, track and field events will continue to provide excitement and enjoyment for spectators and participants for years to come.

SPECIAL DATA: *Time of speech: about five minutes. You could, of course, list the various events in modern track and field as well as giving records. You could also recount stories of the* *greats in the sport such as Bob Mathias and Jim Thorpe. This would make your speech quite long, as there is so much to be said about these famous athletes. This speech gives you some of the basics of the history of track and field, and can be delivered as is or expanded as we suggested before to any length.*

$$\boxed{117}$$

TOPIC: *Gymnastics*

AUDIENCE: *Suitable for any audience.*

It may be more or less general knowledge that gymnastics began in ancient Greece, but if we had a time machine and could return to those ancient days, what we saw would be quite different from what we have come to know as gymnastics today.

To the ancient Greeks, gymnastics included much that has come down to modern times as separate disciplines. Track and field events, boxing, wrestling, and even fencing, for example, were all part of what gymnastics meant to them. In a very crude form, what we might think of as modern gymnastics was used mostly for physical training and conditioning for the more belligerent and combative sports. As the Olympic games progressed, however, some forms of gymnastics were added to the games.

When the Olympic games were terminated in 394 A.D. by the Roman Emperor Theodosius, however, almost all sports entered a decline, gymnastics among them. While the middle ages saw renewed interest in some field sports, gymnastics, the systematic training of the body, was not a part of the scene.

Then came the nineteenth century, and with it, renewed interest in sports of all kinds. Many people began to write papers about the benefits of sports, and very early in that century gymnastics was praised and credited as a means of physical exercise with great merit, since its systematic approach trained the mind as well as the body and achieved both physical and mental discipline. As such, it quickly gained favor.

Suddenly, societies began to spring up devoted to the practice and perfection of gymnastics. These appeared first in Germany and Bohemia, then in France and Switzerland, and gradually, throughout all of Europe.

The 1880s saw a great tide of immigrants coming to America, and it was only natural that these people would bring with them their ideas about gymnastics and gymnastic societies. Soon, gymnastics was established in the United States as well.

At first in the United States, Canada, and Great Britain, gymnastics was accepted mainly for what many considered its therapeutic value. It was used as a rehabilitative tool for people injured in wars, accidents, and the like as well as for those stricken with polio and other crippling diseases. Indeed, certain gymnastic exercises, tailored to an individual's needs, meant greater mobility and a more active life. The incorporation of gymnastic practices into physical therapy programs is a vital part of today's scene as well.

Gradually, these countries came to recognize gymnastics as a sport as well, but all was not peaceful. Two systems developed in the nineteenth century, and both systems had their advocates. There was the Swedish System, developed in the mid-nineteenth century in Sweden and imported to the United States about 1889, which stressed free exercises whose objective was perfect rhythm of movement. Indeed, it was often known as Rhythmic Gymnastics. Then there was the German System that came to the United States at about the same time. This system stressed muscular development and very formally prescribed work on apparatus. The relative merits of both systems were hotly debated by educational experts for the next thirty years.

In the 1920s, a French group, the *Fédération Internationale de Gymnastique*, solved the problem once and for all by advocating competition based on *both* the rhythmic motions of the Swedish System and the more precise emphasis of the German System. It is this combined version that we in America have come to know as gymnastics.

Today, men's competition in gymnastics includes the horizontal bars, the parallel bars, side horse, vaulting, floor exercise, the rings, and the all-around event. Gymnastics was one of the first sports to recognize the advantages of participation by women as well as men, and women compete in balance beam, uneven parallel bars, vaulting, floor exercise, and the all-around. Recently, a women's event called Rhythmic Exercise has been added in which certain floor exercises are performed with balls, hoops, sticks with long ribbons attached, and the like. The beauty and fluidity of movement is highly impressive and scores deeply with audiences. It is very much akin to the Swedish or Rhythmic style.

If those ancient Greeks were to come back today and witness a modern gymnastic competition, they might not recognize it. However, one look at the grace, the strength, the fluid movement, and the vivacity of today's gymnasts would certainly be enough to convince them of the merits of this sport. Gymnastics is alive, it is growing, and it continues to build healthy minds and bodies in athletes throughout our nation and the world.

SPECIAL DATA: *Time of speech: about five minutes. Personally, we feel that gymnastics is one of the most aesthetically pleasing sports. With increased television coverage of both local and international meets, it is gaining in popularity in our schools, and children as young as four and five are taking classes. Add to this speech as you like, possibly making reference to those gymnasts who have become highly visible for their Olympic competition, or use it as it is to give your audience some insight into the development of this quickly growing sport.*

118

TOPIC: *Soccer*

AUDIENCE: *Suitable for all audiences.*

Let's get something straight from the start. While soccer may not be of American origin (only basketball holds that honor), the word "soccer" most definitely is, because, with the exception of Canada, the rest of the world calls it "football" or "association football."

Indeed, there is no doubt that what we call soccer and what we call American football, had the exact same origin. They both came to the United States from Great Britain, although soccer stayed more or less the same as the original English game, and football evolved into the entirely different and separate sport it is today.

Where was the first soccer game played in America? That is very hard to tell, since many places claim that distinction. On the Commons in Boston, Massachusetts, for instance, there is a marker which states emphatically that the first game was played there. There are similar markers throughout the northeastern United States.

It is known that in the mid-1860s, the first intercollegiate "football" game was played between Rutgers and Princeton. That game was nothing like the football we know today, but was actually a version of soccer. The game of soccer, however, retained its identity throughout the ensuing years, and has come down to us today with relatively few alterations.

Soccer is extremely popular throughout the world, more so in other countries than it is in our own. Indeed, soccer is a matter of national or local pride in some countries and has given fans throughout the world much occasion for enjoyment and, unfortunately, for a great deal of violence.

Perhaps because soccer is a relatively simple game to understand and follow; perhaps because the action is non-stop; perhaps because, unlike some other sports, there is little need for expensive equipment, many nations look on it as their national game. Children get together and kick around a soccer ball the way many American children gather on an open field with a baseball. Games, especially championship games, are fantastically well-attended, and excitement rises to a fever pitch. Sad to say, there have been many instances when this excitement has boiled over, and fans have destroyed the field, injured players, and entered into prolonged and bloody battles with each other. Indeed, there are many soccer stadiums in the world where the fans are now separated from the field and the players by barbed wire, moats, and police with attack dogs. Fortunately, such drastic steps have not been necessary on American soccer fields.

While there has always been an interest in soccer in America, its popularity has not been overwhelming, and certainly not in the same category as the interest expressed in baseball, basketball, or football. It is, however, becoming increasingly popular in schools (even elementary schools) and colleges. This may be due to the fact that soccer is, relatively speaking, fairly inexpensive to support, and there are not as many specialized requirements of a physical nature as one might find in football, for example. This can lead to a wide participation by students. Added to the advent of several professional American soccer teams, the continued television coverage of the sport, and the increasing number of young athletes who are physically participating in it, this seems to indicate that soccer will continue to grow in popularity in the United States throughout the years to come.

Moreover, while there are some deviations in American soccer from the international rules, these are relatively minor, and it is not an unwarranted speculation to imagine American teams in international contests, without the attendant violence that is sometimes witnessed.

Ease of understanding, its uncomplicated nature, the continuous action and non-stop pace, the great excitement, and the great physical enthusiasm and vitality exhibited by its players make soccer a game to be enjoyed by players and spectators alike. It is to be hoped that this will continue in the years ahead.

SPECIAL DATA: *Time of speech: slightly over four minutes. If you would like to expand this speech, we would suggest that you look at the speech about American football that began this section. As soccer and football have a common beginning, you might want to bring in some facts about early football to show its similarity to soccer, such as the fact that in the first "football" games, goals were made by kicking the ball under the crossbar supported by two posts. This might bring the comparison and the idea of common heritage into even clearer focus for your audience.*

$$\boxed{119}$$

TOPIC: *Baseball*

AUDIENCE: *Suitable for any audience.*

Let's start out with a quiz. I'm going to mention some words. All you have to do is to tell me what they have in common. Ready?

The words are: one old cat, two old cat, three old cat, four old cat, rounders.

If you said that these were names of games, you would be quite correct. If you said that they were names of games from another century, you would be correct, and if you said that they were games from another century that may have been the forerunners of what we call baseball, you would have been right on target.

In the eighteenth century in England, children were quite fond of playing a game which they called "rounders." This game, which was fully described in books of that time, had another curious name. Since it involved running around and touching certain "bases" after a ball had been hit, it was also known as "base ball;" that's two words, not one.

So popular was this game of rounders with children (adults never really thought too much about it, and it never caught on as an adult sport in Great Britain), that letters, essays, and books of the late eighteenth century contain many references to it, including one in a book by the novelist Jane Austen, in which she describes a character as preferring, "cricket, base ball, riding on horseback, and riding around the country . . . to books." This in a book written in 1798.

Much earlier than that, in 1744 to be precise, a book called *A Little Pretty Pocket-Book* was published in England. The book described 26 children's sports, one for each letter of the alphabet. The letter B in this book stood for "Base Ball." The description indicates that a "batter" hits the ball and tries to run from base to base. The woodcut that accompanies this description pictures boys playing at the sport. It shows a player standing behind a plate holding a bat with a flat end, shaped like a fan; behind him is a catcher. There is also a pitcher throwing the ball. There are two bases which are marked by poles in the ground, with a "baseman" standing beside each of these.

A much more detailed description of "rounders" is found in *The Boy's Own Book*, published in 1828 in London, and republished through many editions because of its immense popularity. Rounders was played on a field shaped like a diamond. Flat stones (rather than the poles of the 1744 book) were suggested for bases. The fourth base or "goal" was where the batter and the catcher stood. A pitcher threw the ball at the batter. If the batter missed the ball three times, he was out. Whenever the batter hit the ball outside of the diamond, he might commence to run around the bases. If the ball went anywhere except over the diamond, it was a foul and the batter might not run. If the ball was hit fairly and caught on the fly, the batter was out. If the hit was a "grounder," then it was caught by a "fielder" who threw the ball at the batter as he ran the bases. If he hit the runner, the runner was out.

Meanwhile, over in the colonies that would be better known as America, the game of "old cat" was played everywhere by boys. "Old cat" seems to be an offshoot of Rounders, which is hardly surprising if you consider that almost all of the original colonists were English immigrants who brought much of their previous culture with them.

In "old cat," a pitcher threw a ball at a batter. The batter hit the ball, and a catcher tried to catch it. The batter had to run and touch a base or bases and return to the "batman's base" before being tagged out by being hit by the ball. The number of bases the batter had to touch ranged from one—"one old cat"—to four—"four old cat." There were also games of "two old cat" and "three old cat." Usually, it depended on the number of people who wanted to play the game what number of "old cat" would be played. Since the batter stayed "up" as long as he could successfully hit the ball, run and touch base, and return, the more bases he had to touch, the shorter his term at bat, generally speaking. "One old cat" could be played by three boys (pitcher, catcher, batter), while in two, three, and four "old cat" the number of players could be increased to 10, 14, or even more. It was extremely simple to play, the only equipment needed was a ball, something with which to hit it, and anything to mark the bases.

Later, the game of "old cat" came to be known as "Town Ball" and its character changed considerably. Teams of men were chosen by various towns or groups within a town, and they played each other. It was played on a field laid out in the form of a perfect square with 60 feet between each base. The batsman stood on the line halfway between first and fourth base with a catcher standing behind him but outside of the square. Any ball that was hit was considered to be fair and playable. Indeed, it was considered to be a great skill for a batsman to be able to hit the ball so that it deflected behind him. The batsman was "out" when he was hit by the ball after it was caught.

Of course, Rounders was also being played throughout the colonies and later the new nation of America. Both Town Ball and Rounders became so popular that clubs were formed for each. In 1833 the Olympic Town Ball Club was formed in Philadelphia, while in 1825 the Rochester Baseball Club was founded in Rochester, New York.

Although the rules for playing Town Ball and Rounders (or "baseball" as it was increasingly being called) were more or less uniform, there were some slight differences from place to place. Many of the games described as "baseball" in those early days of our nation may have been variations on Town Ball and Rounders.

Then came the summer of 1839. In Otsego County in central New York state, in the small village of Cooperstown, an instructor at a military preparatory school who would later become a general in the United States Army, set up a field of new proportions, changed the rules of Town Ball and Rounders somewhat, called it "Baseball," and began what has come to be known as "America's pastime." His name was Abner Doubleday.

The popularity of baseball in America grew and grew, and Town Ball and Rounders were replaced by baseball. Baseball had really caught on. Originally, all players were amateurs who played for the love of it, although it was accepted that certain players of great talent might accept fees for their services to play for one particular team. By the late 1800s, however, professional baseball teams had been formed and were playing schedules of games with complete team competition.

It was at that time, during the 1880s and 90s that a controversy arose that would rise to a feverish pitch and never really be settled to anyone's satisfaction.

Many people believed that Abner Doubleday had "invented" the game of baseball. Many others said that it was just one more evolutionary step from Rounders, Town Ball, and Old Cat. Indeed, many felt that what was known as Rounders in America was so little different from Doubleday's "baseball" that there was a negligible difference, if any, between them. They pointed to the fact, for example, that in Doubleday's game, the player was still thrown out when he was hit by the ball. Indeed, it was not until 1845 that a group established by Alexander J. Cartwright, a surveyor and amateur ball player from New York, drew up a set of regulations for the game that included the "tagging" out of a player rather than hitting him with a thrown ball. There were other rules as well, and these were generally adopted in September of 1845. It was thereafter that baseball, now being played the same way everywhere, began to gain tremendous popularity.

The controversy raged. Unfortunately, by this time General Abner Doubleday was long dead, and he was hardly in a position to give objective evidence. Some were calling Abner Doubleday the father of American baseball while others claimed that title for Alexander Cartwright who had formalized baseball's rules and for Harry Wright who was one of the first professional players and managers.

During the late 1800s, one of the more famous baseball players was a man named A. G. Spalding who later founded the famous sporting goods manufacturing company. In 1907, Spalding established a commission with the directive that they research the origins of baseball and determine, once and for all, how the game developed and who developed it.

The commission took a year. On that commission were politicians, ball players, owners of sporting goods companies, and presidents of various athletic associations. In *Baseball Guide of 1908*, they published their findings. It came down to two statements: First, baseball was an American sport and had *no* connection to rounders or any other game of foreign origin, and, second, baseball and its rules were solely developed by Abner Doubleday in 1839 in Cooperstown, New York.

Immediately, the report was challenged. It was pointed out that the rules under which baseball had developed into a popular sport came from the committee formed by Alexander Cartwright in 1845. They pointed out the game's amazing similarity in those early years to Rounders and Town Ball. They demanded to see the commission's evidence.

Unfortunately, there was a fire, and all the documents that the committee had claimed it used were destroyed, and nothing was left but the final report itself.

Then, as passionate as the controversy had been, it simply cooled down. Perhaps people grew tired of arguing where baseball came from and just wanted to play the game. Perhaps events in the early twentieth century overshadowed the importance of the beginnings of the most popular game in America. Whatever the reason, there was less and less criticism of the Spalding Report, and if people had objections, they stopped voicing them. Baseball itself, unperturbed by arguments about its birth, kept gaining popularity and expanding its scope.

So it was that on June 12, 1939 at Cooperstown, New York, the National Baseball Hall of Fame and Museum was dedicated. There, you will find a memorial to Abner Doubleday, along with memorabilia and commemorative plaques and statues for the greatest players and personalities that American baseball has produced.

Whether baseball was wholly of American extraction; whether it was Doubleday or Cartwright or someone unknown to history who formulated the rules—whatever the case, baseball *is* America's pastime. It is the sport played by more Americans than any other. It does engender more arguments, give more pleasure, and provide a greater source of recreation and enjoyment to the American public than any other sport. Let historians talk. Baseball will not mind, for the game, wherever and however it developed, has captured the minds and the hearts of America.

With such an audience, what can it do but grow and flourish as a mainstay of American culture.

SPECIAL DATA: *Time of speech: about ten to eleven minutes. This is certainly a different approach to a speech about baseball. Almost everyone believes that baseball was invented by Abner Doubleday. Consequently, a speech such as this will be a real attention-getter. Of course, the facts in this speech, as well as in all the others, are well documented. Try this speech and see the enthusiastic response it brings.*

Afterthoughts

You must understand something: we could have easily written a book the size of this one about each separate sport mentioned in this section. The history of these sports is not only fascinating, it is often highly complex as well. Therefore, these speeches contain only the highlights of each sport's history and a few of the many interesting insights into each game. Had we done otherwise, you would have been delivering six- and seven-hour speeches, and we would have done you and your audience a disservice.

The point of our telling you this is that there is much more to know about these sports. If you want to read up on them and add more about your particular sport, that would be fine. You could use the speeches in this section as the bones on which to add more meat. In that way, you could make a speech as long as you wished in order to, let us say, fill a time requirement.

Also remember that while the history of a sport is important and interesting, it is equally important to play the sport and enjoy it. Several personal anecdotes along the way of your personal involvement with the sport will always go over well.

May you become a part of the history of your sport!

part TWO

A Coach's Gameplan for Preparing and Delivering a Speech

As you know, even if we were to cover every speech ever given in a sports or sports-related situation (and we'd need a book ten times the size of this one to do it), that inevitable time would still occur when a coach would have to compose a speech of his own.

Invariably, special circumstances or special events will dictate that a particular speech, perhaps containing specialized information, be composed by the coach. At such a time, preparing a speech can be a very trying occasion, unless some special rules are followed in its composition; rules that have been developed from experience to make composition a relatively painless and efficient process.

Even if, to save your valuable time, you can adapt or deliver one of the speeches in the first part of this book, you must still face your audience and deliver that speech. Most of the time, everything goes well. However, if you speak frequently enough, you are aware that there are some pitfalls that await public speakers and can disrupt any speech, unless the speaker is prepared to deal effectively with them.

Presented on the following pages is a step-by-step guide that has proven effective for us in preparing and delivering speeches. Also included is an invaluable guide in which you will find a great deal of practical advice for avoiding the traps and pitfalls of public speaking; advice that has been gleaned from years and years of practical experience; a guide that will serve you well in every speaking situation.

With these two guides to serve you, you will find it a relatively easy procedure to compose and deliver, free from any drawbacks, an exciting, appropriate, and memorable speech.

We know that these guides will continue to serve you, as they have served us, for a long time to come.

SECTION 11

A Play-by-Play Guide for Preparing and Delivering a Dynamic Speech

If you want to give an effective, stimulating, and memorable speech or presentation, we have found a proven and dependable success formula that has served us well under all conditions. We call it the PREPARE formula. Each letter stands for one building block in the foundation of a good speech.

P — PREPARING AND PINPOINTING YOUR TOPIC

If you were asked to speak on coaching, your first question would be, "What phase or aspect of coaching?" A loose, rambling speech makes an audience restless. Make every effort to limit your topic and pinpoint a specific area that you can cover in depth within your allotted speaking time.

Whenever you are asked to speak, you should ask certain questions:

What is the composition of the audience?

How many people will I be addressing?

Where will my speech fit into the total program for that afternoon or evening?

What event, activity, et cetera is to precede or follow me?

What speaking facilities (microphone, podium, dais, head table/ audience, stage/audience, and so forth) will be available?

How much will the audience know (or think they know) about the topic before I speak?

How does the program coordinator perceive my speech? (Entertaining? Persuasive? Informative?)

What is the maximum and minimum time I will have to speak?

In short, ask any question that you feel might have a bearing on the physical environment and/or content of your speech. This attention to detail will help you prepare the right speech for the right audience at the right time. For example, would you give an hour-long speech if you were speaking just *before* dinner was to be served? Would you give a really serious speech at a parent-child dinner where Santa Claus' appearance was to follow yours? Pinpointing your topic and preparing for the physical surroundings of your speech is your first step on the road to success.

R — RESEARCHING FOR SUCCESS

Obviously, you need to know what you are talking about. Few speakers deliberately try to mislead or misinform the audience, but trusting your

277

memory is risky at best and disastrous at worst. It is at this point that you begin to prepare yourself to meet your audience. Consequently, you will need some information:

What will my audience want to know?

What kind of questions will they ask?

What kind of humor would they like best?

What would antagonize them?

What would please them?

Once you have determined the answers to these questions, you can begin your research.

Compile the information you need. If you are going to speak about a sports figure, for example, find out about him. If it is a current local issue regarding coaching, perhaps you'll want to look at back issues of the local paper. Use Part One of this book and other speech books to select appropriate anecdotes, stories, and humor. Remember that the quality of your research will pave the way to a successful speech.

E — EXAMPLES AND THEIR USE

Good speakers use examples to prove or clarify their points throughout a speech. To get the most out of the examples you use, follow these rules:

1. The example should be appropriate. It must make the point you want it to make. To use an anecdote, however clever or humorous, that has no bearing on what you are saying will only confuse your audience.

2. The example should be understood by everyone. To describe someone as "an alumnus of Phi Slamma Jamma" is fine—if everyone in the audience has knowledge of basketball and the University of Houston. Otherwise, any content of your remark is lost.

3. Avoid inside jokes. Every profession has its inside humor—those anecdotes and stories that are amusing only to those persons in that profession. To use such material before a mixed audience could lead to confusion and antagonism. Therefore, they are better left untold.

P — PRESENTATION AND POISE

Once you have written your speech, you will have to give it before an audience. This phase of preparation is vital. Whether this is your first speech or your one hundred and first, you should rehearse it thoroughly before you set foot before an audience. Lock your door, if need be, and stand in front of a mirror. See yourself as others will see you. Pay attention to your gestures, your eye contact, your use of notes, your posture. Record your speech and listen to it with an open mind. Are you speaking too slowly? Too fast? In a monotone? Are your words distinct? Finally, decide what you will wear that day. You already know what type of function you are attending, so you won't be wearing a sweat suit to a black-tie dinner. Make an effort to select clothes in which you look and feel your best. If you feel good about your appearance, you will project confidence to your audience.

A — ANALYZING YOUR AUDIENCE

When you have arrived at the place where you are to speak, you will have an opportunity to analyze your audience. Look at them, listen to them, and particularly pay attention to their reactions. Is the atmosphere formal or informal? Are they quiet and respectful or noisy and restless? If there were other speakers before you, how were they received? Your analysis of the audience will tell you what approach to take when it is your time to speak. Even a prepared speech can be delivered in several ways. It can be formal, conversational, or even intimate (as friend to friend). Your approach will be determined by your perception of the audience.

Finally, once you begin speaking, you will feel your audience. There is no way to describe this; it must be experienced. Through this rapport— this psychological bond—the audience will tell you what they think of your speech. You must take your cues from them and adjust accordingly.

R — RELAXING AND ENJOYING YOURSELF

In most cases, your audience *wants* you to succeed. They are on your side. If you have done everything in your power to make your speech entertaining, informative, clear, and concise, then you need do only one more thing to ensure your speech's success—relax and enjoy yourself. If you are nervous, your audience will be nervous. If you are uncomfortable, your audience will be uncomfortable. However, if you are enjoying your- self, *so will your audience!*

Speaking before people can be a truly enjoyable experience. If you really believe that and learn to enjoy speaking, then you will be a good speaker. If you don't believe that; if speaking is nothing more than a task, and an unpleasant one at that, then don't worry about it—you won't be asked to do it often. Be at ease, enjoy your audience, and you will be in demand.

E — ENTHUSIASM AND EMPATHY: KEYS TO SUCCESS

Be enthusiastic—believe in what you are saying. If you are, then even if your audience does not agree with what you are saying, they will still respect you as a person of knowledge and conviction. Your enthusiasm can make a lasting positive impression in the minds of your audience. If your speech is to be followed by a question and answer session, you will find that enthusiasm is your greatest ally.

In dealing with those questions from the audience, *empathy* is the keynote. Put yourself in the position of the questioner. If you do this, you will never slough off a question or make light of it or the person who asked it. There will be no need to become defensive, and, because you have done your research, you can answer the question straightforwardly and comprehensively.

This, then, is the PREPARE formula. It has served us well for many years in the preparation and delivery of numerous speeches. May it bring you similar success.

SECTION 12

A Coach's
Survival Guide
for Avoiding
the Pitfalls of
Public Speaking

Public speaking can be an enjoyable experience, but it can also have its pitfalls. What, for example, is the best way to answer a question from the audience so that everyone understands the answer? What if you are faced with a hostile audience? How can you ensure that your charts or graphs will be seen by everybody? What happens if you are asked an obviously hostile question?

These are some common pitfalls to public speaking, but they can be handled to the speaker's advantage. This section offers proven suggestions that will help you overcome the problems and deliver a memorable and enjoyable address.

HOW TO USE VISUAL AIDS TO ADVANTAGE

You can have the best, most thoughtful, most interesting presentation in the world, but it will count for nothing if it remains unseen.

Consider it from the audience's point of view. It is very frustrating to have your attention called to a map, chart, or diagram only to find the visual aid blocked, either wholly or partially, by the speaker's body. What makes it worse is that frequently the speaker is unaware of the problem.

Obviously, this is no problem when you are addressing a small, intimate group and everyone is afforded an unobstructed view of everything, or they may move themselves or their chairs in order to obtain that view. It is when you are appearing on a stage or dais, before a larger audience, that this may prove a difficulty. Surprisingly enough, it is within the physical layout of the stage that your solution to the problem lies.

Most halls or auditoriums are set up so that the chairs for the audience are placed in rows, from just before the foot of the stage backward to the far wall of the room. The chairs on either ends of these rows are usually set up in line with the proscenium arch on either side of the stage.

Therefore, if you can visualize your shoulders as pointers, it will become obvious that your audience will always be able to see you and your display if you keep your right shoulder pointed at the right proscenium arch when you are facing to your left, and keep your left shoulder pointed at the left proscenium arch when you are facing to your right. This affords every member of the audience, in every seat, a clear line of sight to what is happening on stage.

You will also find it useful to gesture with your upstage hand, the hand closest to the back wall and furthest from the audience. If you keep this in mind, you will never reach across yourself when gesturing, which is very unattractive from the audience's point of view and can also block your speech and your display.

HOW TO EFFECTIVELY ANSWER QUESTIONS
FROM THE AUDIENCE

One of the severest tests of a good speaker is the ability to answer questions from the floor in a tight, efficient, and effective manner. If a question from the floor is handled in a halting, stammering, erratic manner, the audience may begin to suppose that the speaker is either unsure of his material or trying to mislead them in some way.

Fortunately, there is a tested and proven way of answering questions that not only conveys to the audience exactly the information that they require but does so in such a precise and effective manner that both the answer and the answerer are remembered.

The method involves two steps. When a question is asked, you should:

1. Repeat the question.
2. Use the AREA formula of response.

Let's examine each of these steps.

When you are asked a question from the floor, the first thing you should do is to repeat the question. This serves two purposes. First, it ensures that everyone has heard the queston and heard it exactly as the questioner intended. Second, it gives you time to think.

Quite often, the only ones to hear the question are the speaker and a few people in the immediate vicinity of the questioner. This may be due to the acoustics of the hall or the soft-spoken manner of the questioner, but it happens more often than not. Therefore, your repetition of the question gives the rest of the audience the chance to hear what has been said. It also ensures that you have heard exactly what the questioner asked, so there will be no confusion later or claims that the question was not answered.

Repeating the question also provides you with time to think and organize your answer. You will be surprised at how even a few seconds provide you with time to get your material in proper order for presentation.

When it comes to actually answering the question that has been asked, there is no better or more effective way of presenting your viewpoint than to use the AREA formula. Each letter stands for one step in an effective answer. They are:

A—Answer

R—Reason

E—Example

A—Answer

First, give your *answer*. Make the point you wish to make. Give the questioner the answer that his question requires.

Next, tell the *reason* for your answer. Tell clearly and concisely why you gave the answer you did.

Third, give an *example* that shows why you gave the answer you did. There is nothing like a concrete example to get across a salient point. Almost anything can be put into the form of an anecdote or story to which the audience can relate, no matter how intelligent you think they are. Everyone profits from a solid example.

Finally, repeat your *answer*. This time, it should be a natural outgrowth of your reason and example. Also, leaving the questioner and, by projection, the audience with an answer gives them something to think about, and something they will remember for some time.

Let's look at how this whole method would be used in an actual situation. Suppose you are speaking, and it comes time for questions. The person you call on asks, "Wouldn't it be better to take everyone who tries out and place them on the team rather than making a selection based on physical prowess?"

"I have been asked," you say to the audience, "if I feel that it is better to accept everyone who tries out for the team rather than selecting only some based on their performance." Now, you turn back to the questioner but make certain that the entire audience can hear you. "Is that correct? It is. I assume you mean better for the students involved, is that correct? It is. Thank you."

You have been addressing the questioner. You now turn and give your answer to the audience as a whole.

"Personally, I do not believe that the best course of action is to take everyone who tries out and is willing or anxious to play. I believe that selection to a team must be based on many other factors that include physical condition and ability. While mental attitude and the desire to play are important elements in a good athlete, all athletics involve a risk of injury to the player. This risk can be minimized, however, if the player is in good physical condition and can play the game well. While many students want to play, not all of them are physically conditioned or talented enough to go out on the field and avoid that risk of serious physical injury. Personally, I would rather disappoint a student by telling him that he is not ready to play than to grant his wish and see him seriously injured as a result.

"For instance, suppose your son tried out for the football team and he weighed one hundred twenty pounds. Let's suppose that he got on the team and, in practice, every time he went to rush or block an opposing player, he did so from a standing position. Suppose no one could break him of this habit. Now suppose that it is the first game of the season, and all at once, your son is faced with a line of one hundred ninety to two hundred twenty pound players. They do not know him, do not care about his physical safety, and come at him from a crouch while he stands upright and unbalanced. Under such conditions, your son might end up in the hospital with broken bones or an even more serious injury. I know that personally, I would not want this to happen, and I am reasonably certain that neither would you.

"Therefore, I believe that it is not wise to use the desire to play as the only criterion for selection to a team."

Notice how, in the example, the question was not only repeated, but a potential area of misunderstanding was clarified before it caused any concern. Then, notice how the question was answered in strict accordance with the AREA formula. Notice, too, that the entire answer was concise and did not ramble.

The next time you watch a televised press conference with any politician, pay attention to how he or she handles the questions asked by reporters. You will see them repeating questions, and, if you pay particular attention, you might just see the AREA formula staring back at you from your TV screen.

While a huge factor in an audience's acceptance of an answer is the personality of the speaker, an important factor is the way that the answer is presented to them. Repeat the question, give your answer, state the reason for your answer, use a solid example, repeat your answer, and you will have answered that question with effectiveness and dispatch.

HOW TO DEAL WITH A HOSTILE AUDIENCE

It is not a far-fetched assumption that you may one day be faced with a hostile audience, particularly if you are addressing groups of dissatisfied alumni or groups of citizens suspicious of the sports program at a particular school. There may come a time when you must face an audience that is not willing and eager to accept what you have to say; that is indeed hostile.

It will not be easy, but it can be made bearable and antagonism can be kept to a minimum if you keep a few rules in mind:

1. Acknowledge in the beginning that there are differences of opinion: "you might not agree with what I have to say tonight . . ."
2. Do not apologize for yourself. Say: ". . . but I believe in what I am about to tell you, and all I ask is that you hear me out."

3. Base what you have to say on hard, cold *facts*: ". . . As I see it, *these* are the facts of the matter . . ."

4. *Never get personal*: To attack an audience's personal beliefs or opinions is the surest road to complete alienation. Let the weight of your argument win them to your side.

5. Be aware of the probability of hostile questions. Handle these questions with tact by stating provable facts, never opinions.

Under any circumstances, facing a hostile audience is a far from pleasant experience. Fortunately, 99 percent of the audiences you face in public speaking will be receptive, but it is a good idea to be prepared for an unpleasant possibility. In such cases, you will survive if you follow the rules above and make every effort to project an image of confidence, assuredness, and calmness.

EFFECTIVELY OVERCOMING THE HOSTILE QUESTION

Does the term "hostile question" really need a definition? It is any question that is designed to put you on the spot. Please understand, we are not talking about a difficult or intricate question that is honestly asked. We mean the "When did you stop beating your wife?" variety that begs the question and whose sole intent is to put you in an unfavorable light.

You can deal effectively with a hostile question if you:

1. Remain calm and treat the questioner with respect and courtesy.

2. Break a question into its simplest parts, both stated and unstated, and then answer each part separately.

Now, let's examine both steps.

First, it is essential that you remain calm. You can think more clearly and you will gain the respect of your audience if you stay rational in the face of hostility. Treating the hostile questioner with courtesy and civility will further aid in swinging the audience's support to your side.

Next, make certain that everyone knows exactly what is being asked. Let's assume that someone has asked you this question: "What makes you so superior that you have all the answers?" (We think you'll agree that that's a hostile question.) Here is a response that exemplifies Step Two: "I'd like to answer that question, but, as I see it, you have asked several questions. I think you're asking *if* I feel superior; *if* I do, then what makes me feel so; and *do* I have all the answers? The answers are 'no,' 'it doesn't follow,' and 'most certainly not.' Now, let's examine each of them in turn . . ."

By handling the hostile question in this manner, you have turned a potentially embarrassing situation into one that will be advantageous to you by gaining the respect of the audience and perhaps the hostile questioner as well.

HOW TO LEARN TO LOVE IT

Finally, let's deal with the single biggest drawback faced by the beginning speaker—nervousness.

Actors call it stage fright; radio announcers call it mike fright. You may call it what you will, but it is that feeling, just before you are introduced, that your knees have turned to jelly; your spine is made of water; your voice has departed for parts unknown; and you would rather be anywhere—from an arctic iceberg to the middle of a desert sandstorm— than where you are. It is something that happens, and it is something that you must deal with. Helen Hayes, that marvelous veteran actress of thousands of public appearances, once reported that she got so nervous before every appearance she made that she would get physically ill. Yet, anyone who has ever had the honor of watching her perform will know that never once was that anxiety communicated to her audience.

What is the solution to this problem? Many have been suggested. We were once told to picture the audience sitting there in their underwear. The picture becomes so ludicrous that you can't possibly be nervous. Another speaker told us that he never looks at the audience, but focuses on the hairline of audience members. This gives the impression of looking directly at them without having actual eye contact.

Each of these solutions has worked for the person who used them. We have never had to. Oh, yes, we have been nervous, but, in those cases, a matter of philosophy has always been our salvation. You see, we have always expected to love every audience to whom we spoke, and we have expected them to love us. We have not been disappointed. Nervous? Certainly we've been nervous, but the minute the first words come forth, we become interested in the audience and we forget about *ourselves, our* problems, and, most important, *our* nervousness.

Try it; it works!

APPENDIX

The Coach's Locatomatic Index of Speech Topics and Occasions

HOW TO USE THIS INDEX

The following index will allow you to automatically locate the correct speech or anecdote for the topic you have in mind, hence its name. It is thoroughly and vigorously cross-indexed, and it can direct you to exactly the material you require in a matter of seconds.

The numbers following the topics in the index indicate the number of the speech or anecdote in which the topic is covered. They are not page numbers. Look up your topic, and you will immediately be directed to the speech or anecdote that contains information on it.

Look for the larger topic first, and see what you can find. Then you may wish to look up some of the topics that are subtopics of the major topic.

For example, suppose you are giving a speech on the retirement of a fellow coach. First, look up "Retirement," and you will be given the numbers of several speeches that apply. But, you might also want to look up "Coach" as you might want to incorporate some of the material under the various subheadings such as "Character of," "As an educator," or "As an inspiration."

Whatever your intent, this LOCATOMATIC INDEX will prove invaluable.

LOCATOMATIC INDEX

NOTE: The numbers following the entries in the Locatomatic Index indicate the number of the speech.

INDEX